Russell T. McCutcheon
Fabricating Religion

Russell T. McCutcheon
Fabricating Religion

Fanfare for the Common e.g.

DE GRUYTER

ISBN 978-3-11-067670-9
e-ISBN (PDF) 978-3-11-056083-1
e-ISBN (EPUB) 978-3-11-055950-7

Library of Congress Cataloging-in-Publication Data
Names: McCutcheon, Russell T., 1961- author.
Title: Fabricating religion : fanfare for the common e.g. / Russell T.
   McCutcheon.
Description: Berlin ; Boston : De Gruyter, [2018] | Includes bibliographical
   references and index.
Identifiers: LCCN 2018024680 (print) | LCCN 2018037923 (ebook) | ISBN
   9783110560831 (electronic Portable Document Format (pdf) | ISBN
   9783110559392 | ISBN 9783110559392(print :alk. paper) | ISBN
   9783110559507(e-book epub) | ISBN 9783110560831(e-book pdf)
Subjects: LCSH: Religion--Methodology. | Religion--Study and teaching.
Classification: LCC BL41 (ebook) | LCC BL41 .M3494 2018 (print) | DDC
   200.71--dc23
LC record available at https://lccn.loc.gov/2018024680

Bibliographic information published by the Deutsche Nationalbibliothek
The Deutsche Nationalbibliothek lists this publication in the Deutsche Nationalbibliografie;
detailed bibliographic data are available in the Internet at http://dnb.dnb.de.

© 2019 Walter de Gruyter GmbH, Berlin/Boston
Dieser Band ist text- und seitenidentisch mit der 2018 erschienenen gebundenen Ausgabe.
Typesetting: Integra Software Services Pvt. Ltd.
Printing and binding: CPI books GmbH, Leck
Cover: "Monk and Baby Elephant," by SantiPhotoSS, used under license from
Shutterstock.com.

www.degruyter.com

This volume is dedicated to Bruce Lincoln, on whose work I have often relied and whose comments on my own early work played no small part in helping me to have a career.

Acknowledgements

I would like to thank the following periodicals and/or publishers for permission to revise and publish in this collection articles that originally appeared elsewhere in the following forms:

Chapter 1 originally appeared in *Numen* (published by Brill of the Netherlands) as "The Category 'Religion' in Recent Publications: Twenty Years Later," 62 (2015): 119–141.

Chapter 4 originally appeared as chapter 5 in Steffen Führding's edited book, *Method and Theory in the Study of Religion: Working Papers from Hannover*. Leiden, NL: Brill, 2017. A French translation was also published as "'L'Homme est la mesure de toute chose...': À propos de la fabrication des religions orientales par l'histoire des religions en Europe" in *Asdiwal* (the Journal of the Swiss Society for the Study of Religion) 11 (2016): 105–126.

Chapter 5 originally appeared in Routledge's journal *Culture & Religion* 18/1 (2017): 34–48.

Chapter 9 originally appeared as chapter 12 in a *Festschrift* for Tim Jensen, edited by Peter Antes, Armin W. Geertz, and Mikael Rothstein, entitled, *Contemporary Views on Comparative Religion* (153–164) and published by Equinox Publishers in 2016.

Contents

Acknowledgements —— VII

Introduction: On Fabricating Religion —— 1

1　　The Category "Religion" in Recent Publications:
　　　Twenty Years Later —— 11

2　　"It's (Not) Easy if You Try:"
　　　The Challenge to *Imagine No Religion* —— 33

3　　A Question (Still) Worth Asking about *The Religions of Man* —— 43

4　　"Man is the Measure of All Things:"
　　　On The Fabrication of Oriental Religions by European
　　　History of Religions —— 55

5　　Identifying the Meaning and End of Scholarship:
　　　What's at Stake in *Muslim Identities* —— 79

6　　Of Concepts and Entities:
　　　Varieties of Critical Scholarship —— 95

7　　Historicizing the Elephant in the Room —— 121

8　　The Magic of the Melancholy:
　　　Shifting Gears in the Study of Religion —— 141

9　　Fanfare for the Common e.g.:
　　　On the Strategic Use of the Mundane —— 161

Author Index —— 181

Subject Index —— 185

Introduction: On Fabricating Religion

I still remember – if I can trust my memory, of course – where I was when the title for my first book occurred to me. It was the published version of my dissertation, and so, to be more accurate, it's a memory of the dissertation's title dawning on me. I wrote briefly about this in the preface to *Manufacturing Religion* (1997: viii–ix), noting the importance that both J. Z. Smith's *Imagining Religion* and Edward S. Herman and Noam Chomsky's *Manufacturing Consent* had on my work. Immersed in those (and, of course, many other) books, the simple combination that resulted in the title occurred to me after I was well into writing it and was standing in the main office of what was then the graduate Centre for Religious Studies at the University of Toronto (an autonomous, cross-disciplinary unit that has long since been demoted to the graduate unit of what was back then the undergraduate Department of Religious Studies). It was my attempt to overcome the possibly idealist readings of Smith's title – readings that undermined what I read as his book's important contributions – by injecting what I took to be the more consequential language derived from Herman and Chomsky, i.e., their interest in how ways of talking about the world made certain sorts of worlds seem to be more credible, persuasive, and legitimate. How using the category religion, defined in a particular way (i.e., as unique, uncaused, irreducible, etc.), played into all this was my interest back then, and the title I came up with seemed to capture it well – at least well enough to use it also for the published version without the publisher's marketing people raising any concerns. (Though the press did veto my suggestion of a cover image from Charlie Chaplain's *Modern Times* [1936], such as the image of a dedicated worker stuck inside the gears while trying to fix them.) I had not gotten to know Jonathan very well at that point, having only met him briefly at an annual conference or two, where I'd tag along with my friends working in Christian Origins, such as when listening in on the November 1995 session entitled "Ancient Myths and Modern Theories of Christian Origins" – the first meeting of what was to be a multi-year consultation of the Society of Biblical Literature (SBL). For I'd already missed my first opportunity to have met him, in Toronto, a few years before (in the spring of 1992, to be precise), when, while a grad student, I wasn't able to attend a colloquium in which he participated and that was dedicated to the work of another famous Wilfred Cantwell Smith. (Although unplanned, that event also marked the end of the Centre since, as of 1 July 1992, it was joined with the department.) Both the papers from that Smith Conference, as it was called, and the papers from the Ancient Myths and Modern Theories consultation were published in *Method & Theory in the Study of Religion* (issue 4/1 & 2 [1992] for the former and 8/3 [1996] for the latter) – a journal with which I was then involved as a co-editor, so I at least got to work on his and others' papers from those two meetings. (Missing the Smith Conference meant it was also a missed opportunity to meet John Hick and Ninian Smart [whom I later met at a conference of the International Association for the History of Religions in Mexico City in 1995], not to mention W. C. Smith himself.)

But I eventually got to know the former Smith, J. Z., a little better and struck up a correspondence (and, I would like to think, friendship) with him – one that continued until his death in late 2017, whether by letter or the occasional email to his wife, asking her to be an intermediary. Although I no longer have a copy of the letter that I wrote to him (perhaps it was when I sent him a copy of *Manufacturing Religion*, as I recall doing), I have what I believe still remains an unpublished essay of his that he sent as part of his reply; originally presented on Nov. 7, 1996, at a conference at what was then Western Maryland College (known, as of July 2002, as McDaniel College), organized by Greg Alles and Frank Reynolds, on the topic of "Reconstructing a History of Religions: Problems and Possibilities." Smith's paper carried the misleadingly simple title, "Why Imagine Religion?" On the top-right corner of the typewritten manuscript, complete with his hand-numbered pagination, Jonathan had written by hand "Russ – see pp. 8–9;" for I'd written him concerning the debt I owed to his own essay collection, *Imagining Religion*, while also noting my more materialist bent in what was then my newly published book – hence my choice to veer away from his language of the imagination.

So, flipping to page 8 of his manuscript, I read as follows (I include the underlining to convey the feel of that typewritten manuscript):

> When I originally drafted what became the prefatory lines of Imagining Religion as a lecture at Brandeis for a conference organized by Jacob Neusner and published by him under the title Take Judaism for Example, a conference which attempted to test out an earlier formulation of mine that the data we study must be taken as exemplary, as e.g.'s, in terms of Judaism as both an object of scholarly attention and as an item in the curriculum, I wrote, and rejected, three other verbs: "invent," "represent," and "fabricate," with the latter surviving through several drafts. I wanted a constructive verb that allowed a parallelism between "their" activity and "ours" and which allowed, as well, an ambivalence as to the status of the endeavor with respect to the fictive and the actual. (Hence the survival of "fabricate" which means both "to build" and "to lie")

Although he goes on to further elaborate the way in which he had tried to use the notion of imagination – such as citing Wallace Stevens' dictum: "imagination is the power of the mind over the possibilities of things" (citing page 136 from the 1951 edition of *The Necessary Angel: Essays on Reality and the Imagination* [New York: Vintage Books]) – it was his comment on the idea of fabricating that was more directly in reply to my point about the possibly idealist connotations to his earlier book's title. For example, in the 1983 book to which he referred above, Neusner's edited volume, *Take Judaism, For Example: Studies Toward the Comparison of Religion* (Chicago: University of Chicago Press), Smith's chapter, "No Need to Travel to the Indies: Judaism and the Study of Religion," phrased it as follows: "I take it as axiomatic that it is by an act of human will, through languages and history, through words and memory, that we are able to fabricate a meaningful world and give place to ourselves. Education comes to life through the tensions generated by the double sense of fabrication: to build and to lie" (217; this essay is a forerunner not just to the now-famous opening of *Imagining Religion* but also his still-useful chapter, "The Introductory Course: Less is Better," in Mark Juergensmeyer's edited book, *Teaching the Introductory Course in Religious Studies: A Sourcebook* [1990]). Here Smith had not only anticipated the practical notion of production that a decade later became important in my own work, but he had even considered how to complicate what I eventually termed manufacturing by using a witty double entendre to ensure that readers mull over both the art *and* artifice of our cultural creations.

Should readers happen to have the main title of this current book in mind, then perhaps it is obvious why I open this collection of essays by citing Smith's unpublished 1996 lecture (let alone why I've opted for a cover image that, though referencing one of the chapter's topics, can be seen as religious *but only if you want it to be*); while I have often relied upon his work in the past and hopefully have made evident the significant manner in which it has shaped much of my thinking on what it means to study religion, I have never forgotten his comments on that wily but, lucky for me, unused title. For here, in a word, we find both analysis and critique: the effort to make apparent the careful *craft* required to make something into an item of discourse as well as the *crafty* inventiveness needed to authorize that creation by erasing any evidence of the manufacturers' fingerprints from their product, to make whatever it was that they had produced seem as if it had arrived under its own steam, as they used to say. (Whether effective or not, my common use of anecdote, always to illustrate larger theoretical points, and my use of the first person singular throughout much of my work are intended as an effort to make apparent our sometimes overlooked smudges on the artifacts, i.e., claims and arguments being offered in our work.) This two-part significance implied by the term fabricate, I know, also influenced my colleague at Alabama Vaia Touna in the titles carried by volumes in a series that she edits for Equinox Publishers. Editions in the Working With Culture on the Edge book series are so far entitled *Fabricating Origins*, *Fabricating Difference*, and *Fabricating Identities* (the first and last edited by myself and the second by Steven Ramey with whom I also work at Alabama). But, as yet, there's not been a *Fabricating Religion* to appear in print, as best I can tell. There's been a *Fabricating Faith*, however, written by Richard Hagenston and published in 2014 by Polebridge Press. Significantly subtitled *How Christianity Became a Religion Jesus Would Have Rejected*, the book takes the sort of normative approach to origins (an approach that counts as data for the authors who contributed to the above mentioned *Fabricating Origins*, by the way) that one might expect from an author writing on religion but who is also an ordained minister (in Hagenston's case, of the United Methodist Protestant denomination). But I would hope that readers of this collection quickly understand that Smith's double entendre must be kept in mind to make sense of my title and contents, since the chapters are, to varying extents, all concerned not just with the techniques of rhetorical and thus social creation but also the legitimization of those creations – seeing this two-step process as fundamental to how we, quite literally, *make sense of the world* and then *try to make that particular sense stick*.

Before proceeding, a few words about the following chapters might be worth offering. More than half of these essays appear here in print for the first time (earlier versions of chapters 1, 4, 5, and 9 have already appeared in print), though everything, to varying degrees, has been revised. (An opening footnote in each chapter provides additional background on the essay, on either its original publication or providing some details concerning its composition.) None have yet been collected into a book of my own and, unlike a recent collection of mine whose contents spanned more than 20 years, all were written within just the past few years. Given their thematic unity, I feel warranted in pulling them together in this collection – for I recognize that there's no reason necessarily to assume that a reader had already found this extended review essay in that journal or that chapter in this book. Though I've been told that I'm in a rut concerning my research interests – a claim that, as I've noted on other occasions, one would never even dream of leveling at specialists in any number of other areas in our, or any other, academic field (telling one something about the sort of rhetoric used to minimize the corner of the field in which I find myself working) – the chapters in the present volume unapologetically continue to press an argument that I've been exploring for some time, one that this book's title makes apparent. For although many today seem to be more than willing to entertain that the worlds that we all inhabit are culturally *created*, I have a nagging suspicion that, when pressed, it becomes apparent that most mean by that culturally *mediated*, i.e., they imply that some sort of real, exterior world is simply re-packaged by our local concepts and historically situated habits. It is the position that I identified some time ago when seeing a host of people apparently willing to consider the category religion to be an historical creation but that they then assumed named some actually religious element in the items so classified – i.e., they assumed that people just naturally were *religious* though they might not all call it *religion*. This tendency to presume that the adjective lurks below the noun (or, as claimed in one chapter, that an actual entity may predate the social concept), with only the latter having the marks of history, strikes me as a troublingly partial application of the sort of critique that some of us have been offering for more than two decades now – a denuded critique that seems to me to be a strategic way to appear to acknowledge the critique while dismissing it at the same time. It's a rhetorical strategy not unlike minimizing a research area with which one disagrees by characterizing it as a rut in which one gets stuck. (That the word rut is thought to derive from the French *route*, naming simply a path or roadway, opened by force [hence its presumed link to the Latin *ruptura* and eventually the English rupture], is a rather nice illustration of the manner in which normative aims can efficiently turn a variety of ways into the one that is authorized and all of its muddy deviations.)

For instance, consider the late John Hinnells's introduction to his edited collection, *Routledge Companion to the Study of Religion* (New York & London: Routlege, 2005); on page 6 we read as follows:

> In my opinion there is no such thing as "religion", there are only the religions, i.e., those people who identify themselves as members of a religious group, Christians, Muslims, etc. An act or thought is religious when the person concerned thinks they are practising their "religion". Organizations are religious when people involved think they are functioning religiously.

On the face of it, this seems to be nicely in step with the sort of analysis that scholars, including myself, have pursued. (Though it's worth noting that his reliance on a philosophically idealist position is certainly at odds with most who champion this position, such as when he writes a little later: "My general position in discussing religions is that people are what they believe they are.") But his resistance to understand the thing called religion as adequately identified as but culture, expressed a few lines later, hints at something else going on. And the suspicion roused by that refusal is confirmed the moment one realizes the list of religions that he so easily goes on to use to illustrate his argument, including not just the already-mentioned Christianity and Islam, but also Zoroastrianism and Hinduism. The problem, of course, is that the Latin-based category religion is native to only one of the four (i.e., to medieval, and later, European Christianity), so it is possible that even if a self-bounded group known as, for instance, the Zoroastrians could be said to exist, its members are not naturally or necessarily thinking (to stick with Hinnells's approach) that they are being religious when they do this or that action (much less that they are performing a ritual). Should their ancestors have had historical contact with, say, incoming Europeans or if contemporaries are internationally mobile and global in their outlook then, sure, they might think that this or that so-called Zoroastrian act was being religious or was a ritual – but maybe not. For maybe it's something that they don't much think about as they do it – like the way readers of this very book likely don't give a second thought to the significance of many of the things that they do throughout the day, let alone concern themselves with classifying them along a continuum stretching from similar to different in relation to all of the other things that they also do daily. That is, Hinnells here nicely represents the problem with the partial critique: the very fact that he organizes part of the world into religion in distinction from other nonreligious parts of the world (which, like many, he terms secular) and then so unselfconsciously is able to group things together so as to include four examples *regardless what their own members might think or say* – which, you recall, was his own criterion for how the category works – is what ought to occupy our attention. For, much like the presumption that the adjective escapes the critique of the noun, he seems to assume that, while the concept religion, in the singular, is invented, the religions, in the plural, are out there waiting to be named and compared.

But please be clear: I've never argued that people can only be studied as they self-designate themselves – if that was the case, then all scholarship would be a form of autobiography and my hope is that scholarship is something other than that. And I've also never claimed that scholars are unable to use their own terms in their studies of others – if that was the case then we couldn't study other people's cultures, given the specifically Latin-based origins of that term, let alone talk about other people's genomes, since not everyone on the planet likely talks that way about heredity, let alone knows what is meant by a haploid set of chromosomes or even our concept heredity itself. Instead, the critique is far simpler – maybe I should say subtle but consequential: scholars, I maintain, have no choice but to use local concepts and concerns, which they apply in unfamiliar situations (we ourselves are situated but do cross-cultural work, after all), opening a negotiation between the expected and the unexpected, whereby their prior interests and assumptions enable them to identify something in the new that's seen by them as either like or unlike that which they take for granted. Meanwhile, the distance between the old and the new opens an opportunity for all sorts of things to happen – such as seeing both the familiar and the strange in a new light (or so goes that old saying in our field about the strange and the familiar). The problem is that the familiar, the local, and the expected are often seen as the norm rather than a heuristic and, when it comes to our field, instead of applying the category religion, knowing the historical baggage and practical implications that come with it and thus knowing that it is how *we* with our concerns, assumptions, and interests are trying to understand the rest of the world, it is ontologized and normalized. The familiar, local, and expected are even "inevitablized" and thereby used as if they name an actual human universal, thereby operationalizing an unarticulated and thus undefended theory of human nature in the midst of such a seemingly innocent thing as describing some group's rituals, myths, or beliefs. The problem, then, is a failure of scholars to see themselves as akin to the people whom they study – as historical, social actors who are always situated and invested (though in different situations with investments of their own, of course); it is a failure to take seriously the so-called self-reflexive turn to which we sometimes just pay lip service, what with the perhaps tempting allure of making universal (yet curiously self-beneficial) claims about the human.

Because my suggestions for how the field *might* work seem always to evade many of my readers – since many of my writings are, improperly I'd suggest, routinely asserted to be negatively deconstructive and never positively constructive (an opposition I do not accept, by the way) – I've added a subtitle to this book that points us in a new direction, outlined in chapters 7 and 8, but explicitly addressed in a concluding chapter that makes clear where I think our field could be moving. For those who wish to retain some immutable specialness in their work (i.e., the adjective lurking behind the noun), then the route that I propose will more than likely be read as sadly insufficient, I know, given that it throws their precious baby out with the bathwater, as anti-reductionists used to say all the time. (But let's just be honest: Eliade reduced religion as much as anyone, it's just that he reduced it to the undefined and supposedly universal experience of the Sacred instead of such mundane things as economics or social forces.) For if the study of religion needs (but for what reason?!) to retain an assumption of inner, transhistorical uniqueness to which only we have access via our unique methods, then the field as I understand and practice it will be utterly unfamiliar, strange, and unappealing to such readers. (Surely, they're the ones who have claimed all along that McCutcheon is out to destroy the field – what I greet as a tired caricature of my work but one which continues nonetheless – whether in published pieces or, now, social media comments.) But for those willing to see our work, as scholars of religion, as being but one component of wider, cross-disciplinary studies of *how people signify their worlds* – and here we return to the two-fold effects so nicely named in this notion of fabrication – then my proposal may be curious and worth considering. For the challenge of the approach that I outline is to be able to entertain that *the rhetoric of specialness is itself rather mundane but effective and thus interesting nonetheless*. For the world is filled with mundane things, but that doesn't stop us from being curious about them – perhaps curious as to why some find it so difficult to see them as anything but extraordinary.

Before concluding, I should express my appreciation for Walter de Gruyter's interest in this set of papers; in the academic study of religion there may be no more important publisher. I have memories of first Mouton books from The Hague (bought by de Gruyter in 1977) and then Mouton de Gruyter and finally

Walter de Gruyter books lining the shelves in the various offices I've occupied throughout the years – from the late Jacques Waardenburg's still-important *Classical Approaches to the Study of Religion* (1973; see also the new edition of his volume one in 2017, which I was honored to open with a new preface) to all of those volumes published in both its Religion and Society and the Religion and Reason series. Though there sometimes can seem to be a gap between the field as practiced in at least Europe and then also in North America, the volumes published under Walter de Grutyer's imprint strike me as having influence regardless where one is situated – thus the honor I feel to find my work joining those who have already been put into print by this still-independent and time-honored publishing house. In fact, there's a bit of a sense of "coming home" in finding my work now published here, since, from 1993–1997, *Method & Theory in the Study of Religion* (*MTSR,* the above-mentioned peer-reviewed journal) was published by what was then their Mouton de Gruyter division, making this publisher the first with which I (one of its co-editors during that time) became formally involved. The small but still significant editorial stipend that the press provided helped all of us to attend conferences in those early years, and we learned much about publishing from our working relationship with their editorial and production teams, and so I'm grateful to still be around and to be carrying out work that their editors are happy to publish.

Also, I should mention the many students with whom I have worked at the University of Alabama – from those in 100-level introductory classes to majors in senior seminars and main office workers who conspired with me on both substantial and fun little projects, as well as our new M.A. students – and also the staff and faculty who have helped to reinvent the department that I have happily called my academic home since 2001. As I have described elsewhere, I was hired to come to Tuscaloosa so that, together, we could revive a public university's department dedicated to studying religion and, although not every initiative has paid off in quite the same way, we have been remarkably successful – a success that, had we done it in a traditional way (one that was premised on the uniquely ineffable quality of our object of study), I speculate that many would have taken notice, since it reinforced a way of talking about religion that's very appealing to people both within and outside of the academy: we need to study religion because it is a *special case*. But we've done it by taking the path less travelled: by assuming that our objects of study are rather ordinary and everyday but, as noted above, fascinating nonetheless – a fascination that is the result of *our* questions and *our* tools. Our method works, though it comes at a price that some are unwilling to pay, for they now must refocus on techniques of classification (i.e., the process of specialization) rather than on the seemingly and already special things that are in fact produced by means of these institutionalized classification systems.

In a word, we must attend to the fabrications – in both senses of the word.

Before closing, though, and after tipping my hat to my copyeditor, Becky Brown (whose in-text comments not only helped shorten some excessively [or should I say impressively?] long sentences but also let me know that members of Gen X know the lyrics to the some of the music with which I grew up), one thing remains: I need to say a few words about my dedication.

Bruce Lincoln, whose work I first started reading, alongside Smith, while writing my dissertation (but whom I had yet to meet in person), turned out to be the external reader commissioned, early in 1995 by Oxford University Press, to assess the manuscript for what had been my dissertation and which eventually became my first book – the book that I mentioned in the opening line of this very introduction. I still clearly recall receiving the email from Cynthia Read, OUP's longtime editor, while I was an instructor at the University of Tennessee, alerting me to the fact that the outside reader's comments were coming to me by mail, for my response – comments by which she was encouraged, she wrote, given how critical of manuscripts this reader usually was. Those who know Bruce might be neither surprised by that line nor that the letter that soon arrived was not anonymous – readers, he noted in the letter, would better be able to gauge the comments in the assessment if they knew from whom they came.

I can imagine plenty of people (some of whom were on my doctoral examination committee, by the way – an exam whose outcome, at least to me, was in question until the very end) who could have read *Manufacturing Religion* and dismissed it out-of-hand (as a few reviewers did, in fact). But Bruce didn't; his assessment was generous, and his critical comments made the re-write far stronger (in fact, the last chapter is there because of his recommendation to write something about where we now ought to be going). Simply put, his own well-deserved reputation – did I add that he was their sole outside reader? – opened a space for me to say something and thereby start to build a reputation of my own. While I have no way to prove it, of course, I've always assumed that the OUP imprimatur on my CV played no small part in some of the good fortune I had early in my career – eventually obtaining a tenure-track job, which took me from east Tennessee to southwest Missouri, being rather high on that list, of course. But it probably also afforded me the opportunity to put some of my energy into a wide variety of other sorts of scholarly projects – i.e., turning attention to writing essays, continuing to edit journals, thinking up anthologies, and co-editing a handbook, even concocting a book series or two – confident that the purists and class-conscious among us might at least be satisfied by that one imprint. And because of that, I've also had the good fortune to have been able to assist a few others to get into print (some for the first time) by means of those projects that I then (and still do) felt free to tackle.

While I would hardly want to trace whatever success I've so far had in my career to any one isolated moment, any singular cause (i.e., beware of monocausal theories), Lincoln's rigorous but kind and helpful comments on that manuscript have surely played a far larger role than I can likely imagine. So while I've thanked him privately, long ago, for his intended and unintended contributions to this thing that I've come to call a career, this collection of essays is my opportunity to say so publicly.

1 The Category "Religion" in Recent Publications: Twenty Years Later

> "[R]eligion" is not the inevitable outcome of an encounter between different peoples; the concept does not automatically generate itself as an anthropological abstraction.
> (Josephson 2012: 71)

Over twenty years have passed since I first wrote a review essay assessing the place of the category "religion" in recent work (McCutcheon 1995; a revised version of that earlier essay was included as a chapter in McCutcheon 1997). Of course, it was not the first academic paper to focus on the category religion,[1] but I think that it was among an early group of publications that attempted to talk about a set of shared assumptions and techniques that we now call the discourse on religion, focusing attention not on debates concerning either the adequacy or inadequacy of this or that definition (as if there was some stable thing in the world against which the adequacy of definitions could be measured),[2] but, instead, on the very fact that

---

[1] For example, see Chidester (2014: 9), where he cites the naturalist William Lucas Distant (1845–1922) from 1877, calling for scholars to "discard the use of the term Religion in anthropological discussions altogether as being an undefined term, and as such not admissible in science."

[2] As I believe I have noted elsewhere on previous occasions, this is the sort of naïve realism seen in those who, for example, cite Buddhism as a part of their critique of definitions of religion as belief in god – "But what about Buddhism?!" they reply. Regardless, the utility of this traditionally idealist definition (slight variations of which are now favored by many cognitivists in our field, e.g., Jeppe Sinding Jensen's current definition of religion as "semantic and cognitive networks comprising ideas, behaviours and institutions in relation to counter-intuitive superhuman agents, objects and posits" (2014: 8), such critics fail to understand definitions as actively stipulative and not merely passively descriptive. How they already knew Buddhism to be a religion and thus a counter example – i.e., that it necessarily ought to constitute a member of the class, a constitution denied by what they perceive to be an excessively narrow definition – is, of course, left unexplored. So what at first appears to be a dispute at the level of data is, in fact, a difference at the level of theory (if we agree that definitions are theories in miniature); such critics are

---

Note: As described in the opening of this chapter, this was originally a follow-up to a review essay published twenty years before this chapter originally appeared in print in the same journal. Implicitly, this marks – at least to my way of thinking – how much more seriously we have come to take those who study the discourse on religion, i.e., the category religion itself as well as its social effects. Given the rather marginal role played by such work in the early to mid-1990s, that this subfield is now populated by a variety of works worth commenting on in the following essays indicates that studies of the discourse on religion have gained considerable momentum (something also evident in the work of those who wish to limit the scope of such work).

some of us think and act *as if* there is such a distinct thing in the world prior to our naming it, a pre-existent and universally recognizable domain in social life, that *requires* naming and study, either to be appreciated, disparaged, or explained.³

That essay – which looked at ten different volumes (monographs, essay collections, conference proceedings, etc.), mostly published in the early 1990s – concluded as follows:

> The fundamental theoretical and methodological differences among the approaches to "religion" examined in this survey carries the message that debates on the adequacy of "religion," and just how one constructs it, will only be productive when scholars become self-critically aware of the theoretical assumptions and tactical agendas that they carry within their studies ... [O]ur continued reflection on definitions and theories of religion, far from being abstract obsessions and examples of navel-gazing, have concrete implications for the future of the institutionalized status of the study of religion. Indeed, Waardenburg is correct: "the current debate about the concept of religion is not as innocent as it may seem" [citing Waardenburg 1992: 226]. (306)

Despite the common way that many scholars now talk about criticisms of the category religion – not dissimilar to the manner in which the terms "method & theory" (once provocatively alien, perhaps even dangerous terms) now routinely appear on C.V.s and in job ads – the question is whether much has changed in the past two decades, other than obligatory references to these critiques. Although discourse analysis has become so commonplace as to seem passé to some, and while many of us claim to be self-reflexive in our use of categories, the world religions textbook market shows no signs of slowing down, the "religion and ..." rubric continues to grow, the turn toward material and embodied religion sounds suspiciously like a reborn form of phenomenology of religion, and the increasing number of studies on secularism seem intent merely to contextualize "the secular" while presuming that the religious (variously known by such other terms as spirituality, faith, belief, etc.) is somehow natural, ancient, panhuman and thus was merely corralled, privatized, and thereby controlled (appropriately so or not, all depends on your own views, of course) by the 17th and 18th centuries' early inventions of this thing we've come to know (at least in English) as secularism.

That is, as I've written on other occasions, we see here a strategically partial approach to the study of binary systems – if, that is, one agrees that such sets as

---

employing (and thereby trying to advance) a competing yet, unfortunately, undisclosed definition and thus theory of religion.

3 Although earlier in my career I was indeed interested solely in what I then termed the discourse on *sui generis* religion, I have come to be interested in any and all uses of the term and not just those that posit religion to be irreducibly unique.

sacred/profane, religious/secular as well as the various attendant pairs of belief/ practice, experience/expression, private/public, and original/derivative are, as with all binary pairs, necessarily co-constitutive, with neither appearing first nor one exclusively anchoring the other. This was a position argued by Bill Arnal and myself in an earlier essay collection we co-authored, *The Sacred is the Profane* (2013). As we phrased it in the introduction:

> It is just this sort of shallow historicization that occurs when historians of the secular naturalize one part of what is supposedly a binary – as if prior to the invention of cooking, we all somehow just knew that our food was raw. When it comes to recent studies of religion and not-religion, what we therefore often find is simply a repackaged version of the old, old story of how the primitive world was once homogenously religious and, with the advent of modernity, was sadly disenchanted – we could go so far as calling this story's rebirth the new secularization thesis. (13)

Despite his influence over many who now write on this topic, I see such a problem in Talal Asad's work which, as most recently described by David Chidester, argued that "this notion of religion as an autonomous cultural system converged with the contemporary interests of secular liberals in confining religion and liberal Christians in defending religion within modern societies. Asad's critique, therefore, was not merely about the validity of Geertz's definition; it was also about the politics of defining religion as an autonomous cultural system" (2014: 308). Religion and secularism, in this approach, seem not to be parasites of each other (as Tim Fitzgerald phrases it [2011: 4]) but, rather, the problem, according to that approach, is in confining religion to a seemingly apolitical, interior domain when, somehow, we all seem to know that religion (or whatever else we call it) is not only real but extends to the whole person, the whole of society, defying the management attempts of what is portrayed as the recently invented secular state.

So it is with this particular set of somewhat suspicious eyes – eyes that have seen their share of critiques of the category that nonetheless employ the adjective as if it still names something distinctive (some authentic, ethereal quality that avoids the much lamented reifications of the noun) – that I looked over a variety of recent works on the category religion. That is, works on the social and political effects of classifying some things *as* religious, the implications of grouping them together as sharing a common, core trait (e.g., although these practices are Hindu and those beliefs are Christian, they're all religious), and then seeing them as being in substantive distinction from all things not categorized in this manner.

As a first example, consider Alicia Turner's paper, published in the inaugural issue of the Irish Society for the Academic Study of Religions' open-access journal, entitled "Religion, the Study of Religion and other Products of Transnational and Colonial Imaginings" (Turner 2014). Despite opening by paying specific attention to the practical uses for and effects of the category religion – for both colonizers and those who were once colonized – it soon becomes clear that her own ability to select certain things in the world *as* Buddhist as well as the assumption that these so-named people and practices are directly relevant to the expertise of the scholar of religion, are not considered further evidence of the category religion's utility and effects. For instance, there is her disagreement with Jonathan Z. Smith's famous (but for some, perhaps Turner among them, now infamous) statement, "… while there is a staggering amount of data, of phenomena, of human experiences and expression that might be characterized as religious – there is no data for religion. Religion is solely the creation of the scholar's study" (Smith 1982: xi). To Smith's claim, she replies:

> I am here to tell you that Smith was flat wrong. 'Religion,' that is the category of religion, is not the invention of the scholar's pen. If only it were – because we scholars of religion do not have that much power and impact in the world. Our books are read by our colleagues, but they tend not to build great bridges or great empires. To claim that the power to imagine and construct the category of religion was contained in the scholar's pen was a bit of academic hubris on Smith's part. (Turner 2014: 14)

Apart from noting that such a reading fails to exhibit much hermeneutic generosity (inasmuch as the intended audience for Smith's 1982 essay collection was surely his fellow scholars, inviting *them* to be cognizant of the effects of *their* classificatory labors), I think that she fails to understand that, being a scholar, her own work itself constitutes but one more example of "the scholar's study" mentioned by Smith – a wonderfully ambiguous phrase, inasmuch as it signifies both our work *and* the space in which we do it.[4] That is to say, while we can discuss further how many people, both inside and outside the academy, now use this surprisingly successful Latin-based classifier to go about the business of making their worlds sensible (perhaps drawing into question Smith's reliance on the qualifier "solely"), it does not take away from the fact that (a) scholars, along with bureaucrats and administrators, deployed this term on the frontier, in situations of contact (as argued by Smith [1998: 275], with regard to the "explosion of data" associated with the colonial era, nicely demonstrated in detail by Chidester [1996]), in an effort to understand what was for them the new, the strange, and the dangerous; but also that (b) her very classification of Buddhism in Burma

---

4 In recognizing the double entendre, I think of James Clifford and George Marcus' still-important essay collection, *Writing Culture* (1986); even those who critique the so-called armchair scholarship of those who fail to do fieldwork carry with them the concepts and assumptions acquired while reading in that armchair in their study or in the library. They then put all of this into practice by means of the questions they post to the Other out in the field.

as something that a scholar of religion has expertise in discussing is itself an instance of precisely what I read Smith to have been examining in that classic quotation. Curiously, scholars of religion who resist the sort of self-consciousness he recommends a few lines lower in that influential introduction assume that their own work is somehow exempt, that they aren't the ones whom Smith was addressing. For it is the very fact that (and thus the practical effects of) these assorted items are all defined and collected together *as* Buddhist and then understood *as* religious, *as* distinct from other affinities and allegiances, and thus *as* meaningful and in need of interpretation, that attracts the attention of a scholar of this category, not simply how an already and obviously constituted group of Buddhists use the category to achieve their own counter-colonial effects (interesting as studying that may be).

I see a similar problem to a recent critique of Smith's well-known claim, this time coming in Kathryn Lofton's untitled article on pedagogy – an article oddly classified by the editors of the *Journal of the American Academy of Religion* as a review essay of Chris Lehrich's edited collection of Smith's writings on pedagogy and the liberal arts, *On Teaching Religion* (2013). "I would not be the first person to observe," she writes after quoting the section in question from *Imagining Religion*, "that there is something dazzlingly absurd about such a claim" (536). But I would counter that it can be judged as "dazzlingly absurd" *only if* we first presume that this thing we now call religion is somehow already there prior to it becoming a discursive object for us or, for that matter, for anyone else, at the moment the term is used, as noted above, to collect and identity just this and not that *as* religious, for whatever desired effect. For if, along with Lofton, we presume that, in critiquing the position represented by Smith, "the thing itself" is somehow lost in his call for rigorous self-consciousness, resulting in "a coldness that often leads readers of Smith to feel he is explaining well the abstract reason behind a ritual, myth, or a community decision, but that he is not capturing anything like their anthropological or psychological reality" (2014: 537), then, of course, the attention to scholarly self-consciousness that he recommends will indeed seem absurd (perhaps even dazzlingly so). In that case, we all just seem to know that (not unlike that proverbial lonely tree falling in the forest) it is there long before we started talking about it. But what if, instead of being concerned in our *analysis* to convey back to readers the anthropological and psychological reality some of them might presume their *practices* to have,[5] our attention was directed toward the way in which some scholars are confident that the thing they

---

5 I am here implying Brubaker and Cooper's distinction (2000: 4) between categories of social and political practice (what we might otherwise term folk categories) versus their retooling as useful categories of social and political analysis.

call religion is indeed really in the so-called believer's mind? Then, much as Jean-François Bayart (2005) recommends studying not identity but the prior identification practices that made this thing called identity appear so anthropologically and psychologically real in the first place, we would then study the continual constitution and reconstitution of just this part of the world *as* religious, *as* real, *as* authoritative, in the very act of using the term. This would be true whether used by scholars or anyone else, for that matter – also recognizing full well that many of the things that count *for us* as religion, that are taught in our classes and included in our books, arise from the actions of people for whom the term continues to be an alien import. In this way, we would be examining the discursive formation of that so-called reality (and the social formation that coalesces with it) rather than lamenting its supposed loss in analytic studies.

What's more, even to those for whom the category religion has become a familiar element of their folk lexicon, I would wager that (akin to what I consider to be the late Frits Staal's still classic study of ritual) *it is highly unlikely that, in the midst of being religious, a person perceives themselves as being religious* – at least as their actions might be defined by the observer, armed with some definition of the term, or perhaps even by the participants themselves but from a hindsight vantage point, reflecting back on the act, for a particular purpose or in response to a specific query from a researcher. Instead, despite our best efforts to just carefully watch and listen and then infer (as Tanya Luhrmann, who is equally concerned with conveying the anthropological and psychological reality of the object for the people we study, describes her skill as an anthropologist [2012: xx]), in the seemingly authentic moment, there's presumably little self-consciousness present or meaning-making taking place. Like all actors immersed in social situations, they're likely absorbed, as Staal phrased it (1979), within the implicit rule system for the situation in which they find themselves, concerned with propriety, i.e., knowing when to stand, sit, kneel, speak, listen, etc. (It is just as I have pointed out before: readers of this sentence are likely not aware of being literate, and whatever that implies, but are, instead, probably just immersed in just using the rules of the written English language. They are completely absorbed and thus unaware that they are engaged in an activity that we commonly call reading – that is, until they read and then process those last few words, at which point *people become readers* and likely perceive their immediately past actions *as* actions for the first time, all due to an unexpected query or poke from a nonparticipant armed with the categories and curiosities that she brought with her.) So, instead of trying to define religion the right way, instead of thinking that our job is just to listen and watch and then later infer, or rather than presuming some sort of reality to attend the so-called immediacy of experience – a reality that our studies must somehow convey or take account of, whether we think it has ontological status or not – our studies could be directed toward examining the constitution of that perceived reality, or what we might just call the interpellative effect (recalling Althusser's work on identity formation [2001], of course).⁶

It is this difference between, on the one hand, those scholars wishing to more adequately represent the realness of the object under study – as either they perceive it themselves or, as is more likely the case, as they presume the participant under study perceives it⁷ – and, on the other, those who are interested in how this so-called realness is created in the first place that defines a longstanding divide in the academic study of religion (a divide at which the longstanding theology vs. religious studies distinction fails to get). In fact, it is a divide evidenced in the work of those strategically partial critics of "religion" who merely wish to *correct* scholars on their so-called misrepresentations of other people's religious lives.⁸ This is why it is so refreshing to come across Brent Nongbri's *Before Religion: A History of A Modern Concept* (2013)⁹; although relatively short (almost half of the book comprises detailed endnotes and references) and offering some arguments that might strike readers conversant with the literature as familiar (and thus it reads more like a survey with an emphasis on our anachronistic approach to the

---

6 See McCutcheon 2012 for my own views on how scholars ought to approach the study of experience.

7 As noted earlier, I read this as also being the interest of the anthropologist Tanya Luhrmann, whose widely published/blogged work (on such topics as the reality of prayer and its practical benefits for the participant) is aimed at taking seriously the anthropological and psychological perspective of U.S. evangelical Christians – doing so "by taking the outsider's perspective into the heart of faith" (2012: xi). It is difficult, however, for me to see this work as anything but a reaction to critiques of religion by calling upon scholars (in a long line of such calls) to "take religion seriously." That taking religion seriously does not necessarily mean simply describing or conserving the participant's own view of their world is, I think, an important point to add. For more on Luhrmann's work, see http://luhrmann.net/my-research/ (accessed Sept. 1, 2017).

8 See the already quoted *Empire of Religion* (Chidester 2014), a book dedicated to Jonathan Z. Smith for a brand new study of the role played by representations of colonial-era Africa in the imperialist foundations of the European science of Comparative Religion. As important as such studies are – and they are! – in making evident that power politics were and remain at the very heart of our academic pursuits, as with *Savage Systems*, it strikes me that the animating force behind the argument is not to examine the creation of the discourse on religion (regardless how anyone defines or employs the term). Instead, it is to make evident how colonial scholars and administrators misportrayed other people's religions, thereby carrying with the argument a presumed norm as to what their religion really was or is if only it was studied correctly. Or, as he phrases it in his preface, "we might still find that the ancestors of the study of religion were wrong, but we will see how they were wrong in interesting and important ways" (2014: x).

9 See also the podcast with Nongbri, posted at The Religious Studies Project, on his book; http://www.religiousstudiesproject.com/podcast/before-religion-nongbri/ (accessed Aug. 14, 2017).

study of classical data[10]), the very fact that enough work has now been done on the category religion to warrant such a synthetic study is, for me at least, rather encouraging. It brings to mind Kevin Schilbrack's "Religions: Are There Any?" (2010; Schilbrack's work on "religion" is discussed in detail in chapter 6) – not because they share the same position (e.g., Schilbrack, in his more recent work, makes evident that, knowing there's something about so-called religions that warrants grouping them together, he's interested mainly in a more precise, better definition, rather than interested in the implications of definition itself [2013][11]) but because they both make evident that there is now in our field a relatively coherent group of scholars who study "religion" and not religion. While Wilfred Cantwell Smith, Jonathan Z. Smith, Talal Asad, Tomoko Masuzawa, Daniel Dubuisson, Tim Fitzgerald, Naomi Goldenberg, David Chidester, Richard King, and others (such as the other members of the UK-based Critical Religion Association[12]) are hardly in agreement on all points, their shared interest in studying the practical effects of scholarly and bureaucratic classification is certainly worth recognizing as a recent development in the field.

Nongbri's book should therefore be distinguished from those that seem to know that religion was already there before we arrived. Unlike many of those who study, say, "religion in America" – a place where the term religion has been so widely adopted as an item of folk discourse that a scholar might be tempted to begin to see the term as naming something universal and self-evident, since everyone is talking about it already – his training is in the study of antiquity (originally

---

10 See McCutcheon 2014: chapter 14, "'As it Was in the Beginning ...': The Modern Problem of the Ancient Self" (a paper first published in 2000), for my own example of the temptation to anachronistically read ancient sources. See also chapter 5, "The Resiliency of Conceptual Anachronisms: On the Limits of 'the West' and 'Religion'" (a reprinted review essay of Daniel Dubuisson's *The Western Construction of Religion* [2003]) and Vaia Touna's introduction to the essay, in Miller 2015.

11 As Schilbrack writes, "And Martin Reisebrodt continues, saying that pure functional definitions dilute the concept of religion 'to the point of futility, considering barbecues with guitar music, soccer games, shopping in supermarkets, or art exhibitions to be religious phenomena. Everything becomes 'somehow' or 'implicitly' religious. Others criticize the concept of religion as an invention of Western modernity that should not be applied to premodern or non-Western societies. In their opinion, Hinduism, Buddhism, and Confucianism are Western inventions that cannot be termed religions without perpetuating colonialist thinking. When soccer games are seen as religious phenomena and the recitation of Buddhist sutras is not, something has obviously gone wrong.' I agree with this complaint. Not every certainty should be called a dogma. Not every falsehood should be called a myth. The study of religions will be best served by a definition of religion that is more precise" (2013: 292).

12 See http://criticalreligion.org/ (accessed Aug. 20, 2017). This group is also discussed further in chapter 6.

the literature around the study of the early Christian rhetor Paul), where it is painfully obvious that no one in the Mediterranean region, back then, was walking around talking about their religion or bundling together those things in their world that *we* now routinely collect together as specifically *religious* things when we study *them*. As Nongbri phrases it:

> If we want to go on talking about ancient Mesopotamian religion, ancient Greek religion, or any other ancient religion, we should always bear in mind that we are talking about something modern when we do so. We are not naming something any ancient person would recognize. ... If we fail to make this reflexive move, we turn our ancient sources into well-polished mirrors that show us only ourselves and our own institutions. (2013: 153)

Nongbri takes the past seriously as a foreign country, and so his attention to this inevitable gap between modern and ancient – or, better put, the modern invention of the ancient – makes the casual insertion of the word religion into translations of ancient Greek, Arabic, or Sanskrit texts, for example, a problem to be studied rather than a commonplace truism to be read over and thereby naturalized.[13] So, while agreeing that so long as one defines it clearly, making the category religion an ad hoc scholarly tool rather than a term thought merely to describe a stable identity or natural kind inhering in the object, there is no reason why it cannot be self-consciously used at the level of redescription (after all, we use "culture" and "ethnicity" to talk about people whether they employ these terms or not in their acts of self-description). He also concludes (2013: 154–159) that studies of the very act of defining something *as* religion (like studying the recent controversy and court case in the U.S. over defining yoga as religious or not[14]) might provide one possible future for the field (thereby citing Smith 2004 as an example). In

---

[13] At a 2016 conference, Vaia Touna sat on a panel reviewing Nongbri's book and made the point that his book's end (which suggests that we may be able to get closer to ancient realities – i.e., see them in a less distorted manner – if we abandon our anachronistic uses of the modern category religion) is somewhat inconsistent with the rest of his critique – a point Nongbri has acknowledged. See his comments at https://religion.ua.edu/blog/2017/03/01/on-religion-words-and-things/ (accessed Sept. 3, 2017). See Touna 2017 for an attempt to rigorously document scholarly anachronisms when talking about the ancient world.

[14] The case involved parents in the Encinitas Union School District in San Diego suing the school for having their young children practice yoga during school hours. The argument their lawyers made was that, as an ancient Hindu practice, yoga is religious and thus its inclusion in the public school's exercises constituted an infringement on their children's constitutional rights. In the summer of 2013, San Diego Superior Court Judge John S. Meyer, however, ruled that it was not in violation of the First Amendment for such reasons as the school removing a variety of elements from the practices that might otherwise make them religious, such as renaming the lotus position as the "crisscross applesauce" pose. As of October 2017, the case is under appeal.

such a case, our field would then share much with others who equally study the curious – perhaps even mundane but no less fascinating – techniques groups use to make their worlds inhabitable and authoritative. These include an early-career colleague in anthropology who wondered why only some immigrants are called "ex-pats," thereby indicating that the study of what we term immigrants is no less lodged in the complicated rhetorics and social interests of those carrying out the studies – people likely with rather different interests than those of the people whose lives are classified and studied in this manner.[15]

So, although *Before Religion* understandably comes well after many of the works that helped to establish this field of study, it's likely the best way into the literature on "religion" for the newcomer (and thus Nongbri's work has the effect of helping to constitute this focus *as* a legitimate specialty). While hardly being a textbook, its shorter chapters and command over a wide literature, coupled with his many practical historical examples, make it very useful in a variety of class settings (whether undergraduate or graduate). Not as useful as a primer but still an important contribution to the scholarly literature, is Jason Ānanda Josephson's detailed study, *The Invention of Religion in Japan* (2012). Somewhat like Turner's previously cited essay, along with a variety of other recent scholars (I think here of Donald Lopez, for example[16]), Josephson's concern is to recover the agency of the Other, in his case the later 19th-century Japanese politicians, administrators, and scholars (those whom Brubaker and Cooper might collectively term "indigenous cultural entrepreneurs" [2000: 24]) who, though operating in a context established by others (i.e., those who brought such alien questions like "What religion are you?" to their shores), responded by creating conceptual linkages and vocabulary representative of their own interests. As he sums up his own book:

> In the late 1860s, most of Japan's inhabitants perceived the following three entities as similar types of supernatural beings and frequently conflated them linguistically: (1) the emperor of Japan (*tennō*); (2) the ox-headed divine king, god of plagues (*Gozu tennō*); and, (3) the four divine kings of Buddhism (*Shi-tennō*). Almost immediately after the Meji constitution came into effect, these three types of *tennō* were differentiated by the official policy of the new regime. Law mandated belief in the divine descent of the emperor of Japan, banned belief in the ox-headed divine king, and deemed faith in the four divine kings "religious," and thus a matter of personal choice. (2012: 251)

---

15 See Mary Rebecca Read-Wahidi's "Expat or Immigrant" posted at http://religion.ua.edu/blog/2014/05/expat-or-immigrant/ (accessed Aug. 15, 2017).
16 Lopez argues that earlier studies of the production of colonial knowledge (such as that of Edward Said) failed to understand that it was hardly a one-sided affair but, instead, the result of "networks of exchange that existed between the Orientalizer and the Orientalized, of the back-and-forth that occurred between Europeans and Asians in which Asians were also agents" (1995: 12).

He immediately goes on to add, "this newfound distinction between fact, superstition, and religion ... was replicated at many different levels of Meji ideology, from laws to textbooks" (251). Josephson argues that the traditional approach to studying binaries does not sufficiently get at the nuance that was actually taking place, inasmuch as that which was not seen as fact was itself further distinguished between those items that were deemed acceptable or tolerable (inasmuch as they did not contest the domain authorized by so-called facts [i.e., that of the state]) and those that were not. Thus the tripartite ideas of secularism, superstition, and religion were co-constitutive in the case of Japan's so-called modernization. Critics of Arnal and my own work in this area – such as Stausberg, who noted that "[t]he co-emergence of religion and the secular and of both with the liberal democratic state is treated as a fact in several places ... but is nowhere elaborated upon in a historical or historicist manner" (2013: 493) – should be very pleased with Josephson's detailed archival work documenting this process, at least in the case of Japan.[17]

Studies such as Josephson's – those that examine classification as a collaborative, situationally specific exercise linked not just to ideas but to social interests, legal systems, and administrative structures (where metaphysics are made concrete, as he observes [225]) – are an important corrective to those who understand situations of contact as merely involving the passive vanquished simply doing the bidding of invading conquerors. Instead, as in all social situations, the creation of significance is a social process, though certainly the power imbalances in any given situation may provide an inducement for scholars to overlook the role played by a wide variety of more marginal actors in the outcome – actors with differing interests and goals, and yes, differing degrees and domains of agency. For, as Josephson notes, "religion [as a concept] takes hold in Japan as a nakedly political category, first considered useful to politicians and put to directly political uses. As a diplomatic category, religion emerged through a process of negotiation, conditioned by competing aims and aspirations" (71). It is for this very reason that I have so appreciated Bruce Lincoln's brief example, in *Discourse and the Construction of Society* (a new edition was recently published), of the way in which Swazi locals in the mid-1930s effectively used a discourse on the authoritative past to prevent the construction of a British airstrip (1989: 27ff.). Their reference to a particular tree where a former Swazi king once supposedly met for a debate, a tree that must therefore not be harmed, used for their own purposes

---

17 It is unfortunate that Stausberg seems to have missed the concluding chapter to McCutcheon 2003, in which this was indeed addressed, at least in the case of Europe. Since it is not news that later writings often build on previous work, it seemed unnecessary to repeat all that in the more recent collection with Arnal.

a well-established European strategy that Durkheim would no doubt find to be a suitable instance of how otherwise mundane things are signified, i.e., set apart and forbidden, for social effect, making this an example of how what we might call the rhetoric of sacrality can cut many ways in any given dispute (something only too apparent nowadays, when arguments citing religious freedom are routinely used in social democracies to promote any number of differing, even conflicting, social agendas).[18]

In much the same way, Josephson's book examines not just the arrival of the category religion in Japan in the later 1800s but, more importantly, the local response on the part of policymakers, all in order to keep the focus not on religions but on the effects of designating certain things *as* religion (or, most importantly as well, *as* superstitious). Like Nongbri, then, he sees the category religion as a thoroughly modern invention (e.g., "There were no medieval religions. This is as true of Christianity as it is for Japanese Buddhism" [258]) but, also like Nongbri, it sometimes seems that the critique has not gone far enough (recall Touna's friendly amendment to his work, noted earlier). Without the modern discourse on religion and, in particular, the discourse on world religions, I'm not sure we would be talking about such seemingly bounded things in the world as early Christianity, medieval Shinto, or, say, Buddhism in the eighth century – whether we call them religions, traditions, or worldviews. For as is evident at a variety of other times in our field when historicizing the idea of religion, it sometimes seems to be a secondary label that is only later placed on what we portray as primary and relatively coherent / stand-alone things that already exist, such as trying to demonstrate how prior things we call traditions were strategically transformed into religions; the problem, of course, is that opting for one word over another (i.e., tradition or cultural system rather than religion) can signal a failure to take seriously how classifications (and the practices and institutions that attend them) are actively constitutive of an identity (think again on Althusser's example of interpellation). Following this alternative line of thought would prompt us not to question how Buddhism was reinvented *as* a religion but, turning that on its head, to examine how, armed with the category religion, social actors were able to invent a seemingly coherent thing called Buddhism (which was then thought to have a history and to be a causal agent) from what might have been a disparate – and thus rather differently organized and identified – collection of prior claims, actions, artifacts, and institutions. For while I'm enough of a realist not to contest that certain acts

---

18 Consider also the example in which a police officer (reported on June 6, 2014), in the state of Utah, is reported to have cited his religious convictions as the reason he declined to serve on duty during a gay pride parade; see http://www.sltrib.com/sltrib/news/58036918-78/jones-police-officer-officers.html.csp (accessed Sept. 2, 2017).

may indeed be quite old, the presumption of their inherent and thus longstanding link to yet other acts may itself be surprisingly recent. Without the designation religion, understood as something set apart from a variety of other practices (e.g., politics or superstition), I am not sure why one would think that a host of (at times) drastically different social groups in existence today, say in the U.S. or in Germany alone, would all be profitably called "Christianity." The thing that we might now automatically see to unite them, and therefore sensibly constitute them all *as* Christian may very well be that we are able to successfully minimize a variety of internal differences by using the category religion to create the impression that they share an even greater or more consequential thing in common (e.g., they're all about the soul or spirituality or are judged apolitical, etc.), a commonality that might simply be an effect of the way that we currently distinguish each from the rest of social life that we then call politics or the secular. That is, drawing on an example I've used before (e.g., see McCutcheon 2015: chapter 5), the perceived internal differences are, at times, great enough for members of some groups named Christian to fight to reserve the designation *exclusively for themselves* (as in either the case of self-named Evangelicals who often deny that Roman Catholics are Christian or the manner in which many would claim that Mormons are not Christian). Or, to press a different example, just because they all have anthems and flags and pledges and armies and uniforms and governments and taxation systems and public schools and, etc., does not mean that we today see all nations as being the same thing (despite the existence of the United Nations – a unifying institution that often seems on the brink of failure).[19] Specific situational conditions and sets of interests lead us to emphasize or deemphasize the innumerable similarities and differences that always simultaneously exist, suggesting that a thoroughgoing study of the discourse on religion will keep its focus on the study of those conditions and interests that made it possible to think Christianity or Buddhism into existence, as having anthropological and psychological reality – as having a history, effects, and a future – rather than presuming their obvious existence and role as causal agents in world affairs. So taking efforts to historicize the category "religion" *seriously* means doing something more than studying labels applied to things in the world but being open to entirely rethinking what it is that we're studying, all in an effort not simply to be paraphrasing, and thereby reauthorizing, how people are already talking about their own lives, affinities, and identities.

---

19 Efforts over the past fifty years or so to nurture the idea of the European Union (EU) – from the invention of a shared currency and courts to the annual Eurovision song contest – constitute a particularly good example to examine the conditions in which the idea of the nation-state is or is not persuasive to us.

I see this willingness in the work of Aaron Hughes (co-editor of *Method & Theory in the Study of Religion*). The controversy that attends some of his writings (for example, his thoughts on how Jewish Studies or the study of Islam, in both of which he is trained, ought to be carried out [e.g., 2007, 2012b, 2014][20]) strikes me as stemming from the way that he takes this sort of critique seriously and the way that it undermines various of the nonacademic interests of other scholars. For instance, in one of his books, Hughes looks not to define the term Abrahamic religions in the right way, to make it more useful to scholars but, instead, examines what's to be gained by anyone even inventing and applying the term to begin with. That's why his little book, *Abrahamic Religions* (2012a) – a short but trenchant critique of using this term as an analytic, scholarly category – strikes me as so important, for it studies the *discourse* on Abrahamic religions, a fairly recent invention linked quite closely to politically liberal discourses on tolerance and what is popularly known as interreligious dialogue, much like the related, and slightly older reliance on the (somewhat less inclusive) term Judeo-Christian. For Hughes, these terms are actively fashioning a certain sort of identity in the present and authorizing it (the two senses of fabricate) by allowing us to presume the term names something real that stretches backward in time – making the use of such categories a form of propaganda or, if that word seems too strong, then perhaps rhetoric – and scholars who use these terms as if they name distinct and naturally occurring groups that exist in the world (much like billiard balls on green felt) are not *describing* (i.e., merely watching and listening) but actively *constituting* and picking favorites; for it should be obvious that not all of those who self-identify as Muslim, Christian, or Jewish will gain membership in this thing yet others call the Abrahamic faiths. And that's where the work of such marginalizing categories as heterodox, militant, extremist, and radical come in – terms that, despite scholars often using them to name non-dominant groups, are more akin to the word cult appearing in a magazine's sensationalist headline. I think here of my colleague Steven Ramey and, to my way of thinking, his important critique of the tendency for scholars to normalize just some elements of the groups they happen to study, as elaborated in his regional American Academy of

---

20 See http://www.equinoxpub.com/blog/?s=reflections+of+islamic+studies (accessed Sept. 1, 2017) for a series of posts related to Hughes' online disagreements with Omid Safi concerning the way Islamic studies should proceed within the academic study of religion. See also http://chronicle.com/article/Jewish-Studies-Is-Too-Jewish/145395/ (accessed Sept. 1, 2017), as well as the various comments posted at the site, for Hughes' thoughts on the state of Jewish Studies. See also chapter 5 in this volume as well as Ramey 2017, where Hughes' work is again a focus of commentary by contemporary writers.

Religion presidential address, delivered in March 2013 at the Southeastern Commission on the Study of Religion.[21]

But Hughes' book is not just a strong argument for why the academic study of religion ought to be something entirely different from the practice of politically liberal consensus-building and dialogue but also an indictment of how many scholars fail to recognize this, what with the prominence of the term "Abrahamic religions" in our own field, among scholars. The degree to which this sort of scholarship – by means of Ramey's accidental (or quite intentional) favorites argument – is actively constitutive of a certain sort of world, whereby (not unlike Josephson's study of how undesirable practices were relegated to the status of superstition), certain ways of organizing ourselves socially are depoliticized, de-historicized, and thereby legitimized, is made evident by Hughes, a technique for overlooking practical differences that are easily found in the historical record in favor of creating an impression of a more ethereal unity for a very particular select group of current practices and institutions.

The explicit geo-politics that, thanks to Hughes, we see in our use of these categories provides a convenient opportunity to mention *Religion and Politics in International Relations: The Modern Myth*, Tim Fitzgerald's study of the geo-political role played by the discourse on religion, especially as found in the work of scholars in International Relations (2011). Since *The Ideology of Religious Studies* (2000), Fitzgerald has become well-known for his own critiques of "religion," the historical development of the category in the work of European political theorists of the past few centuries, along with the practical implications of various elements of its discourse (e.g., the presumption of interiority, civility, apoliticalism, etc.). As was certainly begun with his *Discourse on Civility and Barbarity* (2007a), which was explicitly written for readers across disciplines, *Religion and Politics in International Relations* tackles how the category of religion is the often unacknowledged Other that allows us to conceptualize and then talk about such a domain as politics, world affairs, foreign policy, etc., in the first place. Fitzgerald has long found problematic that our critiques of "religion" were only aimed at our colleagues in the academic study of religion when, in agreement with Chidester and contrary to what Turner argued much earlier in this chapter – "… we scholars of religion do not have that much power and impact in the world. Our books are read by our colleagues, but they tend not to build great bridges or great empires" – Fitzgerald would likely argue that our particular use of the category religion has been handy for scholars across the human sciences as well as bureaucrats and

---

[21] View Ramey's address at https://vimeo.com/64419019 (accessed Sept. 3, 2017) or find it as the afterword in Miller 2015.

politicians from across nations and political preference, who are each interested in creating the impression of a normative social world in contradistinction from all that deviates from it or potentially threatens it. In this way, our work is of immense influence and practical consequence. That only some actions get to count as *religious* extremism or *religious* terrorism, or even religious, private, and ethereal as opposed to political, public, and practical, is a useful way of creating just such a world, much as wearing a so-called discreet cross or a Star of David on a necklace becomes allowable in public, but a Muslim woman wearing any number of different headdresses while carrying out public duties can be turned into something that might potentially be outlawed. (I refer here, not just to France but also to the introduction in 2013 of what turned out to be the controversial *Charte de la laïcité*, otherwise known in English as the Canadian province of Quebec's proposed Charter of Values).[22] So Fitzgerald is interested in how "[t]he unanalyzed [or what I would rephrase as folk] binary opposition between the religious/theological/spiritual aspects of existence and the nonreligious/material/secular ones is built into ... [our] descriptions and summaries [of the world and international events] from the beginning" (120). Getting scholars well outside the study of religion to consider this is, I think it fair to say, a long overdue and thus important goal; far too often theorists trained in other fields, who engage in sophisticated critiques of their own discipline, seem to rely on little more than their own folk, "Sunday School" knowledge when they turn their attention to religion.

Although the general contours of this discourse predate the attacks in the U.S. on Sept. 11, 2001, by at least a few centuries, the manner in which these opposed pairs of concepts (e.g., religious/political, private/public, belief/practice, tolerant/intolerant, experience/expression, etc.) were marshalled and then wielded by reporters, scholars, and politicians to make sense and chart a course forward in its wake is surely one of the factors that has propelled much of the critical discourse on religion over the past decade; speaking personally, seeing the rhetorical labor exerted to determine (or portray?) some Muslims as "safe and allowable" versus those who were "dangerous and extreme" (thereby making the latter legitimate law enforcement or military targets, of course) was among the main motivators for my own little book in this area (McCutcheon 2005). But I am hardly alone in seeing a link. "Especially since September 11, 2001, there has been a proliferation of scholarly books by historians, sociologists, political scientists, religious studies professors, and others exploring the peculiarly violence-prone nature of religion," writes William Cavanaugh, in the introduction (2009: 4) to his

---

22 With the separatist Parti Québécois' defeat in the 2014 provincial election (won by Quebec's Liberal Party), the bill died.

own foray into scrutinizing the work being done by the term religion, either noun or adjective. His *The Myth of Religious Violence* – a detailed study of what he had earlier referred to as his "hypothesis that 'religion and violence' arguments serve a particular need for their consumers in the West" (see his essay, "Colonialism and the Myth of Religious Violence" in Fitzgerald 2007b: 241) – therefore contains much that is familiar to anyone conversant with the growing body of literature on "religion," e.g., the notion that with the advent of modernity the distinction between sacred and secular was slowly refined in order to manage the influence of a set of competing social institutions we call the Church, etc. However, his efforts to demonstrate the advantages to some of portraying that domain known as religious as particularly prone to irrational violence (a critique shared by Fitzgerald [see 2011: chapter 3]) do not strike me as necessarily leading to the argument that the religion/nonreligion distinction is itself a merely (though immensely useful) rhetorical ploy; for example, one of the benefits of "doing away with the myth of religious violence [is that it] would help to eliminate one of the justifications for military action against religious actors" (227). As with some versions of the critique, it only goes part way, for it is not the constitution of anything *as* religious which interests us here but, instead, the way that all religious people have been generalized and misrepresented by "constructing artificial distinctions between religious and secular violence," thereby allowing "types of violence and exclusion labeled secular [to] have escaped full moral scrutiny" (230). Although the other shoe does not explicitly drop in the book, it seems to me to be the first step in Cavanaugh's larger argument – perhaps concerning how, if religion is no more prone to violence than anything else and cannot be distinguished from politics but, rather, informs all of one's life, then despite the media-hype for identifying so-called religious extremism, perhaps what we now see as a holistic religious domain can hold out some promise for "turning some enemies into friends" (as he phrases it in his closing line [230]). If I am correct – and this is, I admit, a speculative reading of his argument's wider or perhaps eventual implications (which would put him in agreement with the sorts of things written on religion and violence by such nonacademic authors as Karen Armstrong [2015]) – then it seems Cavanaugh's book, despite sharing some things in common with the others examined here, deviates rather significantly from the work of Nongbri, Josephson, Hughes, and Fitzgerald.

But, despite this important difference, what is rather satisfying in all of these works – unlike twenty years ago when, writing my earlier review, I mainly had to pay attention to how writers were using the term in their own work on religion, finding few who were themselves examining the discourse on religion itself – is not only that the focus for so many is now explicitly on the category religion but that, in many cases, their work is aimed at a cross-disciplinary audience and its examples are international in scope and historically wide-ranging. It is now clear that the critique of the category has relevance for how we study not just the advent of modernity in Europe, the Americas, and Japan but also in Turkey, India, among Native American groups, throughout Africa, etc. (as evidence in the essays collected by Dressler and Mandair [2011] and also the earlier set edited by Petersen and Walhof [2002][23]). But this should not surprise us, of course, if our argument is that this thing we call modernity, which – with the now worldwide dominance of the socio-economic-political systems that developed within that space over the past few centuries – currently goes by the name of globalization, was made, at least in part, by strategic distinctions and divisions of intellectual and institutional labor that created an impression of private faith in opposition to public fact. No longer is the study of religion – or more particularly, "religion" – exclusively concerned with itemizing a special quality that sets certain actions or feelings apart from all others – for that very focus is now seen to be but one technique of modernity. We have therefore come a considerable distance from Wilfred Cantwell Smith's much earlier interest, following Friedrich Schleiermacher and so many others, to come up with a better way to name the supposedly essential and elusive thing that we sadly misname, misportray, or inappropriately limit as if it were some unified thing called religion (and thereby opting, as we all probably know, for "faith in transcendence" as being the name for the original, personal kernel that is only later expressed publicly, and literally acted out, as the "cumulative tradition" [Smith 1991]).[24] Although I am not so confident as Josephson, who concludes his book by suggesting that "[t]he very critical turn promoted by Asad and others (and indeed this very work) was made thinkable by the collapse of religion as an analytic category" (266), that such a wide variety of scholars are now focusing attention

---

[23] Note that the same troubling ambiguity between an exclusive focus on the discourse on religion, on the one hand, and, on the other, an effort to use this critique to reveal the prior or true nature of religion when not misrepresented by Eurocentrists and colonialists, is present in both of these collections. For example, consider how the discourse on religion as predating the nation informs Petersen and Walhof's opening question: "[W]hat happens to religious ideas and objects when they become the province of the nation?" (11) or Dressler and Mandair's volume being concerned with "the colonial and postcolonial adoption of Western-style objectifications of religion and its dialectical counterpart the secular" and also aimed at "debunking ... conventional ways of conceptualizing religion and the secular within modernist frameworks" (30).

[24] "The cumulative tradition, then, of what has been called religion and each particular religion is dynamic, diverse, and observable. It is, I suggest, historically intelligible. It is even objective ... . Theology is part of the traditions, is part of this world. Faith lies beyond theology, in the hearts of men. Truth lies beyond faith, in the heart of God ... . The traditions evolve. Men's faith varies. God endures" (1991: 168, 185, 192).

on gaps in the comforting story Cantwell Smith once told us about ineffable faith pushed outward is encouraging for those of us who are working toward a truly historical and systematic study of how the intertwined acts of signification, identification, and social formal take place, both locally and globally. Although not yet published, I think here, too, of Naomi Goldenberg's February 2013 public lecture, delivered in my own department, in which she proposed re-conceptualizing "religion" as a naming convention used to manage what she termed vestigial, competing, or former states that yet persist within the midst of the modern nation-state – making the classification religion a form of nationalist rhetoric[25] (a position very much in line with Josephson's analysis). "Religion" and the way in which things so designated can then be managed in law (whether to promote or demote them) then allows the controlling interests of the state to circumscribe and thereby internalize and control all competitors for the affinities of those on whom it exercises a monopoly: the subjects known as citizens – thus linking statecraft and nation-building to how it is that we moderns come to use this Latin-based term in daily life to name things that strike us as having such reality to them. Thus, to build on my opening quotation from Waardenburg with which I ended an earlier review essay in this journal and on the same topic, not only the current debate about the concept of religion but apparently the category itself, is not as innocent as it may seem. That this is now apparent to a wide number of scholars working in an equally wide number of areas bodes well, I think, for the field – if, that is, a self-conscious awareness of situation and the implications of our own practices (i.e., our own fabrications) is desirable.

And so I close this time, over twenty years after first assessing the state of the study of "religion," by quoting from Mandair and Dressler's introduction to their volume (2011: 23):

> It will be interesting to see in which ways the academic discipline of religious studies can respond to the challenges that it will have to face once it recognizes and positions itself more deliberately toward the historical biases that contributed to its creation.

It will indeed.

---

[25] Watch her Feb. 12, 2013, lecture, "Why Do Governments Fear 'Religion,' and How Do They Use It?: An Exploration of the Role of 'Religion' in Contemporary Statecraft" at https://vimeo.com/60792732 (accessed May 26, 2014). See also her podcast at http://www.religiousstudiesproject.com/podcast/podcast-naomi-goldenberg-on-religion-as-vestigial-states/ as well as her following blog post: http://religion.ua.edu/blog/2012/07/the-relevance-of-research-religions-as-vestigial-states/ (accessed Sept. 1, 2017).

References

Althusser, Louis (2001) [1971]. Ideology and ideological state apparatuses (Notes towards an investigation). In *Lenin and Philosophy and Other Essays*, 86–126. Ben Brewster (trans.). Frederic Jameson (foreward). New York, NY: Monthly Review Press.
Armstrong, Karen (2015). *Fields of Blood: Religion and the History of Violence*. New York, NY: Anchor.
Arnal, William E. and Russell T. McCutcheon (2013). *The Sacred is the Profane: The Political Nature of "Religion."* New York, NY: Oxford University Press.
Bayart, Jean-François (2005) [1996]. *The Illusion of Cultural Identity*. Steven Rendall, Janet Roitman, Cynthia Schoch, and Jonathan Derrick (trans.). Chicago, IL: University of Chicago Press.
Brubaker, Rogers and Frederick Cooper (2000). Beyond "ideology." *Theory and Society* 29 (1): 1–47.
Cavanaugh, William (2009). *The Myth of Religious Violence*. New York, NY: Oxford University Press.
Chidester, David (1996). *Savage Systems: Colonialism and Comparative Religion in Southern Africa*. Charlottesville, VA and London, UK: University Press of Virginia.
— (2014). *Empire of Religion: Imperialism & Comparative Religion*. Chicago, IL: University of Chicago Press.
Clifford, James and George E. Marcus (eds.) (1986). *Writing Culture: The Poetics and Politics of Ethnography*. Berkeley: University of California Press.
Dressler, Markus and Arvind-Pal S. Mandair (eds.) (2011). *Secularism & Religion-Making*. New York, NY: Oxford University Press.
Dubuisson, Daniel (2003) [1998]. *The Western Construction of Religion: Myths, Knowledge, and Ideology*. William Sayers (trans.). Baltimore, MD: The Johns Hopkins University Press.
Fitzgerald, Timothy (2000). *The Ideology of Religious Studies*. New York, NY: Oxford University Press.
— (2007a). *Discourse on Civility and Barbarity: A Critical History of Religion and Related Categories*. New York, NY: Oxford University Press.
— (2007b). *Religion and the Secular: Historical and Colonial Formations*. New York, NY and London, UK: Routledge.
— (2011). *Religion and Politics in International Relations: The Modern Myth*. London, UK: Bloomsbury.
Hughes, Aaron (2007). *Situating Islam: The Past and Future of an Academic Discipline*. New York, NY and London, UK: Routledge.
— (2012a). *Abrahamic Religions*. New York, NY: Oxford University Press.
— (2012b). *Theorizing Islam: Disciplinary Deconstruction and Reconstruction*. New York, NY and London, UK: Routledge.
— (2014). *Rethinking Jewish Philosophy: Beyond Particularism and Universalism*. New York, NY: Oxford University Press.
Jensen, Jeppe Sinding (2014). *What is Religion?* New York, NY and London, UK: Routledge.
Josephson, Jason Ānanda (2012). *The Invention of Religion in Japan*. Chicago, IL: University of Chicago Press.
Lincoln, Bruce (1989). *Discourse and the Construction of Society: Comparative Studies of Myth, Ritual, and Classification*. 1st ed. New York, NY: Oxford University Press.
Lofton, Kathryn (2014). Review of *On Teaching Religion*. *Journal of the American Academy of Religion* 82 (2): 531–542.

Lopez, Donald S. (ed.) (1995). *Curators of the Buddha: The Study of Buddhism under Colonialism*. Chicago, IL: University of Chicago Press.
Luhrmann, Tanya M. (2012). *When God Talks Back: Understanding the American Evangelical Relationship with God*. New York, NY: Alfred A. Knopf.
McCutcheon, Russell T. (1995). The category "religion" in recent publications: A critical survey. *Numen* 42 (3): 284–309.
— (1997). *Manufacturing Religion: The Discourse on Sui Generis Religion and the Politics of Nostalgia*. New York, NY: Oxford University Press.
— (2003). *The Discipline of Religion: Structure, Meaning, Rhetoric*. New York, NY and London, UK: Routledge.
— (2005). *Religion and the Domestication of Dissent, or How to Live in a Less than Perfect Nation*. New York, NY and London, UK: Routledge.
— (2012). Introduction. In Craig Martin and Russell T. McCutcheon (eds.), *Religious Experience: A Reader*, 1–16. New York, NY and London, UK: Routledge.
— (2014). *Entanglements: Marking Place in the Field of Religion*. Sheffield, UK: Equinox Publishers.
— (2015). *A Modest Proposal on Method: Essaying the Study of Religion*. Leiden, NL: Brill.
Miller, Monica R. (ed.) (2015). *Claiming Identity in the Study of Religion: Social and Rhetorical Techniques Examined*. Sheffield, UK: Equinox Publishers.
Nongbri, Brent (2013). *Before Religion: A History of a Modern Concept*. New Haven, CT: Yale University Press.
Peterson, Derek and Darren Walhof (2002). *The Invention of Religion: Rethinking Belief in Politics and History*. New Brunswick, NJ: Rutgers University Press.
Ramey, Steven (ed.) (2017). *Fabricating Difference*. Sheffield, UK: Equinox.
Schilbrack, Kevin (2010). Religions: Are there any? *Journal of the American Academy of Religion* 78 (4): 1112–1138.
— (2013). What *isn't* religion? *The Journal of Religion* 93 (3): 291–318.
Smith, Jonathan Z. (1982). *Imagining Religion: From Babylon to Jonestown*. Chicago, IL: University of Chicago Press.
— (1998). Religion, religions, religious. In Mark C. Talor (ed.), *Critical Terms for Religious Studies*, 269–284. Chicago, IL: University of Chicago Press.
— (2004). God save this honourable court: Religion and civic discourse. In *Relating Religion: Essays in the Study of Religion*, 375–390. Chicago, IL: University of Chicago Press.
— (2013). *On Teaching Religion: Essays by Jonathan Z. Smith*. Christopher Lehrich (ed.). New York, NY and London, UK: Oxford University Press.
Smith, Wilfred Cantwell (1991) [1962]. *The Meaning and End of Religion*. John Hick (foreword). Minneapolis, MN: Fortress Press.
Staal, Frits (1979). The meaninglessness of ritual. *Numen* 26 (1): 2–22.
Stausberg, Michael (2013). Review of *The Sacred is the Profane*. *Numen* 60 (4): 492–494.
Touna, Vaia (2017). *Fabrications of the Greek Past: Religion, Tradition, and the Making of Modern Identities*. Leiden, NL: Brill.
Turner, Alicia (2014). Religion, the study of religion and other products of transnational and colonial imaginings. *Journal of the Irish Society for the Academic Study of Religions* 1 (1): 12–25; http://jkapalo.files.wordpress.com/2014/05/religion-the-study-of-religion-and-other-products-of-transnational-and-colonial-imaginings-pdf2.pdf (accessed Aug. 5, 2017).
Waardenburg, Jacques (1992). In search of an open concept of religion. In Michel Despland and Gérard Vallée (eds.), *Religion in History: The Word, the Idea, the Reality*, 225–240. Waterloo, Ontario: Wilfred Laurier University Press.

2 "It's (Not) Easy if You Try:" The Challenge to *Imagine No Religion*

About ten years ago I first visited Pella in north central Greece, touring its archeological site and its old museum (whose collection, as I recall, was then largely in storage, awaiting transition to the newly constructed museum [completed in 2009]). In particular, I recall the large mosaics – some of which were covered outside, to protect them from the summer sun, while yet others, only somewhat smaller, were mounted on the walls inside the museum (all were said to date to around 2,400 years ago). I also remember strolling the meticulously excavated site of the city, walking along its streets and through the blocks that ringed what I imagine (more on that later) to have been its once busy but now empty agora. Arriving at the limits of the site, just as our small group was about to turn around and find a frappé and some shade at a café, we came across a pile – I think that's the correct technical word, meant to convey "heaped disorganization" – of artifacts. Or perhaps I had better term it debris, or maybe just stuff, since, judging from its disarray (at least compared to the mosaics) and the height of the vegetation that was growing in and around it, it had been there for some time. Large pieces of damaged columns and other remains were strewn about in a mound several meters high, where it had all presumably been dumped (aside: I would suggest that "placed" is too careful and intentional a term) on the outskirts of the ancient town (where, come to think of it, we usually find dumps). Judging by what I saw, it was likely comprised of what someone imagined to be the less-than-ideal samples of ancient architecture that, once unearthed, just had to be put somewhere (other than in the museum, of course, where our ideal prototypes find a carefully crafted and artfully lit home among the finds qua exhibits). For there's no doubt that plenty of columns pieces and shattered pots are annually dug up all across Greece – whether on archeological sites or, say, while digging the tunnels for new subway systems. And it's all got to go somewhere, I suppose.

Reading *Imagine No Religion* (Barton and Boyarin 2016) prompted me to recall that pile.

Note: As indicated in the opening note of the preceding chapter, there is considerable distance between critiques of the category religion from two decades ago and the manner in which, today, scholars of note seem to feel obliged to take the criticism seriously and then try to rethink their own approaches. Though in this chapter I will raise problems that I find in Barton and Boyarin's efforts, it is noteworthy that they tackled this topic in their co-authored book. Unfortunately, I was unable to attend the Society of Biblical Literature (SBL) panel on their book at the 2016 annual meeting, though I was fortunate to be asked to review it. Small portions of the following unpublished chapter, then, have appeared in the journal *History of Religions*.

https://doi.org/10.1515/9783110560831-003

Now, before elaborating on what I think links them to each other, let me first state quite clearly: this is a tremendously important book, and if it is only read by those who study religion in antiquity, then it will be a terrible shame. Its topic is, admittedly, a tightly focused e.g. (i.e., how our modern term religion fails to signify the semantic field that once circulated around such ancient Latin and Greek words as *religio* and *thrēskeia*, at least as evidenced in the works of the ancient authors to which we today have access, e.g., Tertullian and Josephus). But the fact that such accomplished scholars have taken the last few decades of critiques of this category so seriously (the work of Tim Fitzgerald mainly stands in here for this body of work) as to produce such a detailed study should send a clear message to those who are equally immersed in other historical or ethnographic subfields. That message concerns how casually (and, perhaps, carelessly, even anachronistically) we translate unfamiliar terms (and also social worlds) by this word of ours, religion, all in our effort to gain command of alien material so as to make sense of other people (those who are removed from us in time or space). But what sense are we making of *them* if this modern word is just *ours*? It's an important question, especially for an academic field in which so many still seem to think that they're studying the *sine qua non* of the human condition (whatever that might actually mean), regardless when and where those people may have lived. For our Latin-based word, religion, is the term that many still use to name efforts to answer the big existential questions of meaning and being that, inasmuch as we're human, apparently demand our attention.

Perhaps predictably, given that this is how plenty use the term today, not many have so far taken critiques of the category to heart – that is, apart from such recent examples as Brent Nongbri's *Before Religion* (2013) and Jason Ānanda Josephson's *The Invention of Religion in Japan* (2012) – both of which are cited in *Imagine No Religion*. (For other relevant works in this subfield, see both my earlier review essay, published in *Numen* [McCutcheon 1995], and also the preceding chapter.) Instead, after ceremoniously tipping their hats to the complexity of defining religion (a now required genuflection, as I've called it elsewhere, that I see often to precede an author's quote of Jonathan Z. Smith's now famous line, from over thirty years ago, about imagining religion), writers often just dive right in to describing all of the colorful features of this or that religion in surprisingly rich detail, apparently (as the old saying goes) knowing it when they see it. (Moreover, in agreement not just with the other Smith, Wilfred Cantwell, but also with Reza Aslan's recent [but now cancelled] CNN show, "Believer," the "it" that they see is often an abiding, personal faith that somehow pre-dates, grounds, and thereby transcends social institutions.) So, to have Carlin Barton (Emerita, the Department of History, UMass Amherst) and Daniel Boyarin (Department of Near East Studies and Department of Rhetoric, UC Berkeley) dig so carefully through ancient texts to try "to remove a mountain" (2016: 15), so as to reconsider how we, today, fit "those bits and pieces … together as 'ancient religion'" (as they quote Nongbri's phrase), is to be welcomed indeed.

The trouble, though, is the presumption that this transfer of dirt will, as with a more careful archeologist digging in the field, lead to a discovery of, as the opening to their first chapter puts it, "a wonderfully interesting world that can only be revealed by its [i.e., the category religion's] removal" (2016: 15).

At this point – the point of revealing and "uncover[ing] a way of life occluded by our conceptions and translations" so as to "reconceptualize a particular set of phenomena in a way that will enhance our understanding of them" (2016: 15) – I return to Pella. More specifically, I return to the curious juxtaposition of that unruly pile of leftovers (more than likely unseen by most visitors) with the contents of that museum's carefully conserved and much-visited exhibits – displays that nostalgically transport visitors back in time *yet do so only because of the strategically unseen curator's choices*. (Note that this contemporary agency is all too evident in the unearthed pile of leftovers dumped out back – and so the spell of authenticity is broken should we happen upon them by leaving the authorized tour and straying too far from our sense of the ancient city's center.) For the book's subtitle – *How Modern Abstractions Hide Ancient Realities* – offers a related juxtaposition of its own. For not unlike other authors who tackle the thorny problem of the past, there is here the clear impression that our job as scholars is to *get it right*, to (as they say in their opening) "listen to and imagine people living in an ancient culture more precisely and richly" (2016: 2). Now, I don't want to hang authors on the choice of a word or two, but the side-by-side verbs *listen* and *imagine* each take me in entirely different directions; even someone who is not in agreement with arguments for the death of the author would likely agree that there's no ancient speaker present when we read a text. So the so-called voice to which we supposedly listen, no matter how carefully, is inevitably imagined by us today; and thus the conjunction "and" that joins the otherwise opposed two verbs in the above-quoted sentence (suggesting two distinguishable moments in scholarly method, perhaps) is rather misleading, for despite lending an empirical feel to the digging of the text specialist, the former is really but a paraphrase of the latter. So, barring time travel and mind reading, it is this word, *imagine*, to which everything returns; yet it is a word that, despite repeatedly appearing as they set up their book's argument, at times seems to disappear (as in the nod toward merely listening more attentively) much as our fabrications benefit from the conservator's hand at the museum being nowhere (yet everywhere) to be seen. (I think here not only of the goal of better understanding the past, presumably on its own terms, and thus free of the preconceptions that come with our term religion, but also of reading ancient texts that occasion speculations on their imagined authors' conscious or unconscious motives.) My point then is simple: in the post-Hayden White world of historiography, how we talk about the past (i.e., how we translate texts to discover what their writers once might have actually meant) deserves more careful attention than we sometimes pay to it. If we take seriously the historiographical problems we've inherited, then the juxtaposition is not between the occluded past and the misconstruing present, but, instead, between those who understand history always and inevitably to be an imaginative construct of always situated and thus interested present actors (think here of the modern curator who proactively distinguishes artifacts from mere debris) and those who instead see the past to be a stable (if obscured) object set apart from the observer. Thus, the observer's task is not so much to mind the gap between us and some posited them but to overcome it by carefully observing the evidence and faithfully describing it, as free as possible from our pre-sorted categories that prompt us to pre-select this or that cultural feature (to borrow from the wording, again in their book's opening).

"Much is systematically occluded," we read, "when the categories of analysis that are mobilized are not produced inductively but simply deployed" (2016: 6). This makes plain the position in this ongoing debate staked out in *Imagine No Religion*. It is a position with which others (if, perhaps, in the field's minority) would differ, however; for, lacking social actors to hear our readings and then confirm or contest *our claims* about *their worlds*, others would contend that scholarly representations of something ancient being hidden and then revealed do not help us all that much since the standards of precision and accuracy are not judged in comparison to an original but, instead, are ours to make and administer (the institution of peer review comes to mind as but one example) – i.e., the standards have no necessary or demonstrable relationship to a long past social situation. They might, of course – just as E. B. Tylor's late 19th-century tale of the so-called savage philosopher, thinking up the theory of animism to make sense of a dream he supposedly had, may also be correct, for all we know (but, as the functionalists who followed him were quick to point out, we have no way of knowing). Even if more evidence is provided in support of a reading (and how much is even enough?), the evidentiary standards and rules of persuasion, argumentation, and documentation *are all ours* (i.e., they are contingent, change over time, and have their limits – and thus we see why parents, sooner or later, just seem to have to retort "Because I said so!"). Of course, should the criteria of precision or accuracy be unproblematically shared by a group (and when is this ever the case?), such as the members of an academic discipline, then the gap between contemporary claims and some originary moment pretty much disappears and we then uncontroversially talk about the importance of such things as careful description and inductive, unbiased observation. But, as I've referenced on a variety of past occasions, even Karl Popper (writing in *Conjectures and Refutations*) understood that induction wasn't merely disinterested description – for one's attention had to be focused first and that focusing wasn't the result of some inner momentum of the inherently interesting object that we are somehow compelled to observe. And thus the seemingly obvious distinction the authors draw between improperly pre-selecting or pre-sorting, on the one hand, and, on the other, more carefully observing the nuance and describing in depth, starts to look far murkier.

So despite finding their book to be a refreshing addition to the literature on the category religion – and it is indeed that – it's just these seemingly straightforward distinctions between past and present, hidden and evident, description and prescription, etc., that I hope we can continue to explore. I do not think that Barton and Boyarin are unaware of the tension between *listening* and *imagining*. (Aside: their unelaborated use of a quotation from J. Z. Smith [on 2–3], in which he argues, at least in my reading, for stipulative rather than, as they seem to support, descriptive definitions, introduced a little more ambiguity as well.) So it's in hopes of seeing how far this investigation into "ancient religion" can go that I provide this one example – sticking mainly here, for convenience's sake, to just their introduction, since it is surprisingly rich for anyone interested in these issues. Opening a paragraph on page 3, we read the following:

> Cultures with elaborate divisions of labor and with the developed hierarchical structures needed to coordinate and rationalize the activities of the participants in that culture often rely for unity on highly simplified covering ideas and symbols. It is exactly the abstraction that sacralizes these ideas, that sets them apart. Each word becomes, so to speak, the head of a hierarchy.

What I found curious here is that, as I read it, what seems presented as a description or fact is, I would contend, a highly theoretical explanatory statement that has proved useful in past scholarly accounts of social life. For while there's been more work on this since Durkheim, of course, it reads to me like an updating of his theory of the totem's social function – an analysis with which I have great sympathies, to be sure – but this makes their statement hardly the description that it appears to be. (I could say the same for talking about cultures, of course – this is a highly theoretical term and not merely descriptive.) It's not that groups "often rely" on this technique but, instead, that some of us who study groups employ a social theory that allows us to read them *as functioning* as such, in our efforts to make sense of others who strike us as curious. For, thinking back to Popper once again (see 1962: 46–47), only if one subscribes to a particular framework would one even talk about the world in this manner, referencing hierarchies and divisions of labor along with the role symbolic abstractions play in facilitating and operationalizing our shared but nonetheless imagined communities (with the appropriate tip of my hat to Benedict Anderson, of course). My point? Description and explanation are not separate methodological moments (despite our using a shorthand that often presents them as such); instead, it may turn out that the latter provides the necessary conditions in which the former takes place. Simply put, as I've noted elsewhere on previous occasions, it's not as if it would be accurate to claim that Marx overlooked, missed, or occluded what Freud later (and, or so one might argue, more accurately) described as anxiety; if we instead understand that their differing theories allowed them to examine, and thereby conceptualize (aka reveal), different things *as* data, then it's not that anxiety lies "hidden" due to Marx's preoccupation with alienation.

Now, while I acknowledge that this might not be such a novel claim, taking it seriously and then applying it to how we sometimes talk about more accurately describing the past, or seeing something as past actors might have seen it, could result in a novel scholarly conversation. For now we might not be so concerned with the correct way to understand this or that word in its original context (or with regard to this or that author's intentions) but, instead, we might focus on why this or that use of a word is persuasive, useful, and, in the end, reproduced (or not). This shift represents a loss, of course, for those concerned with the past *qua* revealed past, such as with reading a text in its supposedly proper context, for example, since delimiting and then understanding that context would now be understood by yet others as irreducibly part of *our* always contemporary scholarly *imaginaire*, doing specific work for us, here and now – something that prevents us from ever getting all that close to those actual human beings who lived so long ago. And here that debris at Pella returns once again. Even the seemingly rough and tumble pile (perhaps akin not just to talking about the authentic or real past without modern preconditions but also to what some now call religion on the ground or, with the University of Erfurt's 2012–2017 initiative in mind, "'lived ancient religion'" which, as defined on their website, "suggests a set of experiences, of practices addressed to, and conceptions of the divine, which are appropriated, expressed, and shared by individuals in diverse social spaces"[1]) was still organized by us. This is true at least as compared to how we might now imagine it, in hindsight, as existing in some natural state, under the earth before it was even found, selected, cleaned, and catalogued, and then ordered to whatever extent – either roughly, outside town limits, or carefully, under soft lights, on velvet, and behind glass in museum cases. Both, inasmuch as they are items of discourse, are *contrived* – a word that, somewhat like "imagine," turns out to

---

[1] See https://www.uni-erfurt.de/en/max-weber-centre/projects/research-groups-ath-the-max-weber-kolleg/lived-ancient-religion/ (accessed March 28, 2017).

be not all that helpful, in fact, since it presupposes some *uncontrived* (i.e., real) alternative which, according to this model, *does not actually exist*. To become an item of knowledge (thinking once again about J. Z. Smith's views on the role played by comparison in cognition), something must be placed, by a third party, into a specific, controlled relationship with something else in order to say something about the world – an imagined relation, of course, such as how we use the notion of fruit to make sense of those things we call apples and oranges (or, come to think of it, how the idea of apples is used to group together otherwise distinguishable red and green things, and so on and so on). But what of the unvarnished past, buried deep in the earth or unread in dusty archives (think of the crate and the warehouse at the end of "Raiders of the Lost Ark" perhaps – an image Borges might have appreciated)? According to this position, such a past lacks that relationship – since one of the items in the comparative pairing (i.e., the actual past) is necessarily absent, given that it is always a product merely of our inevitably contemporary imagination – thereby making the supposed standard against which we measure our sense of the past, utterly unknown and unknowable. Lacking modern pre-conditions and pre-conceptions, there's simply nothing to be said about it – because "it" has no reference.

And this is where the quotation to Smith that I highlighted earlier (from his essay "Trading Places" [Smith 2004]) and which I suggested occupied an ambiguous place in their text helps us a little. I read Smith to be claiming that while it has little use as a descriptor, the category religion, used and defined as a scholars' stipulative tool, may have a role in our disciplined acts of comparative imagination – with scholars always being careful to see it as nothing but their own term and not to see it as somehow synonymous with an inherently human drive or need that exists in the wild, as it were.

So the question we could be asking might not concern how the modern category of religion *obscures* ancient realities but, instead, which sorts of ancient realities does it allow one to imagine. And, better yet, which new ones can be imagined when we drop it! We can certainly imagine different past worlds, by ordering and selecting different items from the archive that the late Michel-Rolph Trouillot once discussed (i.e., which texts can we read inasmuch as they either happen to have survived to our day), and then managing those selections by means of different symbolic abstractions; but now we will have difficulty elevating any of those imaginings to the status of original (since the rhetorics of origins are our *data* not our *method*),[2] for they are now all on a par, as our

---

[2] See McCutcheon 2015 for a more detailed discussion of the inevitably contemporary character of origins discourses.

devices, doing our work – though the work will differ, dramatically, at times. None is therefore any more accurate than another, for precision is now an immeasurable quality inasmuch as the comparison necessary for such a judgment to be made can't take place, given its missing element (i.e., the actual past, the origin, the intention, etc.).

So when we find a list, such as on page 4, of such items as gods, temples, prayers, sacrifices, metaphysical questions, worship, and festivals, it's not that these are the descriptive facts on the ground that we do or do not properly group together *as* religion (i.e., the bits and pieces); rather, it's theory and our imagination, all working to help us make sense of the world, all the way down. And not just at the level of the organizational category religion, for there are those who would argue, to pick but one example, that there's nothing sacrificial about sacrifice – not until someone armed with a theory of sacrifice shows up, becomes curious about what they see as, say, a part given for some whole, and who then does some selecting, ordering, and interpreting of their own. Hoping to accurately understand how the so-called insiders understood their sacrifices and aiming to do so by carefully not overlaying your own preconceptions onto theirs – operating by means of a light touch, as it were – has therefore already naturalized a modern theory and, in doing so, effectively erased the distance between our own situation and their posited worlds – an imperial move that many in the field today criticize while failing to see that their own curiosities and expectations set the mere stuff of the world apart as curious data before they even realized it.

And so, in agreement with Barton and Boyarin, but pressing rather further, what I'm suggesting is that "the apologetic context" (209) of writers – not just Philo and Melito, but *ourselves qua scholars who talk about this thing we call the past* – could attract far more of our attention, that is, if we're going to take historical situations seriously in our work. Rather than bracketing ourselves, as if we are uninterested readers, and proceeding as if we are able, through a more disciplined craft, to ascertain an ancient author's thoughts (e.g., Tertullian [118]), we may come to see that *we*, in our readings of an inevitably imagined *them*, have all along been doing as much as we claim that *they* were once doing, thereby establishing a host of new data domains, in perhaps rather mundane settings, yes, though they may be no less interesting than the ancient authorities that we still seem to feel compelled to study. For, selecting but one handy yet rich example from the book in question, we may now see the important (and, yes, ironic) work happening the moment when, in the midst of making descriptive claims about the regulatory effects of ancient Roman systems of reciprocity, honor, guilt, and shame, we find a socially formative bow inserted in a footnote that, in part, reads: "I am indebted ... to anthropologists and historians. ... There are too many to name, but I would like to give special mention to ..." (220, n. 2).

Thus, reciprocity, honor, guilt, and shame can be studied rather effectively in our own work, without historical speculation.

It should by this point be clear that, as indicated by my essay's title (which, if it wasn't immediately apparent, is slightly amended from the same lyric from which the book's title derives), I maintain that imagining a more accurate representation of the past (one that allows us to listen more carefully so as to better understand peoples removed from us in time because it is somehow free from, or less influenced by, our modern sensibilities) is not as easy as it may at first appear – that is, if we assume that our imaginings are somehow to be judged as a closer fit with some bygone social world – which brings to mind a recent blog post by Nongbri (mentioned in the previous chapter) in response to a variety of scholars who pressed the apparent difference between modern words and ancient things in which he reflects as follows:

> Although the book avoided the term "distortion," I've been convinced by discussions with Vaia Touna and others that *Before Religion* wasn't entirely successful in navigating this cluster of methodological problems. At the conclusion of the book, I wrote as follows:
>
>> ...it is crucial to understand that this is not simply a problem of finding another concept or word that covers the same ground as "religion," of finding a better word for it. The whole point is that, in antiquity, there never was any "it" there to begin with. The different type of descriptive accounts that I have in mind would allow what we have been calling "ancient religions" (that is, the contents of all those books called *Mesopotamian Religion, Religions of Rome, Ancient Greek Religion*, etc.) to be disaggregated and rearranged in ways that correspond better to ancient peoples' own organizational schemes. (*Before Religion*, 159)
>
> I see more clearly now how this final appeal to produce accounts that "correspond better to ancient people's own organizational schemes" raises the same set of questions as those provoked by the notion of "distortion" above. If I could revise the book, I would definitely reconsider the way I use the language of *correspondence*.[3]

And it is this important shift away from claims of occlusion and revelation that prompts me to return to J. Z. Smith's previously mentioned unpublished paper, "Why Imagine Religion,"[4] in which he makes plain his dissatisfaction with the manner in which his now famous book's title had been read by some. With regard to the philosophically idealist bent to some readings of his notion of imagina-

---

[3] See https://religion.ua.edu/blog/2017/03/on-religion-words-and-things/ (accessed March 30, 2017).
[4] The paper, as noted in my introduction, was delivered in November 1996 at what was then Western Maryland College (now McDaniel College) at a conference (organized by Frank Reynolds and Greg Alles) on "Reconstructing a History of Religions: Problems and Possibilities."

tion, Smith notes in that lecture, as I documented at the outset of this volume, that, early on, he had wanted "a constructive term that allowed a parallelism between 'their' activity and 'ours' and which allowed, as well, an ambivalence as to the status of the endeavor with respect to the fictive and the actual" (ms. 8). It makes sense then, as he reports there, why "Fabricating Religion" had "surviv[ed] through several drafts" of the earlier conference paper in which the eventual book's opening lines first appeared. For, as Smith observes, "to fabricate" means both "'to build' and 'to lie.'"

This is just the ambivalence that I see implicit in Barton and Boyarin's book, and it is one that I look forward to seeing explored more explicitly when it comes not just to perusing the exhibits at an archeological museum or even imagining religion but also to imagining the experiences and meanings of absent actors.

References

Barton, Carlin A. and Daniel Boyarin (2016). *Imagine No Religion: How Modern Abstractions Hide Ancient Realities*. New York, NY: Fordham University Press.

Josephson, Jason Ānanda (2012). *The Invention of Religion in Japan*. Chicago, IL: University of Chicago Press.

McCutcheon, Russell T. (1995). The category "religion" in recent publications: A critical survey. *Numen* 42 (3): 284–309.

— (ed.) (2015). *Fabricating Origins*. Sheffield, UK: Equinox Publishers.

Nongbri, Brent (2013). *Before Religion: A History of a Modern Concept*. New Haven, CT: Yale University Press.

Popper, Karl (1962). *Conjectures and Refutations: The Growth of Scientific Knowledge*. New York, NY and London, UK: Basic Books.

Smith, Jonathan Z. (2004). Trading places. In *Relating Religion: Essays in the Study of Religion*, 215–229. Chicago, IL: University of Chicago Press.

3 A Question (Still) Worth Asking about *The Religions of Man*

My first full-time job, a one-year instructor's position at the University of Tennessee in 1993–1994, came with the responsibility to teach three courses each semester. Although I could select the books for two of them (one a thematic introductory course and the other an upper-level course on myth and ritual), I was told to use Huston Smith's *The World's Religions* for the survey of world religions that I was to teach. Although for a couple of years I'd already been a teaching assistant for a world religions class at the University of Toronto, I wasn't all that familiar with this particular Smith's work – for, of the Smiths in our field, I knew the writings of Jonathan Z., Wilfred Cantwell, and even William Robertson far better (and, yes, in that order). The course for which I was one of a small army of TAs had been team taught by the late Will Oxtoby and the late Joseph O'Connell, and that course had turned out to be the proving ground for what later became Oxtoby's still in-print, two-volume edited textbook (as I recall, the students at that time had a course reader produced by Oxtoby and O'Connell).[1] Although I owned a copy, which I bought and first read in 1992 (something evident from the writing I now find inside it and along its pages' margins), Huston Smith's then widely used textbook was still somewhat new to me. When I made the trek south to Knoxville, I was about three-quarters of the way through writing my dissertation – a project that, as with so many of us, eventually became my first book; and so, like almost any early-career person first starting to teach full time, I soon figured out that making the most of teaching prep and experiences gained in the classroom meant sometimes finding in those courses e.g.'s of use in my research and writing. The moral of the story? Thanks to my new department's stipulation that I use Smith, his work made its way into my dissertation and thus first book

---

1 Originally published in 1996, it is now in various subsequent editions, which have been produced, in part, by Amir Hussain, former editor of the *Journal of the American Academy of Religion* – who, just a few years behind me at Toronto, was himself a teaching assistant for that same course, if memory serves me correctly.

Note: A shorter version of this unpublished paper was delivered as part of a November 2017 panel at the American Academy of Religion meeting in Boston, MA, entitled, "Contemporary Perspectives on a 'Perennial' Figure: The Intellectual Legacy of the Late Huston Smith (1919–2016)." Organized by Jon Herman, the panel also included Naomi Goldenberg, Kimberley Patton, Dana Sawyer (Smith's authorized biographer and author of *Huston Smith: Wisdomkeeper* [2014]), and Arvind Sharma. My thanks to Matthew Baldwin, Sierra Lawson, Steven Ramey, Vaia Touna, and Donald Wiebe for reading an earlier draft of this paper.

https://doi.org/10.1515/9783110560831-004

(he is one of three Smiths discussed) – as exemplary of how I thought that the study of religion ought *not* to proceed.

Since the analysis I offered in my dissertation made its way into the published version, I won't repeat all of that here (see McCutcheon 1997: 107–109, 111, 177–181, 187, and 223nn 8 and 10) – though I can't proceed without recalling Smith's Cold War-era rationale for why the staff at Maxwell Air Force base in Alabama might have been so keen on his lectures when he visited there in the late 1950s. In the first edition of what eventually was renamed as *The World's Religions* (an opening section that was retained but shortened it in subsequent editions), he wrote:

> [A]s a unit, they were concerned because someday they were likely to be dealing with the peoples they were studying as allies, antagonists, or subjects of military occupation. Under such circumstances it would be crucial for them to predict their behavior, conquer them if worse came to worst, and control them during the aftermath of reconstruction. (1959: 17; see also Smith 1991: 7)

(I feel that I should say that I am still struck by his remarkably [though perhaps unintentionally] frank and, in my assessment, disarmingly accurate understanding of our field's ongoing relationship to geo-politics – national security being among his reasons for studying religion.[2]) Instead, I'd like to offer some thoughts today on the curiously enduring – even perennial, I guess – nature of his rather early contributions to our field – contributions that, even back in the early 1990s when I first used his book, were made long enough ago that they actually dated to a time prior to the re-establishment of our field in public universities, at least in North America.[3] The educational television course that was to become his

---

[2] Other reasons "to take religion seriously" (1958: 19), and thereby to see the world as others might see it (what he calls "world understanding"), are to understand people so as to avoid war, to help international business to flourish, or simply "the enlargement of one's understanding and awareness of what reality is ultimately like" (19). For, as he elaborates on the same page, "The surest way to the heart of a people is through their religion."

[3] Like a great many departments in public universities in the U.S., ours at the University of Alabama celebrated its 50th anniversary just last year (the 2016–2017 academic year). Like many other colleges, courses on the topic of religion (i.e., such things as theological investigations of the Bible and the history of Christianity) date to the founding of the school in 1831 – something made evident in a public talk on this history given by my colleague Mike Altman during our anniversary celebrations. But it was not until the mid- to late 1960s that public university administrators and faculty felt not just free to establish Department of Religious Studies (the preferred term in North America) but were actually required or at least expected to do so, given that they then felt that the constitutionality of the field in state-funded schools had been settled. A number of factors, of course, played into these decisions in the U.S., from legal cases outlawing such things as prayer in public school classrooms to the interests of private funding agencies (whose grants helped to hire the field's first faculty members) and even Cold War-era geo-politics. See my own

1958 book, *The Religions of Man*, first broadcast in St. Louis in 1955 (within the first year of that station being on the air, in fact) – a full decade, or more, before many public-funded departments of Religious Studies were established in U.S. colleges.[4]

To my way of thinking, this makes for a situation in need of analysis, for not everything from sixty years ago continues to strike people as relevant today. To rephrase, it would not be difficult to imagine something from that era not to have aged all that well; in fact, speaking with the undergraduate students whom I now teach, it's become painfully apparent to me that once-popular films from just a decade or two ago, those that I at least feel are "recent" or "current," are often seen by them as dated artifacts from a bygone time. (There's no feeling like learning that 1999's *The Matrix* now counts for some of them as "an old movie;" as for *The Court Jester* or *The Trouble with Harry* [both popular films from 1955, the year Smith's public television course first aired], who among my students has even heard of Danny Kaye or Shirley MacLaine?) Despite how our youth are force-fed the once formative pop music of aging baby boomers (inasmuch as retailers still reason that the latter group's wallets are thick enough to justify selling Volkswagens, in 2017, using ELO's 1976 hit "Livin' Thing" – that's a song from over forty years ago!), I sometimes might as well be referencing some obscure foreign film if I go to *Citizen Kane*, *The African Queen*, or *It's a Mad, Mad, Mad, Mad World* for a quick illustration while teaching a class. (#generationgap) In fact, I've learned that even off-the-cuff references to *The Simpsons* (which is, as might have been noted on one of those lists that make the rounds before the start of each academic year, a decade older than some of our current first-year students) sometimes evoke the sound of crickets chirping – making the seemingly quick e.g. or analogy a considerable impediment to just making one's argument.

But this is likely as it should be; after all, given that I was born in 1961 and therefore came of age in the 1970s, references to turn-of-the-century fashion or events probably would have struck my teenaged self as obscure items from the murky, distant, and therefore irrelevant past. What did I care back then about what a skinny Frank Sinatra might have sung with Tommy Dorsey's band in the early 1940s, thirty years before we were tapping our toes to Mac Davis' 1972 hit, "Baby Don't Get Hooked on Me" – a song that now, forty-five years later, probably doesn't get much play, even on the so-called oldies stations.

---

discussion of the often-overlooked factors that help to account for the field's mid-20th century rise (or at least its re-establishment at that time) in McCutcheon 2013.

4 The station first started broadcasting on the evening of Sept. 20, 1954, showing "*The Second Opportunity*, a play that dramatized the necessity of free thought in society" (see http://www.ninenet.org/about/history/ [accessed Sept. 16, 2017]).

But for some reason, the book has been continuously in print. The reason why is, I think, still worth exploring, since I'm not satisfied explaining its persistence by appealing to, say, the fact that he just finally got it right and that readers still recognize that. And it's not just the book that grew from Smith's public TV course in 1955; that book has seen multiple editions and formats, from the small 1959 Mentor paperback that I own to a coffee table-sized book with glossy photos to such spin-off volumes as the individually published chapter on Islam (Smith 2001). Not only has this book survived, *but it is still used by some as the authoritative introduction to our field for university students*, thereby setting the table for several generations of students – some of whom no doubt went on to become professors themselves. And, in the process, it sold 1.5 million copies (according to the cover of the 1991 edition that I purchased in Toronto in 1992) – a number that, since then, has increased to 2 million, at least according to the publisher's website for the 50th anniversary edition; according to Smith himself (speaking in a 2010 interview that I'll soon cite), it's sold as many as 2.5 million – a number that's now over 3 million, or so I have been told by the publisher. What's more, as I was also recently told, it is safe to estimate that between half to two-thirds of today's sales are for course adoption.[5] So, unlike saddle shoes of the 1950s, Formica and chrome kitchen tables, and Buffalo Bob Smith and Howdy Doody, this no less dated book – no matter how current its cover may seem – still strikes many people as unironically relevant and thus anything but locked in yellowed amber.[6]

To account for the book's longevity – something that I think is due to more than its less-than-$20 price tag, though that, in part, helps to explain it, I'd suggest[7] – I'd again like to defer to Smith himself. Sometimes, authors tell readers far more than might at first be apparent (which is why the preface to a book can sometimes be so informative). This is evident in my earlier reference to his curiously matter-of-fact linkage of comparative religion to global conquest (a linkage of more consequence to some readers than he may have imaged when first writing those lines, inasmuch as our field was born from out of what Jonathan Z. Smith has termed the "explosions of data" [1998: 275] that resulted from what we once euphemistically called "the age of discovery" – what others today refer to as the age of conquest). Or consider the time, in his textbook's chapter on Confucianism, when Huston Smith tried to convey to his late-1950s – and thus modern – audience how all-con-

---

5 Personal correspondence with Michael Maudlin, senior vice president and executive editor with HarperOne (Sept. 28, 2017).
6 Or, to approach this another way, the book is currently (as of October 2017) number one at amazon.com in their Books > Religion & Spirituality > Islam > Theology category *while simultaneously* number one in Books > Textbooks > Humanities > Religious Studies > Comparative Religion. (My thanks to Matthew Baldwin for suggesting this alternate way to gauge sales.)
7 What's more, the e-book version is currently priced at just $2.99 US.

suming tradition can sometimes be in "their" cultures; after all, as he wrote, "Contemporary Western life has moved so far from the tradition-dominated life of early man as to make it difficult for us to imagine how completely it is possible for human life to be controlled by mores ... ."[8] So, to get across his point, he turned to the much lighter, but still effective, touch that what he called custom likely has on his readers – such as, he suggested, a businessman being seen as "queer, peculiar, different" if he forgets to wear his tie to work. Pressing his analogy, Smith concluded, "[t]here is in a woman's certitude that she is wearing precisely the right thing for the occasion, as some have observed, a peace which religion can neither give nor take away" (1959: 157). The irony, of course, is his inability to see the oddly gendered nature of his examples (i.e., the ruggedly individual male, weathering the storm of his associates' awkward glances, as opposed to the delicate sensibilities and ego of the female who apparently derives her complete sense of worth and identity from knowing that she picked the right outfit). It indicates that, despite what we might try to tell ourselves, "our" so-called customs are no less traditions, in his sense of the term, and are thus no less determinative – making that section of his chapter, inasmuch as it unintentionally illustrates the pervasive 1950s gender ideology of which he and so many others were (and perhaps still are) unquestionably a part, far more useful than he might have imagined, helping one to drive home the point on "tradition-dominated life" – regardless whose they are.

So, in hopes of learning something helpful about his book's curious longevity, consider the already-mentioned 2010 interview that Smith did, at the age of 91, and which was posted online by what was then known as The Center for World Spirituality.[9] Among the various clips taken from the interview is a four-minute segment concerned with the method he reports to have employed to research and write his still-famous book.[10] Describing how he once taught about the "eight authentic, revealed religions" – it may be worth noting, by the way, that there were only seven in the original edition, with so-called "primal religions"

---

8 See McCutcheon 1997: 108–109 for an earlier version of this critique.

9 A variety of clips from the interview, carried out by Marc Gafni and Mariana Caplan, were posted on May 20, 2010. See in particular the one entitled, "Huston Smith on 'How to Study a Religion'" at https://www.youtube.com/watch?v=gNm8FjTFTdI (accessed Sept. 16, 2017). Gafni and Caplan co-founded the Center for World Spirituality in 2010–2011 and today this self-described think tank is known as The Center for Integral Wisdom; learn more at https://centerforintegralwisdom.org/ (accessed Sept. 16, 2017). My thanks to a post on Twitter by John Penniman, at Bucknell University, for bringing this interview to my attention.

10 Though I consider their goals to be shared, Reza Aslan's recent effort to convey to viewing audiences the universal nature of religious faith as something inherently meaningful failed to meet one of Smith's own criteria: not to sensationalize or vulgarize believers (Smith 1959: 19). See https://religion.ua.edu/blog/2017/09/23/two-roads-diverged/ (accessed Sept. 23, 2017) for a brief blog post exploring their differences.

or "tribal religions" (which, he claims, have left their "psychic traces in our deep unconscious" [1991: 366]) being added, in a later edition, to augment what he called "the historical religions" – Smith identifies four methodological principles or strategies that informed the writing of his book on "authentic religion" (1959: 20). Rather than "hol[ing] myself up in a library with books," the stages of his work, according to him, were as follows:

1. "Read the sacred texts of the religion in question."
2. "Search out the human being who I felt ... was the most knowledgeable of that tradition."
3. "I would pilgrimage to the ... , and be like an anthropologist, and live in, with the practitioners of that religion, and I would participate in their rituals, their rites, as well as discussing with the most knowledgeable people ... "
4. "... [N]ever to go to press with anything on any religion without passing it by an authority in that ... , to get his imprimatur or his questions." (See n. 9 for the URL to the online interview of Smith from which this quote is transcribed.)

With this four-fold method in mind (and we might add an implicit fifth, identified in the book itself: conveying all of this in simple prose, doing so in a way that avoided what Smith characterized as a "technical and academic" manner [1959: 20][11] – a method evident in his first edition's appeal to William James' classic notion of religion as an acute fever that must be studied as something alive [1959: 20]), Smith then concludes this segment of the 2010 interview by saying:

> It has paid off; I think it's that approach which accounts for the fact that the book that came out of that, *The World's Religions*, has become the standard introductory text for introductory courses in religion and has sold two and a half million copies.

Whether we should today follow in these steps or not, in trying to identify what Smith there calls the "centrality" of each religion, is, of course, a topic that, in my opinion, is highly debatable – for, unlike Smith, there are those who think that the historical details matter rather more than the supposedly deep meanings that allegedly help us to deal with "such problems as isolation, tragedy, and death" (Smith 1959: 21) – though I would not call it a theory, we see here in miniature his

---

11 This is an approach that, as he acknowledged, prompted him to observe that, "I have deleted enormously, simplifying matters where historical details seemed to clog the meaning I was trying to get at ... . These liberties may lead some historians to feel that the book 'sits loose on the facts.' But the problem has been more complicated than one of straight history. Religion is not primarily a matter of facts in the historical sense; it is a matter of meanings ... ." (1959: 21; this is pretty much preserved verbatim in 2009: 10).

view on the function of religion. But rather than entertaining that question, consider more closely just what he has told us. The success of the book is premised on – if you'll pardon my redescription of his disclosures – offering an orthodox, top-down account that will strike many readers as entirely familiar, thereby providing a scholarly imprimatur to the folk knowledge that readers already possess. (Thus we see his methodological reason for, in his words from the first edition, deleting enormously from the more technical historical record.) But the book's impressive command of elite cross-cultural folk knowledge hardly qualifies *today* as a scholarly approach. For instance, contrary to many of the people who may read or use them, as scholars we know that things do not just become "sacred texts" of their own accord. Instead, they do so through long periods of disputation and editing, by groups with vested interests, such that certain texts (i.e., certain textual communities) are reproduced and authorized while others are contested, marginalized, maybe even burned (along with members of some of those communities) and then suppressed and forgotten instead of enshrined and venerated. So the act of identifying a text *as* sacred, let alone reading it *as* a sacred text (whatever that may mean, in comparison to how we read any old text), as if it is somehow representative of a community called a religion, is, as we hopefully know today, rather more complicated an act than what Smith seems to suggest. In fact, simply reading texts *as* sacred could be understood to implicate such a reader in reproducing the rather specific social world from which that text arose as well as the world for which it may today act as an authority or touchstone – but I'm guessing that this was not the critical concern of his first methodological point. In fact, steps two, three, and four seem to preclude any sort of critical scholarship whatsoever, inasmuch as the work of a scholar in this Smith's tradition seems meant to authorize itself by means of the legitimacy granted to it by the already authorized, and thus authentic, people being studied – a rather small number of elites, no less, with whom the scholar has made acquaintance.

So, what happens if we approach the book in *this* manner, seeing it as offering not an accurate account but, instead, an entirely familiar and thus safe account for those who may have a vested interest in the material? After all, even the things included that might be new to a reader are nonetheless still represented as instances of the sort of transhistorical wisdom and meaning relevant to all human beings. With this approach, we may see in his later comments on its success a perhaps unintended explanation for why a piece of scholarship that is sixty years old and strikes me as bearing all of the now-outdated marks of its time (no less than R. C. Zaehner's once widely adopted but now largely forgotten textbook, for example – which originally dated from 1959, making it slightly more recent than Smith's!) strikes yet other contemporary scholars as still relevant and thus timely (helping those sales numbers to continue to climb by means of their textbook orders) – leading to readers who might be surprised to learn that they're reading a book older than their professor.

Whether or not the book played a crucial role in the establishment of the field, by engaging new audiences and providing a new generation of faculty with a simple and straightforward resource on which to draw when inventing the field in the mid- to late 1960s, is something that we can discuss and something to which I might even agree. To be sure, the field, let alone our own society, was a different beast sixty years ago, as I presume will always be the case – after all, which thriving academic field is still pursuing the questions and using the methods – let alone the textbooks – from over half a century in its past? Sure, I sometimes have students read Müller and Tiele, among others from the pre-history of our field. This very semester, I'm using Jacques Waardenburg's 1973 anthology, *Classical Approaches to the Study of Religion* in one of my upper-level undergraduate classes – but we're using it to provide us with a way to talk about from where our field came and the incredible distance between us and them, as opposed to seeing in those writers a model for what we are now doing or ought to be doing tomorrow. In fact, even Waardenburg's own lengthy introduction to the volume, first published over forty years ago, reads to me now as a product from another era, when members of the recently emerged field (again, at least in North America) seem to have needed a narrative of origins and canonical set of readings/authors to go along with it. It was a time when, at least in Waardenburg's estimation, European and North American scholars could use a common understanding of the direction in which they should be moving and shared vocabulary, all based on a developmental narrative begun with Müller and Tiele. Thus, a careful reader will come to that text thinking not that it tells them all that much about religion, the study of religion, or even about each of the authors included, but, rather, they will hopefully approach it knowing that they see 1973 writ large in its pages, a time in the field's history when the production of such a canon made sense. Waardenburg's book – as with all texts, no? – is therefore a socially formative work and not, as some might see it, a merely passive description of other things, for (hearkening back to canons of so-called sacred texts) as editor he has chosen, ignored, emphasized, organized, etc., all based on interests of relevance to him – *when I was 12 years old*. So more than likely the interests that those choices helped to operationalize are no longer concerns today – which doesn't mean that we won't read the book, of course, but we'll likely use it far differently than how readers came to it in the mid-1970s, back when it was an orange-bound hardcover published by Mouton of The Hague.

If this applies to how we read Waardenburg's anthology, let alone reading our late-19th century predecessors, then does it not it apply to reading the subsequent editions of *The Religions of Man* as well? Is this text itself not an historical, primary source that may deserve reading and careful study today but, as argued just above, *not* as an introductory textbook and *not* as an innocent description of actual realities in the world, such as what Christians think, what Buddhists do, and how these things some call primal religions endure? Instead, it's as a socially formative artifact from a previous age whose persistence we can explain inasmuch as many readers, as well as many professors to this day, come to a class in the study of religion in search of confirmation for what they've thought all along: e.g., that individuals come before groups; that meaning is internal and dynamic and only secondarily pressed out into the world; that private and personal sentiments known as faith and belief animate outward action; that value is timeless and transcendent; and that some parts of the human are pure and special and thus elevated among the polluted others. Investing in a resource that helps to confirm all that, especially in a classroom setting where readers might be concerned that some of their cherished folk truths may be challenged or undermined (such as our still widely shared presumption of the self-evidency of "the essential similarity of human nature" [Smith 1959: 19]), may well pay off. Despite having little analytic utility and representing a moment in our current field's pre-history that some of us have long put behind us, Smith's understanding of religion as "a matter of meanings" (1959: 21) and thus "the clearest opening through which the inexhaustible energies of the cosmos can pour into human existence" (1959: 20), concerning "conditions of the soul that words can only hint at" (1959: 21), still has its share of advocates, plenty of whom are within the academy. I assume that very few of those buyers are like me, finding that 1893 edition of Müller's *Lectures on the Science of Religion* in a used bookstore, happy simply to own an historical artifact from a prior time (in fact, I bought the 50th anniversary edition of Smith's book in preparation for writing this paper). I also doubt that – as with undergrad students in our department's world religions courses with my colleague, Steven Ramey[12] – they're using it critically, inasmuch as students will eventually make whatever textbook they're using their object of study, and thereby examine the very category of world religions itself.[13]

And so I conclude by citing here a question recorded in the back of my own now-tattered 1991 edition of the book, written (when I was a doctoral student)

---

[12] Though he regularly changes the books he uses, this semester Ramey is using *Religion is Not One* by Stephen Prothero (2010). See https://religion.ua.edu/courses/rel-102-001-religions-of-the-world/ for information on Ramey's particular approach to the world religions course; see also http://www.religiousstudiesproject.com/podcast/would-you-still-call-yourself-an-asianist/ for an interview concerning his approach to the study of religion (accessed Sept. 25, 2017).
[13] See Cotter and Robertson (2016) for a collection of essays, approximately half of which set as their goal a thorough critique (i.e., historicization) of "world religions" rather than aiming to expand it even more by debating what else ought to be admitted to membership in that family.

on one of its final blank pages, when first reading Smith's bestselling book twenty-five years ago:

> Is reprinting a wide-selling 1958 general publication in comparative religion reason for interest in 1992? When that publication largely reproduces, relatively intact, the patterns of thought and habits of an era gone-by, then there is great reason for interest.

Given that the book is still in print and still being bought and used in classes across this country, reproducing the 1991 edition verbatim (now with an added transcription of a 2002 Theosophical Society lecture by Smith along with a *Shambhala Sun* magazine interview with him from 1997),[14] it seems a question still worth asking – a question that concerns not Smith or his work but us and how we read it. Longstanding critiques of simplistically dividing the world between West and East, problems with the theologically motivated notion of Abrahamic religions (Hughes 2012), problems with presuming that the category "historical religion" actually is helpful to our work, problems with examples and suggested readings that are at least thirty years old, let alone problems with the very notion of world religions itself, are all irrelevant to this text – perhaps as it should be, given its age. But they ought *not* to be irrelevant to current readers of the book, since our object of study is the doings of historical human beings and both they and the field that studies them, unlike fossils, are not locked in amber. So, to repeat: *why*, we should ask ourselves, continue to use it today and, if we do require students to purchase it, then *how* are we employing it and in the service of *what* ends?

References

Cotter, Christopher R. and David G. Robertson (eds.) (2016). *After World Religions: Reconstructing Religious Studies*. New York, NY and London, UK: Routledge.
Hughes, Aaron (2012). *Abrahamic Religions: On the Uses and Abuses of History*. New York, NY: Oxford University Press.
McCutcheon, Russell T. (1997). *Manufacturing Religion: The Discourse on Sui Generis Religion and the Politics of Nostalgia*. New York, NY: Oxford University Press.
— (2013). "Just follow the money": The Cold War, the humanistic study of religion, and the fallacy of insufficient cynicism. In William E. Arnal and Russell T. McCutcheon, *The Sacred is the Profane: The Political Nature of "Religion,"* 72–90. New York, NY: Oxford University Press.
Oxtoby, Willard G. (ed.) (1996a). *World Religions: Eastern Traditions*. New York, NY: Oxford University Press.

---

[14] This bi-monthly magazine is now called *The Lion's Roar* and remains devoted to, according to its cover, "Buddhist wisdom for our time."

Oxtoby, Willard G. (ed.) (1996b). *World Religions: Western Traditions*. New York, NY: Oxford University Press.
Oxtoby, Willard G., Roy C. Amore, and Amir Hussain (eds.) (2014). *World Religions: Eastern Traditions*. 4th ed. New York, NY: Oxford University Press.
Oxtoby, Willard G. and Amir Hussain (eds.) (2010). *World Religions: Western Traditions*. 3rd ed. New York, NY: Oxford University Press.
Prothero, Stephen (2010). *Religion in Not One: The Eight Rival Religions that Run the World*. New York, NY: HarperOne.
Sawyer, Dana (2014). *Huston Smith: Wisdomkeeper. Living The World's Religions: The Authorized Biography of a 21st Century Spiritual Giant*. Louisville, KY: Fons Vitae.
Smith, Huston (1958). *The Religions of Man*. New York, NY: Harper & Brothers.
— (1959) [1958]. *The Religions of Man*. New York, NY: Mentor Books.
— (1991) [1958]. *The World's Religions*. New York, NY: HarperCollins.
— (2001). *Islam: A Concise Introduction*. New York, NY: HarperSanFrancisco.
— (2009) [1958]. *The World's Religions*. 50th anniversary edition. New York, NY: HarperOne.
Smith, Jonathan Z. (1998). Religion, religions, religious. In Mark C. Taylor (ed.), *Critical Terms for Religious Studies*, 269–284. Chicago, IL: University of Chicago Press.
Waardenburg, Jacques (2017). *Classical Approaches to the Study of Religion*. 2nd ed. Russell T. McCutcheon (foreword). Berlin, DE: Walter de Gruyter.
Zaehner, R. C. (ed.) (1967) [1959]. *The Concise Encyclopedia of Living Faiths*. Boston, MA: Beacon Press.

4 "Man is the Measure of All Things:" On The Fabrication of Oriental Religions by European History of Religions

For over a decade, my university (like many, maybe most, in the U.S.) has been mindful of the need for professors to develop clearly stated and measurable outcomes for each of their courses; in fact, entire departments must now have such outcomes for the programs that they offer, stating what a student will be able to know or do upon the completion of their degree. Once simply called goals (as in a syllabus stating something like, "In this class students will learn to describe and compare ... ," etc., etc.), what we now term "learning outcomes" are accompanied by "assessment measures," i.e., ways of determining whether or not the various outcomes have, in fact, been achieved. For why list the ambition of teaching students to describe and then compare two things if you don't have some way to determine if they have actually acquired these skills and been able to use them correctly? Ideally, or so faculty are regularly told, these assessments are not just broad-based (such as a final grade earned at the completion of a course, or even a grade earned on any one assignment) or merely anecdotal reports on how the professor *thinks* the students have done. Instead, they must be particular and quantitative, thereby itemizing, in a factual manner, how many students were able to carry out this or that specific skill, at this or that specific moment in the course, based on their performance on this or that specific assignment or test question. And, depending on whether the intended outcome was achieved (e.g., at the start of the course I might

---

Note: While the subtitle derives from the occasion and setting when this lecture was first presented (speaking to a class at the University of Zurich on this topic [on Sept. 29, 2015]), the main title – to be further discussed below – is the common translation of Plato's *Theaetetus* 152a, a well-known line attributed to the pre-Socratic philosopher and so-called Sophist, Protagoras (c. 490–420 BCE). The line is also quoted by Sextus Empiricus (d. 210 CE) in his *Against the Mathematicians* (*Adversus Mathematicos*) Book 7.60: "πάντων χρημάτων μέτρον ἐστὶν ἄνθρωπος, τῶν μὲν ὄντων ὡς ἔστιν, τῶν δὲ οὐκ ὄντων ὡς οὐκ ἔστιν" ("Man is the measure of all things: of the things that are, that they are, of the things that are not, that they are not"). I greatly appreciate Professor Christoph Uehlinger's invitation to lecture to his class, devoted to the impact of oriental religions on the history of religions. The main reason for my visit to Switzerland was to participate in a master class devoted to the work of current doctoral students at the Universities of Basel, Bern, and Zurich, involving the following participants: David Atwood, Felizia Benke, Anne Beutter, Benedikt Erb, Philipp Hetmanczyk, Vanessa Lange, Stefan Ragaz, Lilo-Marie Ruthner, Maria Wedekind, and Barbara Zeugin, My thanks to Anja Kirsch, at the University of Basel, for arranging my visit and hosting me while there.

https://doi.org/10.1515/9783110560831-005

aim for 80% of students knowing the capital of France by the end of the semester), there's a place in what we call an assessment report for communicating what revisions you'll make the next time you teach that class, either to ensure that more students meet your goals or, perhaps, to adjust your expectations and thus increase your standards so that students are seen to be continually improving. After all, why not aim for 85%, maybe even 90%, of your students to know about the City of Lights?

If you've been following U.S. politics at all over the past decade or so, then you might know why we, in the university, now talk about assessment, outcomes, and measures; it has a great deal to do with a federal act, called No Child Left Behind, that was signed into law by President George W. Bush in January 2002 (it was, in fact, simply a reauthorization, and revision, of the Elementary and Secondary Education Act of 1965). The U.S.'s current focus on so-called standards-based education is hardly uncontroversial. It emphasizes regular standardized testing across the country and the implementation of measurable outcomes. It also empowered the U.S. Department of Education to set annual progress markers (that, if unmet, can eventually result in the school being closed, taken over by the state, or its duties farmed out to a private company – what we call "charter schools"). And although it was *not* aimed at universities, we are now the inheritors of a generation of students who, all throughout what we term their elementary and also their secondary schooling (i.e., grade school and then high school), were taught using this method. Although it took about a decade for standards-based education to work its way up the ladder, it is now well-ensconced in American higher education, something that is especially evident in public universities. Unlike private colleges, the budgets of public universities can often be largely dependent on government funding (whether from their state or the federal government) and a key ingredient in obtaining that support is for a school to be regularly evaluated by a regional credentialing organization. So although there may be no direct way for the federal government to intervene in a university classroom, or to require a professor to, for example, implement quantifiable outcomes and so-called assessment rubrics (for instance, stating clearly and systematically, for students, what counts as a B+ on some assignment and the specific ways in which that differs from an A), the routine and day-to-day financial needs of any university make obtaining certified status with one of the federally recognized credentialing agencies a necessity. Failing to do so risks those federal dollars flowing to your school. And so, inasmuch as the credentialing agency (whether assessing an entire university or any of its individual degree programs [which happens every decade or so]) expects measurable outcomes (because, in turn, the U.S. Department of Education expects them), then whole departments and professors alike, much as in the case of public elementary school teachers, are now expected to report on their classes' measurable outcomes.

And thus was born the so-called assessment initiative on U.S. university campuses.

But why am I telling you all this?

I've decided to open this chapter in this way for two reasons. First, whenever an opportunity presents itself, I like to make apparent that if we take the critique of *sui generis* religion seriously (a topic on which I focused my early work in the field [McCutcheon 1997]), then that means that those claims, behaviors, and institutions formerly known as religious or spiritual or sacred turn out to be ordinary things that have become interesting *for us*, as *scholars*, only because those wielding the category religion have decided to select certain of them and then link them up, *as if* they have always been inherently related and obviously set apart from all other things. So, to press this very point, why not start an essay in *Religionswissenschaft* by making seemingly arbitrary references to the state of public higher education in the U.S. – something obviously not religious whatsoever, no? The second reason is directly related to this point concerning how our observation and organization of the world constitutes that world in certain sorts of self-beneficial ways – a constitution that, I would argue, we often merely describe and thereby fail to recognize as our own creation. I begin in this manner because the curious thing about measurable outcomes is that, despite their emphasis on the quantifiables in student performance ("Just the facts, ma'am," as the detective in an old TV police drama used to phrase it, when questioning witnesses), the empirical result that you obtain and then report is actually a product of the standard that you had set – or should I say, *happened to have set*. (And with that subtle introduction of happenstance, by which I mean contingency, human interest, and thus situated social circumstance, you may see where I'm heading by starting my essay as I have – for the quantitative may be far more qualitative than we care to imagine.) Case in point: at the conclusion of a course, one might report something like "80% of the students correctly identified Switzerland on a map of Europe" – an especially good result if, on the first day of class, you offered a pop quiz, as we say, and only 35% knew where it was and, even better if you'd originally hoped for at least 60% to learn it by the end of the semester. (Congratulations! You surpassed your goal!) But despite the seemingly tangible, factual nature of such a report – after all, 80% of twenty-five students are twenty flesh and blood bodies that you can count, which bump into each other, and who all know where Switzerland is – this claim about your students is the product of an authority figure. Perhaps it's a professor, or the U.S. Department of Education, or maybe even a professional association with an interest in maps, such as the Association of American Geographers, which could demand this performance of the Departments of Geography that it credentials annually. But this authority figure happened to decide that, of the virtually innumerable things students would be learning that semester, the location of (to stick with my arbitrary example) this one European country was not just something worth paying attention to but should also be seen as representative of what success in a course meant.

Not only that, but, as already suggested, the reported success rate of 80% can only be judged by its relationship to whatever goal happened to have been set at the start of the semester. Did it surpass a goal of, say, 60% ("Well done!") or have we failed to meet an even more ambitious goal, such that our 80% result is instead characterized as a sadly disappointing performance by our students and which might be indicative of our poor teaching techniques? So, not only is the act of grouping those twenty successful students together a product of someone else's decision to signify them as similar in this one regard (i.e., they are a group only inasmuch as someone cares about them knowing Switzerland's location) but, following from this, in and of itself, that seemingly empirical, quantifiable, tangible, factual 80% is meaningless (i.e., so what twenty of twenty-five students have this one thing in common – surely we could cut that twenty-five-student pie in innumerable other ways since they have innumerably different things in common, no?). In order to give the impression of that group's stable boundaries, its members must be signified by being placed into a controlled, comparative relationship, likely not of their making, that's measured against some ideal that, again, is possibly alien to the members who end up being assigned to the group (do they even care where Switzerland is?!). It's an ideal that is itself hardly an empirical or brute fact but, instead, as suggested above when I introduced this notion of situated happenstance into the analysis, it is the result of – to stick with our arbitrary example – a particular professor's changeable hopes and dreams. For, thinking back to the No Child Left Behind federal law, despite how proud you might be with the results you've obtained, only if that 80% falls within the parameters of the Department of Education's annual progress markers will it be judged sufficient or not – i.e., as should be obvious, 80% can be a failing grade if the bar is set high enough.

But, leaving all this aside for a moment: let's say we play this game correctly. Let's say we do such things as submit our assessment reports on time (as I have done on many past occasions, inasmuch as I have often acted as my department's so-called assessment coordinator) and in the proper format, using the correct terminology (such as saying "outcome" rather than "goal"). Let's even suppose, if you'll excuse me, that we *not* question why knowing Switzerland's location on a map is something worth knowing, *not* ask why 80 or 85 or 90% is a goal worth attaining, *not* look into why having some students fail to attain the goal is undesirable (after all, perhaps not everyone should meet a standard in university), and *not* wonder why we should have confidence in the credentialing agency in the first place (for asking "Who credentials the credentialing agency?" opens a worm hole of philosophical problems worthy of earnest, late night conversations among slightly inebriated undergrads[1]). If we do all these things, acting in the correct and proper fashion (with a nod to a quote from Slavoj Žižek [who was himself quoting Louis Althusser] that I've often used on a variety of past occasions[2]), that will allow us all *to come to believe* that the goals and methods of standards-based education say something *real* and of *value* about the world. The change it tracks will then count as progress that is *tangible* and *significant.* And those twenty students will be seen as *naturally* and *necessarily* grouped together, inasmuch as we take for granted – and in taking it for granted, thereby reauthorize – how someone, somewhere else, not only defined what counted *as* knowledge and *as* success but, in doing so (at least in the case of the five who didn't master this geographic skill), also defined what counted as membership within the group of those who failed to meet our expectations.

Correction: it is not *the* outcome but, rather, *our* outcome or *theirs*. For, I would argue, ownership matters.

As we consider the impact of Oriental religions on Europe as well as on the academic discipline known as the History of Religions, this is all worth mulling over for a moment, I believe. We have a very nice illustration of the often-overlooked, qualitative factors that determine what counts as a quantitative consequence worth measuring. As I've just suggested, if we do this all correctly then, of the innumerable ways that those twenty students *might* be arranged in terms of similarity and difference (and calling those biological individuals all "students," and thereby uniting them into that single constituency, by seeing

---

1 For example, consider that in the U.S. there are six main regional credentialing associations in higher education (the Southern Association of Colleges and Schools [SACS] being the one in my part of the country). They are in turn legitimized by two bodies: 1. the U.S. Department of Education, which, of course, is a legitimate authority only inasmuch as the very people who either attend or work for the schools it oversees or whose children attend them vote for the party that leads it; and 2. the Council for Higher Education Accreditation (CHEA), a group comprised of roughly 3,000 member institutions, which certifies the credentialing agencies that, in turn, judge these very institutions.

2 The quote reads as follows: "Religious belief, for example, is not merely or even primarily an inner conviction, but the Church as an institution and its rituals (prayer, baptism, confirmation, confession...) which, far from being a mere secondary externalization of the inner belief, stand for the very mechanisms that generate it. When [Louis] Althusser repeats, after [Blaise] Pascal: 'Act as if you believe, pray, kneel down, and you shall believe, faith will arrive by itself,' he delineates an intricate reflective mechanism ... that far exceeds the reductionist assertion of the dependence of inner belief on external behavior. That is to say, the implicit logic of his argument is: kneel down and you shall believe that you knelt down because of your belief – that is, your following the ritual is an expression/effect of your inner belief; in short, the 'external' ritual performatively generates its own ideological foundation" (1997: 12–13).

their shared significance in terms of their placement within our setting of higher education, could just as easily have been our example here), *only one* will seem to stand out. It's not only the difference between saying "*the* outcome" as opposed to "*our* outcome," but *that very phrasing*, this way of conceptualizing the issue, as if some feature has agency and can *stand out* on its own, is part of the problem that we need to re-consider if, instead of just behaving "properly," we're trying to pay more careful attention to *how propriety works*, or, in this case, how the process of identification works. Knowing the location of Switzerland on a map and using that criterion as a means for isolating the five people who failed at this task (and, in the process, constituting the twenty who succeeded) hardly proclaims itself, of its own volition, as a criterion to which we *ought* to give consideration. Simply put, despite the seemingly descriptive, passive nature of our language, it does not *stand* on its own, and saying that it does obscures *our* ownership by means of *our* role in proposing and then propping up that one feature. The contingent, even arbitrary nature of a course's subject matter (i.e., the students could have enrolled in another course instead, studying something else entirely), as well as the standards for success that we set, along with the role of a professor, a professional association, or a nation-state in not just setting but authorizing those standards, conjures this particular groupness into existence at this particular site, for the purposes of the one doing the conjuring.

So, as I've tried to make evident, this apparently tangible, shared group identity of those twenty geographically gifted students can also be seen as contextually and thus historically specific. Such an outcome would make little sense in a calculus class and, even if the class was on modern European geography, it's just as likely that the criterion could have been Italy's location on a map (and, being an easily identifiable boot, perhaps we would have aimed for 100% success on that one – "Well done!"), making their knowledge (or lack of it) concerning the Swiss of no relevance whatsoever. What's more, should we decide to increase standards next year, or perhaps put a finer-tuned measure in place by expecting students, for instance, to name all of the neighborhoods of any one of Zurich's twelve districts, well, some of those who might have met last year's assessment goal will suddenly find themselves excluded from the group of high achievers who passed, maybe giving the Department of Education the impression that our class's performance has dropped sufficiently to call its very existence into question. They do close schools, after all.

My point?

Failing to historicize (by which I mean finding the actors, in specific settings, who made the standards and set the definitions, and thereby recovering the ownership, rather than leaving it – as Lincoln has phrased it – implicit and masked [2014: 140]) the situated and interested means by which social life is regularly constituted and reconstituted lends the impression that the groups of which we claim membership – or of which we claim that others are members – are naturally occurring phenomena with clear, stable boundaries. While I am firmly committed to the notion of social life as being a necessary and foundational component of existence, that this or that *particular* social group (or, better put, sub-group) exists is, however, not necessary at all; instead it's an ongoing work in progress. So, theorists interested in the intertwined processes of identification and social formation – what I've been discussing so far but at a site seemingly removed from our field – have much to be curious about when studying the means by which groups (any groups) are constituted and continually re-constituted. Unlike those who focus on that hypothetical class's 80% success rate, as if this outcome has obvious value, I think it is far more interesting to ask questions about who gets to set the standard in the first place. Answering that will tell us a great deal about the interests that may lie behind, and the consequences entailed by, our presumption that there's an identifiable group of successful students in distinction from those who sadly failed to meet the mark (or, better put, *our* mark). Or, to put it in terms that apply to myself, it seems to me to be far more interesting to ask questions about how, in my own case, Canadian identity is even possible then to take it as a settled fact, as if it has a force of its own and thereby focus merely on talking about, say, Canada's role in the world or discussing Canadian cuisine or Canadian literature. Focusing on the latter topics without also entertaining the former – that is, without first considering the formation of that object that subsequently is thought to have a variety of effects in the world – risks failing to entertain the continuous feedback loop that exists, as Émile Durkheim once phrased it, between those things that we commonly call beliefs and practices. It doesn't even touch on how that interconnected ideal and material network conjures into existence the social formations we often mistake for naturally occurring objects that need only to be described, appreciated, or sometimes criticized. Canadians and the Swiss certainly have effect in the world – I won't be so silly as to argue with that; but that's only because we all think and act *as if* there's such a thing as a Canada and Switzerland as well as presume that uniform traits are instilled in those living there – something that is confirmed by my acting like others might all hope a Canadian would act (e.g., saying "please" and "thank you" and "excuse me" and "sorry" often enough to persuade you that I'm not, perhaps, British or American – or at least how one might think a caricatured Brit or Yank might act). And it is this continual, mutual self-constitution – i.e., an observer's self-interested expectations fabricating objects and subjectivities that, in turn, are thought to exert influence on those who presume themselves to be but disinterested observers – that, I would argue, needs to be taken far more seriously in our field (let alone in our efforts to judge a student's performance in our course).

All of which leads me back to the topic of the class into which I was so kindly invited to speak when offering an earlier form of this chapter as a public lecture. What makes me curious is how, despite having read our Said and despite having read our Foucault, so many in the field still wish to discuss the impact or place or history or future of so-called Oriental religions, or, in an effort to be politically correct, what we might today instead call Asian religions (still presuming, despite the name change, some unifying element to them all that distinguishes them from what, Occidental or Western religions?). All of this leads naturally to discussions of such topics as immigration, diaspora, syncretism, multiculturalism, interreligious dialogue, and globalization, to name but a few topics that now populate so many of the courses and the books in our field. I tend to think, however, that such an approach (one that posits the prior existence of things called Hinduism or Buddhism, Sikhism or Taoism and Shinto, over there, that subsequently exert some influence on us, over here. [The interesting thing, by the way, is how I knew what to put in that list! Question: Is Islam any longer an Oriental religion? And if so, then *to whom*?]) has it rather backward – even if one makes the seemingly provocative move to acknowledge that, though they're out there, they're not stable but, instead, in a constant state of flux. (We all likely know how popular it now is to replace the singulars with plurals, such that we now study Hinduisms and not Hinduism, no?) As you may by now have surmised by my problematizing of outcomes and assessments, and by coming to see them not as merely *descriptive* of stable states of affairs but, instead, as indicative of invested situations that *constitute* the very notion of a good or a bad student or a good or a bad school, some state of affairs that we think ourselves to merely be describing is, instead, actually being constituted by the lens (or set of criteria) that we opt to use. It's *our* decision, after all; the question is whether we can *own* it. And it's a lens employed not just to look at this or that pre-existing group of people in some new way but, rather (recalling those twenty good students), that we use to see just these people *as* comprising a group that's worth looking at. I therefore approach the study of identity (as in the act of identifying something *as* a religion that is then thought to affect us or do things in the world, like motivate people to act in this or that way) as the tip of usually unseen icebergs with which we ourselves, as the so-called observers, are in fact intimately involved.

Perhaps my reason for choosing the main title that I did for this chapter – an ancient saying attributed to the pre-Socratic philosopher Protagoras (d. 420 BCE) – is becoming a little clearer?

Let us return to my analogy in a domain far from our field but where I've invited you to think through some of the issues that I see to be of relevance to our field, where some routinely talk about orthodox Hindus and extremist Muslims. This idea of a good or a bad student is something other than an innocent description of a matter of fact. It makes me think back to a quotation from the famous linguistics scholar Noam Chomsky, as phrased in the 1992 documentary film *Manufacturing Consent: Noam Chomsky and the Media*, in which he discusses recollections of his own elementary education:

> And I also had the advantage of having gone to an experimental progressive school, to a Deweyite school, which was quite good, run by a university there, and, you know, there was no such thing as competition. There was no such thing as being a good student. Literally, the concept of being a good student didn't even arise until I got to high school. I went to the academic high school, and suddenly discovered I'm a good student.[3]

This is an instructive example, for we have here a moment of hindsight self-reflection in which a person considers how he was integrated and socialized within – or, in keeping with Althusser's theory of identity formation, perhaps we should just say interpellated by means of – a classificatory system that created certain sorts of identities within individuals by means of authorized criteria and the social relationships that resulted from their continued use. The identity that is created – i.e., in this case, that of "being a good student" but could we also not add "being a good Hindu"? – can now be understood as resulting *not* from an inevitable or authentic self-expression based on an innate quality but, instead, as an effect of an imposed structure that is representative of interests other than the person's own. It's a structure that allows us to see, for example, the child *as* a student or the person *as* a Hindu, let alone *as* a good or a bad one. And now, taking seriously the imposed nature of this structure, the seemingly ethereal, private thing called subjectivity or self or identity can be understood as evidence of prior historical events and social acts (what I mean by an imposed structure). Like all other products that human beings manufacture (inasmuch as products derive from the refinement and assembly of prior, raw – i.e., pre-, or better put, differently signified – materials), that self-conception we call subjectivity now can be understood to come with a production date subtly stamped somewhere on it, indicating the social situation in which it came into being. And, being a contingent, as opposed to a necessary or totalized, product – one that was made in a specific location by specific productive factors, and which therefore has effect in a particular situation for particular purposes – necessarily means that, like everything else we call historical (such as jugs of milk that eventually go sour), it also has an expiration date.

---

3 See the 30:20 point of the documentary (*Manufacturing Consent: Noam Chomsky and the Media* [1992], directed by Mark Achbar and Peter Wintonick). "Deweyite" refers to a school influenced by the work of U.S. pragmatist philosopher John Dewey (1859–1952) and his thoughts on student-centered education reform.

So when it comes to studying social formations, or what we might also call identity formations – of which the things we call religions or world religions are but examples, alongside people who feel themselves to be either good or bad students – you may now see why I favor a scholar such as the French social theorist Jean-François Bayart. As made evident, I think, by the many case studies assembled by those writing at the blog for Culture on the Edge (edge.ua.edu), his work (such as his 2005 book, *The Illusion of Cultural Identity*) helps us to understand the sociology and politics of the so-called experience of having and expressing an identity (whether an individual or a group). It's an experience that participants no doubt feel to be real, affective, deeply lodged, personal, and thus private, but it can be described as being the result of what he terms *operational acts of identification* – acts on the part of themselves and others as well. As a form of action (such as the classificatory act of separating this student's name in a grade book from that one, placing the letter A beside one and F beside the other), this experience is necessarily an historical and thus public item that can be examined.

And so, after this long preamble – though it is my hope that readers understand the utility of thinking a problem through in one domain before applying it to another – I finally come to the subtitle of this chapter: The Fabrication of Oriental Religions by European History of Religions.[4] You may now understand my reason for saying that the widespread presumption that religions from *there* have effect on us *here* could be seen to be rather ironic. It's not difficult to make a case for our (or at least our intellectual ancestors) having been the ones who not only first named these things *as* religions but, more importantly, who also first assembled the particular sets of claims and practices and institutions together *as if* they were coherent and necessarily related items (i.e., our disciplinary predecessors were the ones who put the -ism in Buddhism by seeing otherwise diverse and discrete behaviors as inherently linked). Consider that this action done before eating and that action done at a funeral were somehow thought to be essentially related, both expressions of the Oriental mind, as it might have once been phrased. So, to repeat, here too we are hardly disinterested observers intent on innocent description. We not only named and treated those things *as* religious, but we were the ones who selected and grouped their constitutive parts that, once collected and animated by us with an apparent agency of their own, created the impression of

---

4 As already indicated in my introduction, the utility of the double entendre of "fabricate" – both to build as well as to lie – is highly useful here and intended to add some depth to our thinking about what it is we do when we talk about objects in the world – i.e., we create them, through discourse, while disowning them as our own creations (thereby telling lies about their origins and autonomy).

distinct organizations doing distinct things and thus in need of distinct names (and, in the case of our field, distinct methods for their study so that we understood them properly).

So, to scrutinize the impact that, for instance, Hinduism now has on our nation or on our intellectual pursuits – or, better yet, the impact of the larger genus to which we assign that which we call Hinduism, i.e., so-called Oriental religions – risks overlooking *our* constitutive role in creating and maintaining these objects in the first place. Our role is both historic, with reference to the labors of our late 19th-century scholarly predecessors, and contemporary, with regard to each time we teach a world religions class, each time we hunt through a publisher's catalogue, every time we read a news story on, say, Hindu/Muslim violence today in India, and every time we use the results of a census which asked people to classify themselves. That this discursive object, once instantiated in authorized literature, once legislation and the force of coercive violence ensures that it becomes a judicial and thus political reality, then seems to exert influence of its own on the world cannot be overlooked, of course. Failing to see ourselves as complicit in its apparent agency conveniently removes *our own agency* from the discussion (like talking about "*the* outcomes" instead of *ours*), representing ourselves merely as passive recipients of the Oriental religions' enduring effects. And thus we arrive at a situation in which the historicity of these so-called religions, these social formations which we have brought into existence in our efforts to catalogue all human beings according to what we take to be an interrelated system of panhuman disembodied beliefs and ritual practices, is erased. It leaves them with no manufacturing history and no expiration date, and thereby represents the social formations we've fabricated (in both senses of that English word) as if they were ahistorical, totalized systems that were here long before any of us arrived – which is the myth of origin that virtually every world religions textbook perpetuates in the opening pages of each chapter.

Although I'll elaborate a bit more on this later, the same goes for this idea of Europe, of course, for it, too, has a manufacturing history – something painfully evident, perhaps, in the gaps and disagreements that have recently become so profoundly apparent. I think here of some nations' reactions to the so-called Greek financial crisis. Or perhaps we should refer to either Brexit or the recent contest over whether to call the Syrians who entered Europe *refugees*, who are welcomed, as opposed to those classed as *migrants* and who are then returned home? Despite the success of Eurovision (and yes, I watch it each year), the possible failure of this supposedly transnational idea to address longstanding national disagreements and divergent national interests indicates that this idea, too, likely has a "best before" date inscribed on it somewhere, the bitter taste of which some are now experiencing.

To provide an example from our own field of how this all works – how we portray items that we constitute *as if* they are found objects that exert an influence of their own on the world, thereby removing our own fingerprints from the impact we conclude that *they* have on *us* – I could make a more detailed reference to earlier eras of scholarship's creation of Hinduism or Buddhism, for example. Perhaps I could cite what I consider to be Philip Almond's classic 1988 study, *The British Discovery of Buddhism*, in which he concluded that:

> It was the Victorians who developed the discourse within which Buddhism was circumscribed, who deemed it a worthy focus of Western attention; it was they who brought forth the network of texts within which Buddhism was located. And it was they who determined the framework in which Buddhism was imaginatively constructed, not only for themselves, but also in the final analysis for the East itself.[5]

Or, as already suggested, I could reference Said's now canonical work on the creation and reproduction of an Orientalist discourse in Europe (and elsewhere, of course). Perhaps I could even going so far as to examine how European-based discourses have been so successfully deployed that social actors worldwide now seem able to think themselves into agency only by means of such imported rubrics as the nation or world religions, whereby all of us understand ourselves *as* citizens (I needed a passport to get here, after all) or *as* having a religion that must be respected and studying appropriately. But I'd rather provide a more current

---

[5] I admit that I take the thesis concerning the European invention of these so-called Oriental religions, such as Hinduism, as now credibly established, therefore not worrying too much about such responses as Pennington's (2005). For when he states, in his introduction: "It would be a severe historical misrepresentation (albeit a faddish one, to be sure) to suggest, as many have, that Hinduism was the invention of the British. Adapting to the colonial milieu, Hindus themselves entered a dialectic space in which they endorsed and promoted the British publication of ancient texts and translations, resisted missionary polemic, and experimented with modifications, alterations, and innovations in Hindu religious forms" (4), it strikes me as deeply problematic that he fails to distinguish a group of people at that time called Hindus from, say, residents of the Indian subcontinent or, perhaps, pundits, or any number of other ways of characterizing the people who either collaborated with or actively resisted colonial rule – i.e., classifying them in a way that they themselves would have recognized instead of exporting our organizing concept, "Hindu" backwards in time so casually. This strikes me as just as improper as calling them citizens of India (inasmuch as the nation-state had yet to be invented). In other words, in response to the invention of Hinduism thesis, Pennington simply re-asserts (rather anachronistically, I'd suggest) that the people of the subcontinent already thought of themselves as Hindus, as well as having something called a religion, prior to the colonial encounter. Lamenting that the position with which he disagrees "erases Hindu agency" (5) is, I would therefore conclude, a judgment of which we're capable today, most certainly; but whether it would have been a common or sensible way of conceptualizing the situation 300 years ago is the issue for careful historians.

example, in part to ensure that we do not see self-implicated fabrications as being something only carried out in an historically distant and thus alien era when, or so the argument goes, scholars were either sloppy and too easily influenced by politics, or perhaps just not as nuanced as we see ourselves as being today. (This is often the argument I hear when current scholars critique their predecessors – sooner or later we learn not that the colonialists invented, say, African religions, but, rather, that they *misunderstood* or *misrepresented* them [which is what I read in Chidester's otherwise important work (e.g., 1996)].) So consider, if you will, a European research consortium in whose inaugural conference I participated as a respondent (in October 2008). Taking place at Ruhr University in Bochum, Germany, the conference was entitled, "Dynamics in the History of Religions Between Asia and Europe."[6] Funded generously by the German Federal Ministry of Education and Research (i.e., *Bundesministerium für Bildung und Forschung*), the results of the consortium members' individual research and its conferences (to which they have regularly invited international participants) are being published in a series with Brill of the Netherlands; the first conference's volume, including an essay of my own, appeared in 2012.

The description of the consortium's book series, which closely parallels what I understood the inaugural conference to be about, opens as follows:

> The so called world religions and other religious traditions are not, and have never been, homogenous, nor have they formed or evolve[d] in isolation. Trying to overcome cultural stereotypes and their ideological misuse, the series *"Dynamics in the History of Religions"* focuses on the crucial role of mutual encounters in the origins, development, and internal differentiation of the major religious traditions. The primary thesis of the series consists in the assumption that interconnections of self-perception and perception by the other, of adaptation and demarcation are crucial factors for historical dynamics within the religious field.[7]

What at first might seem to be part of the now ongoing critique of the world religions category (evidenced by the insertion of that qualification "so called") turns out, on further inspection, to be a far more traditional approach – interested merely in fine tuning our understanding of how these already existing things called "major religious traditions" interact. As suggested earlier, such terms as syncretism, diaspora, hybridization, and creolization, not to mention dialogue, encounter, and transgression, have, for some time, been categories of choice for

---

[6] Portions of the following discussion of this consortium – renamed the Käte Hamburger Consortium in 2010 – are adapted from McCutcheon 2014: chapter 13.
[7] Find the full series description at http://www.brill.com/publications/dynamics-history-religions. For more information on the research consortium itself, see https://khk.ceres.rub.de/en/publications/dynamics-history-religions/ (both links accessed Aug. 14, 2017).

those who wish to present social life as far more dynamic than we might have previously thought (thus few of us opt for the singular noun "society" anymore). And so, predictably perhaps, such terms occupied a prominent place at the conference.

Now, I admit that, when it comes to carrying out research that requires significant external funding from such bodies as, say, the nation-state or private corporations, especially multi-million euro/dollar grants that are above and beyond what the universities already cost the state to run,[8] I become, if not a suspicious hermeneut, then at least a curious one concerning what is going on at such events and what new knowledge and action they might make possible. I therefore find it helpful at such times to think about some of the "destabilizing and irreverent questions" posted in one of Bruce Lincoln's well-known "Theses on Method" (1996: 225), specifically number 4: "'Who speaks here?' ... 'To what audience? In what immediate or broader context? ... With what interests?'" For example, what in the life of the EU in general, or a country like Germany in particular (or, say the Netherlands, whose Organization for Scientific Research [Nederlandse Organisatie voor Wetenschappelijk Onderzoek] "generously funded" [de Vries 2008: xiv] "The Future of the Religious Past: Elements and Forms for the Twenty-First Century" research initiative[9]), would prompt those who control the (always limited) resources of its various granting agencies to fund so heavily, in the early 21st century, such an elaborate, multi-university, scholarly consortium, devoted to, of all things, understanding religions as internally diverse and thus heterogeneously in motion and invariably in contact with one another? Or, why would a Ministry of Education, charged with setting and attaining the educational conditions for a nation's youngest citizens, be interested in seeing religions as more dynamic than some of us might have once pictured them? Breathing new life into the German humanities programs, and raising their reputation in the world, as well as to promote interdisciplinary cooperation, are among the stated reasons (e.g., Krech and Steinicke 2012: 1). But I suspect that there may be more to this than might at first meet the eye, since they could have funded any number of other things, for far less money, to achieve those goals.

I think the context of that 2008 event at Bochum might help us to answer this question concerning the consortium's own conditions of possibility. For in and around the time that I was at the first of these conferences, the issue of immigration across Europe was (and, in recent months, still is, of course) very

---

[8] The grant, from 2008–2014, was worth a total of 12 million euros.
[9] For a description of this 2002–2012 project, which aimed to ascertain the new forms that so-called traditional religions will take in the future, see http://www.nwo.nl/en/research-and-results/programmes/the+future+of+the+religious+past (accessed Aug. 16, 2017).

much in the news, especially the, to some (then and now), questionable role played throughout the EU of this thing simply called Islam. Consider the once much-publicized and debated laws concerning women's headscarves in France to the Danish cartoon controversy (of September 2005) and now the more recent *Charlie Hebdo* attacks in Paris (of January 2015), as well as past debates over the role of publicly funded Muslim religious education in Germany. (As I understand it, religious education is constitutionally mandated, and thus state-supported, in many of Germany's sixteen federal states, in which religious bodies provide the content and the training for the teaching, though both must be approved by the state – although students can opt out for an "ethics" course instead, as I recall.) All of this comes in the wake of the post-9/11 discourse within almost all liberal democracies concerning what constitutes legitimate versus illegitimate forms of Islam (think of newspaper or magazine headlines, not to mention an array of scholarly books, concerning Islam being a "religion of peace" as opposed to, or so it is commonly phrased, the "radicals" and "extremists" who have "hijacked" it). The place of Islam in general, and Muslim immigrants and citizens, in particular, in the future of various nation-states remains a topic very much on the minds of politicians and academics. It is also on the minds of many throughout the public who do not identify as Muslim – and this is not just in Europe; consider the prominent place the topic of Islam had in the run-up to the 2016 U.S. presidential election. For example, at a campaign event, one member of the audience, while posing a question, went so far as to say, "We have a problem in this country and it's called Muslims; we know our current president is one; you know he's not even an American."[10] This is also an issue of importance to those who identify as Muslims themselves but who nonetheless also seem to share significant economic and political interests with many others in these widely diverse liberal democracies, thereby putting them in what might seem to be a curious opposition to any number of ways that yet others identify *as* a Muslim. "How to deal with the problem of Islamic radicalism?" is therefore the question that all of these groups seem to be asking, employing the common designator "radical" to name versions of the social formation seen to be in competition with their own taken-for-granted norms of modern, national life (one of which is the so-called separation of church and state, in which belief or conscience, no matter how

---

10 See http://www.theguardian.com/us-news/2015/sep/18/trump-fails-to-correct-questioner-who-calls-obama-muslim-and-not-even-american (accessed Sept. 18, 2015). This was part of an opening question posed to then Republican candidate Donald Trump at a campaign event on Sept. 17, 2015, in New Hampshire. Subsequent press focused on Trump's failure to correct the questioner.

sincerely they are claimed to be held, are understood to be apolitical and thus strictly private sentiments).

Although it was not stated explicitly (and I would, of course, need far more evidence to make this claim in any manner other than speculation at this point), I left that conference wondering if this so-called problem of Islam – or, far more widely, what is commonly called fundamentalism or extremism (terms that at first seem merely descriptive but which, like the notion of a good student, end up telling us much about the one doing the naming once we examine them a little more closely) – was the undiscussed elephant in the consortium's room, as we might say. That is, the event struck me as an example of how scholarship can develop and deploy (whether consciously intended by us or not) techniques that are conducive to the interests of the nation, and, in the process, fabricate the impressions of allies and foes of our choosing (somewhat akin to late 19th-century scholars developing tools to study "superstitious primitives," perhaps – intellectual tools and scholarly findings that certainly did not hamper the worldwide spread of colonial "civilization"). The tools that the consortium aimed to develop struck me as being very useful to identify and then divide and conquer – thereby effectively countering, by isolating, some people's claims concerning their own supposedly uniform and oppositional nonstate identity. It would turn people into a veritable kaleidoscope of potentially competing sub-interests and slipping sub-allegiances (and this is where we return to that now popular choice of studying plurals, e.g., not Islam but the many Islams). And some of these allegiances, despite first impressions, or at least as some might hope, may turn out to be aligned with the interests of the nation itself.

But I don't think this is all complete speculation on my part. For example, consider Guy Stroumsa's contribution to the consortium's inaugural volume: "The History of Religions as a Subversive Discipline: Comparing Judaism, Christianity, and Islam" (2012). After echoing the conference's theme, inasmuch as his paper's premise was that "[w]e should seek to avoid perceiving religions as monolithic entities and rather look for the constant dynamic between religious attitudes and beliefs" (150), he concludes by stating rather clearly just what the practical effect of this stance is. Stroumsa writes:

> I started by emphasizing the subversive character of our discipline. I hope that by now, what I mean by this adjective is a bit clearer ... . [T]he very practice of our discipline represents a powerful rebuke to the pretensions of orthodoxies to be the sole keepers of truth. (158)

Here we find the divide and conquer strategy named earlier; for I read this to be saying that the task before the history of religions is *to contest orthodoxy*, both diachronically and synchronically, by making evident not only the path that some self-proclaimed normative center has actually taken, from the past to the present (thereby deauthorizing the orthodox by seeing them as contingent and blended and not, as some might claim, necessary and pure) but also by identifying its merely relative place among a variety of other present-day alternatives, each of which is vying for local authority. Now, while agreeing with the method – i.e., what I would call a rigorous historicization capable of studying constant dynamics – I fail to agree with his motive or the desired effect of his scholarship. I do not see our work as intended to subvert or rebuke the people whom we study, or to identify and then correct what the consortium's book series calls "ideological misuses." If anything, my aim is to challenge *scholars* who, as Stroumsa seems to do, wish to dabble in social engineering by picking the winners and losers among the people they study. I therefore see us to be playing an entirely separate game from that which is played by the people about whom we write our books or among whom we do our fieldwork. In fact, this distinction (which Stroumsa seems not to make) between studying social worlds and reproducing them suggests to me why the work of some scholars of religion can be greeted so harshly by the people about whom they write. For instance, I would argue that protests are inspired by the work of some scholars when participants (in my opinion, sometimes understandably) read scholarship to be implicitly or explicitly contesting (subverting and rebuking, to appeal to Strousma's preferred terms) their own self-representations and thereby minimizing their own first-person interpretative authority (i.e., their ability to say what they think they mean, what they think their texts are saying, what the effect of their practices are, etc.). Yet setting out to contest *what we consider to be* a group's more conservative or orthodox elements – not unlike scholars of fundamentalism, who seem incapable of studying their subjects without, sooner or later, winking to the reader concerning just how wrong these people are – says everything about *us* and the sort of social world *we're* trying to normalize. It's evidence of a situation in which scholars feel confident making ambitious existential – rather than just modest professional – claims about the world, since they somehow seem to know that the orthodox are mistaken and pretentious, leading such scholars to chastise them publicly in their work, by telling them, for instance, what their own texts *really mean*. This couldn't be further from what I think the academic study of religion ought to be. That *my* reading of a participant claim fails to match the claim itself is obvious to me (and likely to any of the people whom I might study, should they ever even read my work [and since I study my own field, my research subjects often do]). But the curial point here is that, unlike scholars such as Stroumsa, I do not think that we should aim to correct their reading (since, for example, we're not in the business of saying what the Bible or the Qur'an *really* says or *really* means or *really* ought to prompt us to do with our lives – *that* we leave to the people for whom those texts are influential, no?). Instead, my aim is simply to offer an alternative way of understanding some item of culture that coheres with the rather different definitions and assumptions about the world that are presupposed by the social theory that animates my work. My claims, then, are premised on my assumptions and so are not normative judgments about how the world ought to work that compete with those of the people whom I study. Instead, any normative claims that I might offer always concern how our *field* ought to work, such as arguing that we should carry out our research and writing not to either discipline or support the faithful (whomever that may be and whatever they may say or do), but to provide other scholars, who equally wish to understand some element of the social within the parameters of our work, with one possible model for how to develop and communicate new knowledge about the world.

But if, instead, our desire is to dethrone the orthodox so as to promote versions of the groups we study that are in step with our own interests (what we might otherwise call nation-building) – and, as scholars who work in universities that are often funded and therefore run by (and thus for) the nation, this is where the state re-enters our conversation – then this divide and conquer strategy can be quite effective. To pick but one example, if there is not one but, instead, many Islams, then some forms might be argued to be more legitimate or original and thus authentic than others. If so, then those elements of this larger, abstract identity which oppose us (and whatever our strategic interests happen to be today) now can be represented quite effectively as being isolated and thus alone on the illegitimate fringe – with some variants being so far removed from what *we* wish to authorize as the legitimate center that we won't even call them by the name of the larger group (think of all those people in media or government, at least in North America, who still say such things as "the so-called Islamic State"). Thus, by having scholars complicate the seemingly uniform identities that are in competition with our own – and doing this by emphasizing their dynamic interconnectedness and their adaptations, their differentiations and encounters, thereby recasting other people's efforts to standardize what *they* claim counts as legitimate Islam or original Judaism or authentic Hinduism – well, it may be possible to create conditions in which what *we* value as mutually beneficial alliances can develop, between what are no longer perceived to be monolithic and opposed parties (alliance-building that, in our field, often goes by the name of interreligious dialogue). Now, much as in how nations often conduct foreign policy, a segment of the Other's world can be brought in line with the only monolithic identity that remains unchallenged: the nation itself. In the work of the consortium that I witnessed, it seemed that the nation, or this idea of Europe, constituted the foundational melting pot within which all other identities were presumed to be ad hoc, private, dynamic, shifting, playful, and necessarily changeable (I think here of Naomi Goldenberg's work on the category religion as being a management tool used to name and thereby domesticate what she refers to as vestigial states that still exist within the nation [2015]). It was from this one stable center that we, the conference attendees whose travel, food, and hotels were paid by the consortium's impressive grant, examined (as the introduction to its first volume phrased it) the "inter- and intra-religious cross-over areas of reciprocal perception and denial, delimitation and inclusion, tolerance and rejection" (Krech and Steinicke 2012: 3). After all, while the nation is the source of the funding and thereby provides the secure position from which we talked about the fluid Other, the participants hardly dissected *that* (i.e., *our*) possibly ambiguous and ad hoc identity, in search of *its* internal contradictions, convergences, adaptations, and competitions.

Because members of the nation-state find the category "religion" so good to think and act with (a point argued throughout much of my own work), I find this sort of partial theorizing (and by partial I mean how we often historicize *them* but not *ourselves*) not just at that conference but all over our field today. For example, despite the apparent progress (over those who once portrayed it as utterly unique and thus special in the turn-of-the-era world) made by considering early Christianity to be a *syncretistic movement* – as it was once provocatively theorized to be – the two sources from which this new, blended mix was thought to originate (i.e., Judaism and Hellenistic culture) were nonetheless presumed themselves to be homogenous, autonomous items that, once colliding, produced their new offspring. The more provocative approach would be to see it as *syncretism all the way down*, inasmuch as this thing called Judaism as well as that other thing, Hellenism, are themselves understood to be abstract constructs that stand in for no less dynamic and ambiguous social worlds that are only tamed – that is, constituted – *by our use of those very categories*. That makes plain that "syncretism" itself is a rather unhelpful analytic term inasmuch as *all* identity and social formation is now understood to be inevitably blended and thus derivative, ensuring that we, as scholars, can talk about such things as sources and origins – not unlike my earlier comments on standards and progress – *only inasmuch as we self-reflexively own up to the fact that we created each for our own purposes* (a point I worked to make in my own contribution to that 2008 conference that I mentioned earlier [McCutcheon 2012; see also 2015]). Without those social interests and the criteria that we devise to manage an unruly world in ways that suit us, each supposed source is but the destination for some prior dynamism that, for whatever reason, has been left unexamined and thereby dehistoricized. But, in my experience, this is *not* the approach taken by studies of syncretism or diaspora (inasmuch as a static and authoritative origin/orthodoxy is a necessary postulate for us to then be able to judge what counts as change or movement away from it).

But let me stop here and remind you where we have been so far: I have offered an analogy between, on the one hand, the way we approach talking about good students and, on the other, the way we approach talking about people's religions. In both cases, I think it is not difficult to demonstrate that what, on the face of it, seems like a disinterested description turns out to be an invested prescription that actively constitutes a particular social world conducive to the interests of the observer. Failing to see how these actions form the foundation of our world leads to our mischaracterization of that world as coming already packaged and sorted – a view that, I would further argue, disempowers us, its creators, by portraying social actors as passive respondents to a world already steeped in meaning and significance. Instead, I've argued that definition and designation implicate the observer in the constitution of their object of study (whether it is Islam, Buddhism, or the idea of being a good student). As applied to the topic at hand, we would better challenge ourselves, as scholars, if we focused not on the effect of Oriental religions on Europe or on the History of Religions, as some might conceive of their project but, instead, to examine, as my subtitle suggests, the processes and circumstances whereby these things known as "Oriental religions," along with "Europe" and "the History of Religions," are co-constituted as mutually informing identities. Such a study, I'd further argue, empowers the people in this story, inasmuch as it understands definition and distinction to be world-constituting activities driven by human labor and practical interest, ensuring that we, as scholars – the ones who are, in many cases, doing the defining and the describing – see ourselves as historical subjects no less embedded in dynamic social worlds than anyone else whom we might study.

Which is why that quoted (as opposed to asserted – the difference is crucial to note, I maintain) phrase in my main title, credited to Protagoras, strikes me as so useful. It makes plain not only that the world, unlike our food in grocery stores, does not come pre-shelved, but that the position, viewpoint, and interests of the one doing the shelving – in this case, the man – is made abundantly clear. (Paying attention to the shelves in grocery stores will make the interests of the manufacturers and distributors, along with the stores themselves, apparent, too, by the way.) Despite obvious criticisms of the androcentric nature of such a phrase, much of the knowledge that we today possess of the world, and many of the actions in which that knowledge allows us to engage, was indeed gained precisely from that point of view. Therefore, Protagoras' position makes plain, in a way that we ought not to minimize if we value historical context and detail, the situated nature of all claims about the world – doing so not only in a way that makes it very difficult to remove the fingerprints from the world as we've made it but, in making plain its own situation and investments, opens room for those activities that we call disagreement, negotiation, compromise, and revision. In a word, it is discourse.[11] Unlike disengaged, universalist claims about "Hindus thinking or doing this or that" or authoritative claims about what counts as educational standards, progress, and excellence in our classrooms, this ancient saying, despite whatever shortcomings you may think it has, is preferable to me. It keeps our eyes firmly focused on the speaker along with the occasion of the claim and its many possible implications, rather than on the things about which we see fit to speak, as if they're inherently interesting and already signified. So regardless of how others may interpret my title, for me it is a strong reminder that representations of the world are *people's* representations of the world, representations that produce a world in their effort to express it (appealing to a line from Roger Chartier, in reference to the work of Pierre Bourdieu [2015: ix]) – that they are always situated and interested representations that, whether they like it or not, always invite us to pose Lincoln's "destabilizing and irreverent questions" to each other.

Afterword

And so, taking my own words seriously prompts me to close with a brief self-reflection of my own. What might be increasingly evident in my own work is a situation not often disclosed, if by disclosure we mean the explicit trace of intellectual influences that we often find only by digging through footnotes and citations. The situation to which I refer is the influence of Bourdieu's work on my own (something evident in my first book, for those who could see beyond the many references to the works of, for example, Michel Foucault and Jonathan Z. Smith) and his effort to devise a self-reflexive sociology – one in which, to appeal to Roger Chartier again, fellow scholars are sometimes critiqued "for unduly universalizing their categories of analysis and insufficiently questioning the social and historical construction of partitions and classifications that they too often took as natural objects" (xvi). In a conversation with Chartier, first broadcast on the radio in France in late 1987 and early 1988, Bourdieu phrased his efforts as follows:

> I believe that one of the contributions of my work ... has been to turn the scientific gaze onto science itself. For example, to take occupational classifications as the object of analysis instead of using them without hesitation or reflection. The paradox is that historians [and, I would today add, scholars of religion] ... often show an extraordinary naivety in their

---

11 I allude here to a line from the introduction to Burton Mack's *A Myth of Innocence* in which he argues that the inevitable gap between the displaced ideal, as articulated in a group's myths or rituals, and "the actual state of affairs experienced in the daily round," provides the space in which social life takes place (1991: 20).

use of categories. For example, it is impossible to conduct longitudinal statistical studies comparing the status of medical doctors from the eighteenth century through to our day – perhaps I'm inventing this example – without being clear that the notion of a 'doctor' is a historical construction that has constantly changed. It is the very categories with which the historic object is constructed that should be the object of a historical analysis.

The same pertains in relation to the terms with which we speak about reality. 'Politics', for example, is completely a historically constituted notion, constituted very recently; the world of what I call the political field is practically an invention of the nineteenth century. You could discuss – I don't want to go out on a limb, being faced here with a redoubtable historian – but I believe that all these notions, all the words and concepts that we employ to conceptualize history, are themselves historically constituted; and strangely, historians are actually the most apt to fall into anachronism since, whether to seem modern or to make their work more interesting, or out of negligence, they employ words that are currently used to speak of realities within which these words were not current, or else had a different meaning. I believe that this reflexivity is extremely important. (11–12)

It is important, I would argue, only if we hold on to the hope that the articulation of an identity can, in some crafty way (if we are working within the bounds of agreed-upon disciplinary rules that govern our field), be distinguished from an understanding, to whatever extent, of the way that this identity is made possible in the first place – the conditions of the possibility of being Buddhist, of being Canadian, of being European rather than just claiming *to be* a Buddhist, a Canadian, a European. That my very argument for a way of doing scholarship that somehow differs from simply reproducing the worlds we happen to study (such as examining the means by which the notion of a good student is made rather than just aiming to be a good student) can itself be characterized as but one moment in the ongoing constitution of scholars as a group who are somehow set apart from the people whom they study is, I acknowledge, an irony buried in the heart of our scholarly pursuit. But, as Bourdieu himself argued, while the sociologist is no less social than anyone else, it does not mean that the study of social life is an impossibility. (In fact, the applicability of the tools to the one who uses them speaks to the device's utility and not its limitations.) It just means that, for those convinced of this shift in focus, we never take it too seriously if someone informs us that we're a good student (though we'd be wise to run as far as we can with whatever coin this designation provides). So I hold out a hope that, while we agree that objectivity is a mythic goal toward which we no longer aim, we nonetheless continue to work to put in place those conditions that make it possible, in a setting such as this (i.e., that institution known as the university), at a moment such as now, to talk about the world in disciplined and generalizable ways that can be applied and tested in other locales.

Whether my work has helped to move us in this direction is, of course, for others to judge. But to assist them in that pursuit, I've not only cited my sources (as Lincoln wisely advised [1999] in his effort to distinguish myth from scholarship – inasmuch as the latter has footnotes) but also tried to make plain all along that, like anyone else, I have interests, investments, and a viewpoint – i.e., I do not speak from no place. And this admission should, I think, makes their efforts to critique me all the easier.

Vive le discours.

References

Almond, Philip C. (1988). *The British Discovery of Buddhism*. Cambridge, UK: Cambridge University Press.
Bayart, Jean-François (2005). *The Illusion of Cultural Identity*. Steven Rendall, Janet Roitman, Cynthis Schoch, and Jonathan Derrick (trans.). Chicago, IL: University of Chicago Press.
Bourdieu, Pierre and Roger Chartier (2015) [2010]. *The Sociologist and the Historian*. David Fernbach (trans.). Cambridge, UK: Polity.
Chidester, David (1996). *Savage Systems: Colonialism and Comparative Religion in Southern Africa*. Charlottesville, VA: University Press of Virginia.
Goldenberg, Naomi (2015). The category religion in the technology of governance: An argument for understanding religions as vestigial states. In Trevor Stack et al. (eds.), *Religion as a Category of Governance and Sovereignty*, 280–292. Leiden, NL and Boston, MA: Brill.
Krech, Volhard and Marion Steinicke (eds.) (2012). *Dynamics in the History of Religions between Asia and Europe: Encounters, Notions, and Comparative Perspectives*. Leiden, NL and Boston, MA: Brill.
Lincoln, Bruce (1996). Theses on method. *Method & Theory in the Study of Religion* 8 (3): 225–227.
— (1999). *Theorizing Myth: Narrative, Ideology, Scholarship*. Chicago, IL: University of Chicago Press.
— (2014) [1989]. *Discourse and the Construction of Society: Comparative Studies of Myth, Ritual, and Classicization*. 2nd ed. New York, NY: Oxford University Press.
Mack, Burton L. (1991) [1988]. *A Myth of Innocence: Mark and Christian Origins*. Philadelphia, PA: Fortress.
McCutcheon, Russell T. (1997). *Manufacturing Religion: The Discourse on Sui Generis Religion and the Politics of Nostalgia*. New York, NY: Oxford University Press.
— (2012). A response to Robert Ford Campany's "Chinese History and Its Implications for Writing 'Religion(s).'" In Volhard Krech and Marion Steinicke (eds.), *Dynamics in the History of Religions between Asia and Europe: Encounters, Notions, and Comparative Perspectives*, 295–305. Leiden, NL: Brill.
— (2014). *Entanglements: Marking Place in the Field of Religion*. Sheffield, UK: Equinox Publishing.
— (ed.). (2015). *Fabricating Origins*. Sheffield, UK: Equinox Publishing.
Pennington, Brian K. (2005). *Was Hinduism Invented? Britons, Indians, and the Colonial Construction of Religion*. New York, NY: Oxford University Press.
Smith, Jonathan Z. (1996). Why imagine religion? Unpublished lecture presented as part of the "Reconstructing a History of Religions: Problems and Possibilities" conference (on November 7) at Western Maryland College (later renamed McDaniel College), Westminster, MA.

Stroumsa, Guy (2012). The history of religions as a subversive discipline: Comparing Judaism, Christianity, and Islam. In Volhard Krech and Marion Steinicke (eds.), *Dynamics in the History of Religions between Asia and Europe: Encounters, Notions, and Comparative Perspectives*, 2149–2158. Leiden, NL and Boston, MA: Brill.

Žižek, Slavoj (1997). Introduction: The spectre of ideology. In *Mapping Ideology*, 1–33. London, UK: Verso.

5 Identifying the Meaning and End of Scholarship: What's at Stake in *Muslim Identities*

All of this, however, takes place against a murky backdrop in which memory and desire, fact and fiction, collide.
(*Hughes 2013: 18*)

On Feb. 21, 2016, Robert Jones (onetime Missouri State University faculty member and now founder and CEO of the Public Religion Research Institute[1]) appeared on the MSNBC television network to try to help explain the support that Republican candidate Donald Trump was then receiving from so-called evangelical voters. How could someone who, as described in a Feb. 27, 2016, article in *The New York Times*, is "[a] twice-divorced candidate who has flaunted his adultery, praised Planned Parenthood and admitted to never asking for God's forgiveness,"[2] be so successfully courting this group of voters in the primaries? For although he seems not to possess their "values," they nonetheless support him inasmuch as – or so Jones claimed – he successfully appeals to their sense of a bygone time in American history when their interests were dominant and unquestioned. (But is this a memory or a myth? – that's the key question, of course.) As Jones phrased it, "White evangelical voters are showing themselves in this cycle not to be values voters, the way many of us have kind of been trained to think of them, but really

---

[1] As described on its website, the PRRI "is a nonprofit, nonpartisan organization dedicated to research at the intersection of religion, values, and public life" (see https://www.prri.org/about/ [accessed Feb. 25, 2016]).
[2] See the opening paragraph to http://www.nytimes.com/2016/02/28/us/politics/donald-trump-despite-impieties-wins-hearts-of-evangelical-voters.html (accessed Feb. 28, 2016).

Note: Given the prominent place the work of Wilfred Cantwell Smith still plays for some in the field of Islamic Studies, let alone the academic study of religion (e.g., a recent editor of the *Journal of the American Academy of Religion* cited him as among his own major influences), I thought it was fitting to opt for a title related to one of his own but in an essay that called into question the approach represented by his work. This chapter originally appeared as part of a review symposium devoted to a recent book of Aaron Hughes' (2013), but since it tries to address the place of his work within a much larger setting, it seemed relevant to this current collection of essays. The review symposium, published in *Culture and Religion* and which also included essays by Tim Jensen, Göran Larsson (who organized the set of papers), and a reply from Hughes himself, was organized in place of a review panel set for the 2015 world congress of the International Association for the History of Religions (AIHR) – a panel which, unfortunately, did not take place due to Hughes' and my own inability to attend the meeting.

to be what I call nostalgia voters." Elaborating, he made clear that, contrary to how we usually think, those whom we call evangelical Christians in the U.S. may not vote merely based on single-minded attention to a small number of so-called religious issues (e.g., same-sex marriage, abortion rights, etc.). Instead, the interest among this subgroup in a candidate who focuses on illegal immigration, building walls, saying it "like it is," and the ever-present danger of "others," to name but a few topics discussed at his rallies, suggests to Jones that they might be better redescribed as a "disaffected group of voters … who feel their kind of cultural world in many ways is passing from the scene."

Whether Jones' analysis is persuasive or not, what I found particularly interesting about this interview was the host's response. For, as soon as he finished his initial comment, NBC reporter Tamron Hall commented as follows:

> And a cynical person, Dr. Jones, would say, then, what you're just saying, in a more harsh way, is that religion, perhaps, does not matter but the white culture and the preservation of what they saw as a nationalist attitude, or nativist attitude, is what matters more, and so they're looking for a guy who can win it for them, and putting religion and faith aside. That's what a cynical person would say about what you're describing here.[3]

Jones' reply?

> Well, I think these things are wrapped together; and so if you believe that the best thing for America is for a kind of conservative, Christian moral outlook to be, to kind of rule the day and kind of be dominant in the culture then this is not cynical at all; this is actually, in a kind of roundabout way, it's pushing for values.

This exchange is instructive – if we can even call it an exchange, since, in a way, they're actually talking past each other, or at least the reporter is spinning Jones' comments to suit her own narrative about race supplanting the importance of religion (a narrative that, evidenced in his reply, Jones thinks is far more complex). We see here two models of how we often talk about religion: Jones adopts one in which items that we classify as religious are but part of an always hybrid cultural, historical situation (and so they inevitably mix and blend with innumerable other items, possibly gaining or losing significance, let alone the designation "religious" or "sacred," at almost any point along the way). On the other hand, Hall – exemplifying a classic binary logic that reflects the commonsense use of the term – seems to understand religion to be a distinct and separate identity that one either does or does not possess (i.e., issues either are or are not religious). And so the

---

3 These quotations were transcribed from the web version of the interview; see the four-and-a-half-minute interview at http://www.msnbc.com/tamron-hall/watch/why-did-white-evangelical-voters-choose-trump-627694659803 (accessed Feb. 25, 2016).

puzzle for those adopting this latter approach is why religious voters are interested in what some might call an irreligious politician. But for the scholar who assumes the former, there is no puzzle to self-described evangelicals supporting Trump, for their so-called religious identity is presumed to intersect at a variety of points with, say, their economic and political, even nationalist and racial, interests.

I open this chapter by referencing this episode not to preoccupy us with the sport known as American politics or to exemplify the challenges that face any academic with dreams of becoming a public intellectual; instead, I cite the reporter talking past an approach that takes seriously classificatory ambiguity and multiple social interests, who sees (and dismisses?) this starting point as "cynical," as an example of an attitude that is just as present within the academy as anywhere else. Yet while possibly being understandable when coming from a television news reporter – whose training hardly touches upon things with which the nuanced, historically oriented scholar of religion is often said to be concerned – seeing scholars reject as cynical, overly critical, reductionistic, dismissive, and disrespectful, etc., any approach that fails to reproduce and thereby sanction a people's own commonsense view of the world, is troubling, to say the least. Yet today, in a variety of the study of religion's subfields, the stance of this reporter remains far more widespread than the stance of this scholar and claims that scholarship that historicizes the commonsense way people talk about their own worlds – i.e., their goals, their past, and the sense that they and not others constitute a specific sort of "we" – is inappropriate because it is seen as demeaning (i.e., it fails to take religious people seriously) are not difficult to find.

What's lamentable to me, then, is that aiming simply to describe (aka summarize and paraphrase) some people's own self-understandings sometimes passes as the end (in both senses) of scholarship, thereby bypassing any form of higher-order analysis (or redescription, in the language of theory).

Among the subfields I have in mind is Islamic studies – at least as it is often practiced in the academic study of religion. I should say, from the outset, that it is hardly unique (despite some claiming this to be the case[4]) in being an area where scholarly advocacy for normalizing a specific sort of discursive object (variously known as authentic Islam, lived Islam, progressive Islam, or Islam on the ground) is portrayed as not just an acceptable model among others but generally seen as the only legitimate way to study how people actually talk, act, and organize. That few who carry out such work would likely see it as advocacy (calling it, instead, engaged scholarship) also deserves to be noted, of course; for they might portray

---

4 I think here of Juliane Hammer's recent reference to what some refer to as "Islamic studies exceptionalism" (2016: 26) in a set of *JAAR* papers to be discussed below – an assumption contested by Brockopp (2016).

their work as a species of postcolonial ethnography that allows the Other to speak for him or herself. That such work fails to treat all Others comparably and that it fails to engage in any sort of explanatory analysis and, instead, is deeply invested in documenting just some participants' views of the world either as the people might talk about it themselves or, better yet, as the scholars themselves wish to talk about it (after all, it's the scholars who arrive and ask all the questions, for their own purposes), is something that we cannot overlook if we're serious about the so-called reflexive turn in the field. Over the years, I've discussed these problems at a variety of sites across the field, to be sure (e.g., consider how scholars often dehistoricize and spiritualize almost anything to do with what we know as Buddhism [see McCutcheon 1997: 167ff.]). And with regard to the study of Islam, it is something I've explicitly addressed at least twice before (i.e., all throughout McCutcheon 2005 and also in McCutcheon 2012 – the latter of which focused explicitly on the controversy around Hughes' recent work on Islam).[5] Inasmuch as the problems have not gone away, this chapter provides an occasion to visit the topic once again

Now, what makes Hughes' work controversial to some – traits present in his own introductory book *Muslim Identities* no less than in his other recent works on Islam (e.g., Hughes 2007, 2012c, 2015, and I would also include his critique of the concept Abrahamic religions [2012a]) – is that he refuses to play favorites (to borrow an apt phrase from Hughes' co-editor at *Method & Theory in the Study of Religion* [Ramey 2015][6]). Instead, derivation and difference play a leading role in Hughes' work – a role we would reasonably expect of any scholar who takes the historical details (i.e., the contingent, the happenstance, the situated, along with competing human interests and unintended consequence) seriously. But this is hardly the approach of most introductions since, as Jonathan Brockopp has recently (and rightly) observed, "[m]any textbook writers follow this lead" of popular (and not just, I would add) writers on Islam who often "aim to present a clear story without getting bogged down in details" (2016: 29). Case in point: consider the opening to Jane McAuliffe's section on Islam in volume 2 of *The Norton Anthology of World Religions* (2015 – though certainly

---

5 McCutcheon 2012 details the story behind the appearance in *MTSR* of one of Hughes' essays on the current state of Islamic studies within the study of religion – an essay originally submitted to and then rejected by the *Journal of the American Academy of Religion* (for which I served as one outside reader – part of the backstory I disclose in the article) because, as Hughes was told, one of the anonymous reviewers thought that it was too controversial.

6 Ramey's term, already referenced elsewhere in this volume, is not unrelated to what Jonathan Brockopp refers to as "incidental normativity" – such as the often unarticulated scholarly "presumption that Islam is unique among the world's religions" (2016: 28–29). "This view," he then goes on to comment, "is a parallel to the apologetic claim that Islam was perfect and complete in Muhammad's lifetime."

not a textbook, it is pitched at the introductory reader all the same): predictably, it adopts an exclusively descriptive voice, telling readers how various (though mostly authoritative) Muslim actors understood their own worlds. While this is not unimportant at the level of data, failing to move a reader to any sort of analysis is a severe shortcoming.

As an example, consider her section entitled "The History of the Qur'anic Text," which begins as follows:

> Conventional accounts of the history of the qur'anic text ordinarily begin with its oral conveyance in the Prophet's initial preaching. Then they move to the period after his death, the decades of the early caliphs. During this era, the Qur'an was "collected" from the memories of its first recipients and from whatever written fragments could be found. A small team of scribes set down the collected portions in an assemblage of chapters, or suras, arranging them roughly from longest to shortest. (2:1379)

You will find in her text no other account of the Qur'an's origins; for, contrary to how one might read her opening line ("Conventional accounts ... ordinarily begin with ..."), as if it sets up an eventual description of, for lack of a better term, an alternative and thus unconventional or unordinary (i.e., analytic or scholarly) account, no redescription is offered and thus there is no change in authorial voice – the other shoe never drops. Instead, readers learn what influential participants think of their own text and that's all. Interestingly, David Biale's introduction to his section on Judaism, in the same Norton volume, is careful to distinguish the presumption of some participants for how the Tanakh was produced from how scholars discuss it: "it is the product of many hands, including even the Torah, which tradition holds to have been written by Moses," he writes (Biale 2015: 56). In fact, he proceeds to inform readers that the Book of Deuteronomy, for example "written most probably at the end of the seventh century B.C.E. ... [w]as composed *in the form of* a speech by Moses before his death ..." (57; emphasis added), giving a nod to a few centuries worth of scholarly work on the compositional history of the text (a viewpoint significantly different from those who yet maintain that Moses actually wrote it). And Lawrence Cunningham's introduction to the same volume's section on Christianity (notably the shorter introduction to his initial sub-section, entitled "The Apostolic Era, 4 B.C.E.–100 C.E.") presupposes the Markan priority thesis, thereby giving a nod of his own to no less serious scholarship on the compositional history of the New Testament and, in particular, the first three Gospels (2015). It's an approach that produces a story rather different from the conventional view of many Christians (let alone from those scholars who still prioritize the text of Matthew). But unlike Hughes' intro book, which ensures readers are familiar with "a very different account of the emergence of Islam" (2013: 34) – i.e., the work of such scholars as Patricia

Cone, John Wansbrough, Michael Cook, etc., and not just, as he puts it, "[t]he customary presentation" (2013: 20) – McAuliffe's text never entertains that a scholarly apparatus is needed to make sense of how participants themselves talk about their worlds. Instead, inasmuch as these origins stories – "[l]ike the myths of Moses receiving the commandments on Sinai and the death and resurrection of Jesus" (Hughes 2013: 34) – are just that, *origins narratives*, and as scholars we should presume that they represent the interests of later generations (their "backward projections," as Hughes phrases it [23]), developed in their effort to define themselves and, by means of a discourse on the past, authorize that self-understanding (on the politics of origins see McCutcheon 2015a). The tales are therefore not just to be reported on; but this shift in the camera angle, one that allows us to see the local account as itself being curious and deserving of study for reasons not necessarily shared by those who tell the tales, is a shift that McAuliffe (like many others) failed to make here.

That Hughes more than acknowledges the stakes of taking the details seriously, and the temptation for scholars not to make this critical shift, can't be overlooked (see the very first words of his preface, for example); in fact, he consistently tips his hat at the conundrum. So, with this in mind, he makes plain from the outset that the book is written for those who "are unused to or uncomfortable with speaking about religion using terms and categories normally relegated to explicating more mundane phenomena" (xi). So *Muslim Identities* aims to reach what he characterizes as a middle ground by not only offering careful description of how some (maybe even many) participants themselves might discuss a topic, such as Islamic origins – recounting a tale of the Prophet's migration from Mecca to Medina, etc. – but also including the sort of analysis that we would undoubtedly expect of scholarship on virtually any other human act or organization. It's work that presses beyond certain insider views of homogenous or monolithic social life developing along a linear path and, instead, recovers evidence from the archive (as we happen to have it) of what the social theorist might characterize as a more meandering historical trail of debate, disagreement, compromise, unanticipated result, etc. And that's what sets Hughes' work apart from many of his peers. His intro texts can include technical, social theory terminology, such as myth (defined as something other than a lie, of course), social formation, inheritance, innovation, anachronism, not to mention origins and authenticity (both seen as contestable claims made by situated social actors rather than as descriptive realities[7]), along with the names of such theorists as Benedict Anderson,

---

[7] For example: "Accounts of Islamic origins, like the accounts of religious origins more generally, are largely projections by later groups attempting to read their own agendas into or onto the earliest period with an eye toward legitimation" (36).

Jean-François Bayart, Pierre Bourdieu, and Bruce Lincoln. These appear nearly as frequently as do an insider discourse of transliterated Arabic terms and the names of various theologians thought by many to be important to this thing called "the tradition." And it is the fact that both are present – not just a recapitulation of the emic discourse but also an accompanying etic analysis – that, although making Hughes provocative to some, ensures that, from where I sit, his work is essential reading. Although this book is an introduction to the study of Islam alone, we would do well to have a comparable volume for each of those groups studied in the typical world religions class. For example, we'd benefit from an introduction that did not just tell us about ancient cross-legged engravings and ancient peoples living along the Indus River Valley (as if they lead irresistibly to modern-day Hindus) but which, as well, made plain the role played by colonial era bureaucrats and scholars (the ones who came up with that tale of the Indo-Europeans [see Arvidsson 2006]) in ensuring that we today feel so confident to talk about some supposedly unified thing in the world called Hinduism. While the latter thesis is now hardly controversial for some scholars (case in point, consider Josephson's already discussed book on the invention of religion in modern Japan [2012]), it has yet to fully make its way into the introductory classroom – a place where students all across the disciplines are still generally told the (admittedly, appealing) story of pristine origins and linear development (a point documented in McCutcheon 1997, chapter 4; see also McCutcheon 2018 for further reflections on the introductory course).

But, as noted above, the trouble is that simplistic narratives are not only present in textbooks (suggesting that, though an intro book, Hughes' *Muslim Identities* could profitably be read by a far wider audience). As another example of the endemic nature of this problem in our field's study of Islam, I'd like to consider some of the papers published at the start of 2016 in the *Journal of the American Academy of Religion* (*JAAR*, our field's widest circulated scholarly, peer-review periodical – self-described on its website as the premier journal in the field). Originating at a session at the 2013 annual meeting of the American Academy of Religion (held in Baltimore that year – a panel to which, as I recall, Hughes was originally asked to respond, though he did not attend the session; no response from him appears with the subsequently published AAR papers[8]), the papers assess the current state of normativity in Islamic Studies, at least as carried out in our field. And almost all of which, I'd argue, at least implicitly situate themselves in relation to Hughes' work – that is, it's not only that without

---

8 Instead, Anna Gade (2016) responds; described as a scholar of eco-Islam, she is a Chicago-trained historian of religions who is professor at the Nelson Institute for Environmental Studies at the University of Wisconsin–Madison.

his unremitting critique I doubt such a panel would have been organized, but that several of the papers cite his programmatic *MTSR* essay (2012b) while one goes to lengths to critique it.⁹

The tone of this collection of essays is set from the start in Juliane Hammer's introduction, where the papers' overall theme is described as involving a discussion of "the elusive boundary between theology and the study of religion" (2016a: 26).¹⁰ For Hughes and others, there is nothing at all "elusive" about this boundary and to claim as much already skews the conversation away from his position significantly, as if the starting point is that these two pursuits (the articulation and defense of, for lack of a better term, the faith as opposed to studying those who articulate and defend it) are somehow easily conflated. This skewing of the issue is further accomplished in her opening paragraph where she claims the debate is between normative and prescriptive studies, at the one end of the spectrum, and "*supposedly* more critical scholarship" at the other (2016a: 25; emphasis added; see the following chapter for further comments on this qualifier, "critical"). This "supposedly" does much work, of course, for the seemingly broad spectrum has just been flattened considerably, inasmuch as, upon closer look, critical scholarship may not be so critical after all, and thus akin to the very thing it tries to disallow from admission to the academy. (This, too, is the point argued in Bazzano's paper in this same set.) It's a key move, this flattening, when scholars are intent not just on studying religion but (as was Eliade's inaugural issue when he described his "new humanism" back in 1961 of *History of Religions*) also on normalizing and authorizing specific social worlds by means of the information they gain and control as scholars. This is something Hammer herself engages in when, as she phrases it in her introduction, she asserts that "all scholarship is based on normative claims and assumptions," an assertion that she then describes as "an important step in reclaiming the humanities as a tool for change in contemporary society" (2016a: 26–27). While I have no idea from whom she wishes to reclaim

---

9 I have in mind Zareena Grewal's essay, which makes the interesting move to characterize Hughes' critique of the field as an emotional reflex characteristic of defensive posturing prompted by anxiety (2016: 46; see Gade's response to this set of papers for a similar characterization about this "old anxiety in religious studies" [2016: 113]).
10 In her own paper in the set, she elaborates: "The position of the objective scholar as free of positionality and/or religious commitment has been thoroughly debunked as a patriarchal as well as white normative construction that restricts access to the secular academy" (2016b: 99). That her project for "making societal change both a moral and intellectual imperative for scholarship" is anchored in a quote from the work of a bearded white male (i.e., Karl Marx [100]) is either ironic or demonstrates the hegemonic nature of the good toward which she thinks her work moves us.

the Humanities (as if it has been hijacked?)[11] or, at this point, what sort of societal changes she wishes to enact (this becomes more evident in her own paper in the set), a strategic move is being made here, one also made by Zareena Grewal (in her own *JAAR* paper) when she conjectures, "If we understand normativity to mean any and all claims directing people to ways they ought to act or think, then *all* scholarly activity is inevitably normative and interested" (2016: 45). But what if this oddly (or should I say strategically?) broad definition is *not* how we understand normativity? In other words, such a move vacates this term "normative" of specificity by universalizing it, such that now everyone is normative – and thus, as the old argument goes, no one is normative, thereby opening the proverbial big tent of our field to any and all approaches, since they're all apparently no less normative.

To rephrase: seeing normative claims about how, for example, society ought to work or concerning the existence and features of powerful, invisible beings as indistinguishable from, say, normative claims concerning plagiarism or how to go about doing comparison in the university classroom (what Thomas Lewis, appreciatively cited by Grewal, calls the "norms for scholarship itself [2011: 171]) is the first step to allow such a flawed project to get off the ground. And I say it is flawed because those offering such critiques (not unlike those so expanding the term religion, by making claims about such things as the religion of secularism, that the term becomes rather meaningless) fail to understand what I would characterize as the difference between what are sometimes termed methodological reductionism and metaphysical reductionism. As I phrased it in an earlier work, "because I presume this natural world to be a complex place of competing judgments and interests, I also presume that no human community knows what is *really* going on in it" (2003: 151). "Metaphysical reductionism," I then concluded, "simply makes no sense to me as an explanatory option." Instead, our conclusions – as evidenced in the quote above – are premised on assumptions, on shared scholarly conventions, etc., always forming a conditional "if/then" argument: if you grant me X then I'm able to say Y about the world. We are therefore careful to note that our claims are not anchored in a correspondence to the real world (i.e., we are not competing with the people we study when it comes to the claims we make about the world, for we are playing entirely different games); instead, they are

---

11 The manner in which a normative origin or source is necessarily presupposed (and thereby implicitly reinforced) by means of rhetorics of "hijacking" something was the topic of a June 7–11, 2017, conference at the University of Bonn (organized by Adrian Hermann, Leslie Dorrough Smith, and Steffen Führding); for more information see https://www.fiw.uni-bonn.de/religionsforschung/forschungsprojekte/konferenz-hijacked (accessed Sept. 2, 2017). The conference proceedings are presently being edited for publication with Equinox.

a function of our interests, assumptions, tools, theories, etc., and, for instance, should you share those interests, then you may find the claims that I make helpful in going about your own work (and thus we arrive at scholarly research traditions, schools of thought, departments, disciplines, etc.). In the case of the academic study of religion, this is a game suited to be played within the public university and within any domain where we work toward making rational and persuasive claims about a complex world that we presume to be inter-subjectively available. Nothing is premised on an ontology and so, contrary to Lewis, who notes that "we make normative claims whenever we try to identify '*what is really going on here*'" (175; emphasis added), scholars of religions whom I have in mind as models for the profession – Hughes foremost among them – never aim to make such a metaphysical (i.e., normative) statement; and thus, strictly speaking, they are *not* normative in the way that those whom they study are (i.e., those making claims about, say, the origins of the universe, its ultimate meaning, or what is really going on). It's therefore not news to us that our claims are always partial and limited – of course they are. How could it be otherwise?[12]

What is ironic to me, then, is that the flattening of our understanding of normativity that this flawed project requires doesn't, as Hammer puts it, expand the boundaries of the debate at all. As with that set of *JAAR* papers completely lacking the voice of someone like Hughes to counter and thereby contest their authors' claims, it ensures that the boundary around this one subfield is shrunk and policed all the more tightly. It's not that all approaches are now possible (as these writers maintain) but, instead, approaches once ruled to be significantly out of bounds (inasmuch as they were engaged in what we once termed theologically constructive projects internal to one or more religions and not interested in the empirical, historical, cross-cultural study of religion) are now admitted and those who engage in what we once called *Religionswissenschaft* are marginalized in what they once considered to be their own field (their work is characterized in this one set of papers as old, ill-considered, unprincipled, etc.). Case in point: the entire issue of *JAAR* that started off 2016. We not only find a series of articles advocating for the admission of theologically normative approaches to the study

---

[12] I have in mind here Gade's reply to the *JAAR* set: "the discipline of the academic study of religion offers tools that are useful, but, ones that are nevertheless limited and acquired only with some effort" (2016: 114). In the hands of some, this limitation is a way to, in turn, argue for the need to supplement such tools by those that offer a bigger or the whole picture. This secondary move is one that I would resist, for it conflates two reductions mentioned in my main text. Scholars of religion whom I have in mind do not set out to offer the whole picture because they (i) own their questions, methods, and thus findings while (ii) seeing rhetorics of the whole as being just that – socially efficacious *rhetorics* rather than descriptions of actual states of affairs.

of Islam (e.g., Bazzano's paper on furthering interreligious dialogue by means of comparative studies of Qur'anic exegesis [2016][13]), but we also have the new editor oddly characterizing the field as "our effort to divine what marks humankind's adventure with mystery, meaning, and community" (2016: 2 – "mystery" seems a curious code word to appease those who see the field as being about more than just studying human beings). Then, there's the immediate past AAR president discussing a scholar of religion's specific duties to help solve global warming (Zoloth 2016)[14] as well as an article that offers lessons from Christian missiological studies and other "theological or religious ways of knowing" to assist the study of religion in grappling with issues of self and other (Lybarger 2016: 151).

If anyone is going to argue for a field being hijacked, it might be those who worked so hard, over the past generations, to establish the academic study of religion.

And this is where I return explicitly to my opening, for the gap between these two ways of approaching our material ensures that those who wish to do something other than study Islam (or Judaism, Buddhism, Hinduism, etc.) as, for lack of a better term, a variegated socio-historical social identity – nothing more and nothing less – create institutional space for themselves by characterizing what I would consider a scholarly approach as if it were "debunking ... Muslims' normative beliefs and claims" (Grewal 2016: 46). Grewal elaborates:

> To adopt a definition of criticism and reflexivity that is so narrow as to require a scholar to have a skeptical and perhaps even hostile relationship to the normative beliefs of Muslims is to posit religion as beyond the realm of reason, as that which cannot be argued about. ... Furthermore, Hughes' position elides the fact that all scholars of religion have normative investments of their own by unnecessarily resurrecting the perennial religious studies debate about insiders/outsiders, or believers/nonbelievers. (46)

At this point I feel I've sufficiently addressed, here and elsewhere, the spurious moves made in such a critique and can therefore simply add that it seems to me

---

13 Of course, the divide between Muslim and non-Muslim scholars dwindles if we not only begin from the point of view of promoting interreligious dialogue but also if we focus on studying the *meaning* of a text; that not all scholars of religion might wish to recover the meaning of the Qur'an, however, seems not to be entertained.
14 See chapter 8 of McCutcheon 2015b – "And That's Why No One Takes the Humanities Seriously" – for my own thoughts on what I read as Zoloth's overly ambitious presumption that scholars of religion, inasmuch as we study religion, have "a role specific duty" (as she phrased it in her call to AAR program unit chairs, in advance of the 2014 meeting) to help solve the global warming crisis. See also the chapter "Perhaps (Not) Love" in McCutcheon 2018 for a similar critique of the 2016 presidential theme for the American Academy of Religion's annual conference.

that, not unlike my opening's reporter talking past the scholar, such writers are – as we say in politics (especially during presidential primaries here in the U.S.; so-called Super Tuesday 2016 is the day on which I wrote parts of this chapter's first draft[15]) – now simply playing to their base, with no interest in a substantive engagement with interlocutors who may question the merits of their arguments. (What's more, Grewal's claim that "Hughes himself remains committed to the possibility of 'real' scholarship about 'real' Islam," an approach that reifies the category belief [2016: 47], prompts me to wonder how carefully critics have even read him over the years.[16]) For only if one thinks that a scholar of religion's task was to nurture the object of study would one refer to Hughes' careful efforts to pay attention to the historical details as aiming to debunk Islam or be hostile to it. (Yet if one is working to limit what legitimately counts as Islam, in order to highlight a particular strand, then I could indeed see Hughes' interest to pay attention to a broad range of Islamic argumentation and social organization as undermining one's own ends.) This sort of thin-skinned rhetoric, to my way of thinking, is an indictment of those who use it, as it betrays a bit of a scorched earth policy whereby one's aim is to cast all adversaries beyond the pale – hardly the sort of move one would expect from a field that revels in, as Hammer phrased it above, "expand[ing] the boundaries of the debate." Instead, much like calling someone a heretic in an earlier era, it stifles debate and thereby marks the end of discourse and thus scholarship as many of us have come to know it.

What is particularly concerning is that even Jonathan Brockopp, whose contribution to the *JAAR* roundtable is rather critically minded in many regards (e.g., recognizing just how little material evidence from the early years of Islam that we have), also presents us with claims that deserve closer attention. Case in point: while observing that "literary accounts of early Islamic history are no longer read as simple mirrors of the past" – a view that suggests a far more complex

---

15 For those not already aware, this is the day when eleven states hold primaries for the Republican nominee for president and thirteen for the Democratic nominee, making it a significant day for sorting out possible front-runners.

16 That she assumes that an approach somehow giving us access to how Muslims *think* and their *ideas* rather than what they *believe* (49) offers a difference of any consequence is itself rather interesting but not nearly as interesting, I maintain, as her advocacy for a discursive approach that somehow allows us to "engage in the knowledge schemes of Muslim subjects without imposing our own epistemological framework and calling their ways of knowing into question" (57–58; although worrying over imposition is also a theme of Eltantawi's paper on this panel [2016: 63], she seems not to mind asking what our terms modernity and postmodernity "mean" to Nigerians, as if these are commonsense designators of significance to local discourses there) – as if the discursive method was itself somehow transparent and in step with reality itself. Such advocacy for a consequence-free method should strike readers as rather suspicious.

view of the past than we find in the work of some scholars of religion – he then proceeds to claim that "rather, they reflect the *imaginaire* of the moment in which those accounts were written" (2016: 36). But I'm not sure what gain has been made here – and thus whether this amounts to the shift in the field as Hughes might make it – since in both cases a text is presumed to be a gateway onto some unified, originary moment in the past (whether in the mind of an author or the *imaginaire* of a group). This is a presumption that I critiqued in an earlier chapter for its failure to understand texts as historical artifacts, i.e., as the product of countless possibly disconnected social actors, in a variety of settings, working for any number of different ends, that result in producing an item that we, long after them, name and read as a unified thing called a text. After even just a passing glance at the Barthean or Foucaultian discussion on the death of the author (but are these the sorts whom scholars of religion regularly read?), we can at least acknowledge – no? – that texts do not necessarily "reflect" (a term used by Brockopp that's remarkably close to the notion of mirroring that, or so he claims, we supposedly no longer subscribe to, by the way) their time of origins or their author's assumptions about the world, let alone anything about a supposedly coherent group that's behind them.

In yet another example of this tendency to diminish the critical insights that seem at first to be offered, he later argues that "Islam itself had rather fuzzy boundaries in the early centuries, with Muslims and Christians worshipping at common sites" (36); contrary to Hughes' discussion (e.g., see chapter 1 of *Muslim Identities*), in which it is clear that modern notions of distinct identities are routinely (and more than likely incorrectly) read back onto an emergent period, Brockopp does history by presuming the distinctions we today take for granted, going only so far as to portray them as "fuzzy" back then. If indeed he is correct when he later argues that "there was a Qur'an by the late seventh century, and it was a book, but what that book meant and how it was used … still remain unclear" (37), then on what basis can we presume a coherent group with an *imaginaire* (fuzzy boundaries and all) lurking behind the text?

The problem, as argued in chapters 2 and 3 of this volume, is that it is *we* who are building, in his words, the "contextual framework to place what little evidence we possess into a developmental scheme" (Brockopp 2016: 35, 37) – a modern, inevitably anachronistic, and always self-serving constructive activity that lacks any experimental control since it is referencing a period for which we have, as he acknowledges, so little historical evidence. (We determine what counts as evidence!) So what's to govern our fabrications other than the contemporary interests that we may happen to have? For, as already argued as well, we cannot compare our work to an original, a template, to see how close we got it. Even when studying contemporary social actors whose own assessments can most certainly judge our scholarly constructions, this is still a problem, of course (as more careful anthropologists have long told us). We can't afford to overlook that people's claims and answers are to the questions *that we've posed* and *the situations in which we have put them* (i.e., making interview subjects of them – what Louis Althusser called interpellation) – questions and settings reflective of *our* curiosities and not to be confused with naturally occurring facts on the ground, as it were. And so into these unavoidable historical and social gaps we have no choice but to inject ourselves (here Brockopp's useful notion of incidental normativity re-enters the discussion, exemplified nicely in the usually unrecognized problem of anachronism in historical writing[17]). This is the moment when Hughes' interest in documenting and taking seriously what the epigraph to this article described as social formation's inevitably "murky backdrop in which memory and desire, fact and fiction, collide" offers us a way to moderate the accounts we hear; it is a moment when, inasmuch as we start out by assuming that no anchor can stabilize this murky backdrop, attempts to anchor these otherwise shifting identities can be made evident, allowing us to recover the often overlooked, contingent circumstances, finding those moments when alternatives were present and possible. Studying that anchoring activity itself, i.e., the processes of derivation and how human beings across time have grappled with difference, is what *Muslim Identities* tries to address for a novice reader – a focus which obviously resonates with me. Unlike Grewal's claim, then, I would argue that it is not an aim that "distracts us from the fact that the object of our study, Islam, is also the source of scholarly disciplines, with norms of study, research, and criticism" (2016: 46). On the contrary, her plural nouns need to occupy us – disciplines, norms – thereby inviting us to look for agreements and disagreements, differences and, yes, even contests, in telling the story of how it is that so many today casually talk of this thing called Islam (not to mention Christianity or Shinto, etc., etc.).

To tell such an alternative tale, as is evident from the reception of Hughes' work, is to swim upstream, no doubt about it (as the state of the field, at least as represented in that *JAAR* issue, should make plain). But his is an approach that's tough to ignore, both because of the way it takes the details seriously (and not just the ones with which we happen to agree) and because of his untiring optimism that at least some readers will be up to the challenge of seeing the end of scholarship as something other than what the people whom we study are already

---

17 For instance, consider how we casually name early Islam "a religion" and see it as inherently comparable to those other things we call religions (i.e., Judaism and Christianity), each conceived as itself being internally homogenous, regardless acknowledgments that their borders may have been porous.

saying about themselves. To significantly repurpose Gade's generally affirmative response to what I find to be a deeply problematic roundtable (2016: 125), I can borrow and revise her response's closing words to say that it is reassuring to see Hughes writing an introductory book that challenges the apparent consensus that all along we have been doing the best job we could when it comes to how we study religion. If this is the best we can do, and if the *JAAR* roundtable represents what most of us think the meaning and purpose of scholarship ought to be (whether on Islam or any other topic in the study of religion), then I have serious concerns for the future of the field.

References

Arvidsson, Stefan (2006). *Aryan Idols: Indo-European Mythology as Ideology and Science*. Sonia Wichmann (trans.). Chicago, IL: University of Chicago Press.
Bazzano, Elliott (2016). Normative readings of the Qur'an: From the premodern Middle East to the modern west. *Journal of the American Academy of Religion* 84 (1): 74–97.
Biale, David (2015). "Judaism. Introduction: Israel among the Nations." In Miles, *Norton Anthology of World Religions*, 2: 55–68.
Brockopp, Jonathan E. (2016). Islamic origins and incidental normativity. *Journal of the American Academy of Religion* 84 (1): 28–43.
Cunningham, Lawrence S. (2015)."Christianity. Introduction: The Words and the Word Made Flesh." In Miles, *Norton Anthology of World Religions*, 2: 737–766.
Eller, Cynthia (2016). Editor's note. *Journal of the American Academy of Religion* 84 (1): 1–2.
Eltantawi, Sarah (2016). What does "modernity" and "postmodernity" mean to northern Nigerians? *Journal of the American Academy of Religion* 84 (1): 60–73.
Gade, Anna M. (2016). Roundtable on normativity in Islamic Studies: A response. *Journal of the American Academy of Religion* 84 (1): 113–126.
Grewal, Zareena (2016). Destabilizing orthodoxy, de-territorializing the anthropology of Islam. *Journal of the American Academy of Religion* 84 (1): 44–59.
Hammer, Juliane (2016a). Roundtable on Normativity in Islamic Studies: Introduction. *Journal of the American Academy of Religion* 84 (1): 25–27.
— (2016b). To work for change: Normativity, feminism, and Islam. *Journal of the American Academy of Religion* 84 (1): 98–112.
Hughes, Aaron W. (2007). *Situating Islam: The Past and Future of an Academic Discipline*. Sheffield, UK: Equinox Publishers.
— (2012a). *Abrahamic Religions: On the Uses and Abuses of History*. New York, NY: Oxford University Press.
— (2012b). The study of Islam before and after September 11: A provocation. *Method & Theory in the Study of Religion* 24 (4/5): 314–336.
— (2012c). *Theorizing Islam: Disciplinary Deconstruction and Reconstruction*. Sheffield, UK: Equinox Publishers.
— (2013). *Muslim Identities: An Introduction to Islam*. New York, NY: Columbia University Press.
— (2015). *Islam and the Tyranny of Authenticity: An Inquiry into Disciplinary Apologetics and Self-Deception*. Sheffield, UK: Equinox Publishers.

Josephson, Jason Ānanda (2012). *The Invention of Religion in Japan*. Chicago, IL: University of Chicago Press.

Lewis, Thomas A. (2011). On the role of normativity in Religious Studies. In Robert Orsi (ed.), *The Cambridge Companion to Religious Studies*, 168–185. New York, NY: Cambridge University Press.

Lybarger, Loren D. (2016). How far is too far? Defining self and other in religious studies and Christian missiology. *Journal of the American Academy of Religion* 84 (1): 127–156.

McAuliffe, Jane Dammen (2015). "Islam. Introduction: Submission to God as the Wellspring of a Civilization." In Miles, *Norton Anthology of World Religions*, 2: 1377–1408.

McCutcheon, Russell T. (1997). *Manufacturing Religion: The Discourse on Sui Generis Religion and the Politics of Nostalgia*. New York, NY: Oxford University Press.

— (2003). *The Discipline of Religion: Structure, Meaning, Rhetoric*. New York, NY: Routledge.

— (2005). *Religion and the Domestication of Dissent, or How to Live in a Less than Perfect Nation*. New York, NY: Routledge.

— (2012). The state of Islamic Studies in the study of religion: An introduction. *Method & Theory in the Study of Religion* 24 (4/5): 309–313.

— (ed.) (2015a). *Fabricating Origins*. Sheffield, UK: Equinox Publishers.

— (2015b). *A Modest Proposal on Method: Essaying the Study of Religion*. Leiden, NL: Brill.

— (2018). *"Religion" in Theory and Practice: Demystifying the Field for Burgeoning Academics*. Sheffield, UK: Equinox Publishers.

Miles, Jack (ed.) (2015). *The Norton Anthology to World Religions*. 2 vols. New York, NY: Norton.

Ramey, Steven W. (2015). Accidental favorites: The implicit in the study of religion. In Monica R. Miller (ed.), *Claiming Identity in the Study of Religion Social and Rhetorical Techniques Examined*, 223–237. Sheffield, UK: Equinox Publishers.

Zoloth, Laurie (2016). 2014 AAR presidential address: Interrupting your life: An ethics for the coming storm. *Journal of the American Academy of Religion* 84 (1): 3–24.

6 Of Concepts and Entities: Varieties of Critical Scholarship

> The word "religion" and its discursive associations are often – if not always – freighted with a great deal of normative baggage, even in apparently academic or scholarly treatises that purport to be merely descriptive.
> (*Martin 2015: 297*)

From the outset, let me state how pleased I was to see Kevin Schilbrack's "Religions: Are There Any?" (2010) appear in print. I've known Kevin for a long time (having first met, as I recall, at a regional conference in the U.S. Southeast, sometime in the late 1990s); we have differences of opinion on some aspects of the field, but on other matters we agree (or at least complement each other's views). So when I learned that he had published an article that took critiques of the category religion seriously (instead of dismissing them, as many did back then – some, in fact, still do), and then attempted to mount a realist defense of the term's utility nonetheless, it was something worth noticing. Although the essay was published back in 2010, articles take time to work their way through external review once they are submitted to an academic journal, not to mention the length of time that it takes to write them in the first place – which means that his essay was about a decade ahead of some current efforts to think through and respond to the critiques of the category that have increasingly been appearing for the past twenty years or so. (I have in mind both some of the more recent critiques, as outlined in chapter 1 of this volume, as well as chapter 2's example of at least one current response to them.) That Schilbrack has, since then, further developed his thoughts on applications of what some term critical realism to the academic study of religion (e.g., Schilbrack 2012, 2013, 2014a, 2014b, and 2017b) makes plain that anyone interested in the implications of the category religion should take his work into consideration. What's more, the luxury of having one's critique addressed in detail ought to be repaid in kind. And so, it seemed to me high time to offer Schilbrack some thoughts in reply – thoughts more systematic than the occasional conversation that we've been able to have on the topic.[1]

---

[1] I think here, more specifically, of conversations we had during Lehigh University's "Collaborations: Directions in the Study of Religion" conference, (Oct. 28, 2014), at which he presented a paper on the discourse on religious experience (2014a) – a paper which more closely agreed with my own approach than I had anticipated (for example, see McCutcheon 2012).

But before addressing his 2010 essay, it occurs to me that the qualifier "critical," in his chosen approach's name (i.e., critical realism)[2] first needs to occupy us in some detail, if for no other reason than to plot his approach with regard to other similarly named options in the field. For we also find the term used in a recently founded journal in the field, *Critical Research on Religion*[3] (along with both its affiliated Center for Critical Research on Religion[4] and book series with Brill[5]), not to mention its appearance in the UK's somewhat older research collaborative, the Critical Religion Association.[6]

For instance, as described by the latter group (on their site's home page):

> [W]e examine religion from a positive critical standpoint, with a view to showing how open to re-interpretation or re-conceptualisation [sic] the term 'religion' is today in our intellectual, social, and cultural spheres. We try to do this in ways that seek out and identify the limits of the language we employ (whether this be 'religious language' or language about 'religion' or 'religions' etc.), so that we can move beyond these limiting terms and concepts.

Noting that some of my own work has contributed to the foundation on which they build, the UK-based research group also names such other scholars as Tim Fitzgerald, Naomi Goldenberg, and Talal Asad (the former two are listed among the members of the group). Focused on determining the "internal limits" of the category religion in what they characterize as the post-secular 21st century, the group asks, "How far can the concept of 'religion' take us before it must, perhaps necessarily, leave its own conceptual framework behind?" (see "What is Critical Religion?" on the already-noted site for the group). Yet this usage differs significantly, in my estimation, from *Critical Research on Religion*'s use of the term – one that is much more in line with a Marxist tradition (influenced,

---

[2] As he notes (2010: 1113, n. 3), this approach is traced to the British philosopher Roy Bhaskar (1944–2014) – in my reading, it tries to steer a middle course between outright positivism and postmodern critiques of it.

[3] Established in 2013 and published by Sage, it is currently edited by Jonathan Boyarin and Warren Goldstein, with Rebekka King editing book reviews.

[4] Find their website at http://www.criticaltheoryofreligion.org/ (accessed July 7, 2017); a series of affiliated scholars are listed on their site.

[5] See http://www.brill.com/publications/studies-critical-research-religion (accessed July 10, 2017).

[6] Find their blog at https://criticalreligion.org/blog/ (accessed July 7, 2017); see Stack et al. 2015 for a recent example of the work of some of those affiliated with this initiative and see also Fitzgerald 2007 for an earlier collection, originating at a July 4–6, 2003, conference at Stirling University ("Religion-Secular Dichotomy: Historical Formations in Colonial Contexts"), which involved a variety of writers who came to be affiliated with this association.

as the founders of that journal note, by Frankfurt's critical theory tradition). For in the journal, we see not a focus on the origins, effects, and limits of categories, as with the UK group, but, instead, the term "religion" is simply used to name what are taken to be religious things, in an effort *not* to identify the ideological nature of religion *per se* (as, for example, with earlier, so-called vulgar Marxist thought), but to distinguish better religion from worse, all in the service of achieving the group's self-described emancipatory agenda. The journal's mission is described as:

> A critical approach examines religious phenomena according *to both their positive and negative impacts*. It draws on methods including but not restricted to the critical theory of the Frankfurt School, Marxism, post-structuralism, feminism, psychoanalysis, ideological criticism, post-colonialism, ecocriticism, and queer studies. The journal seeks to enhance an understanding of *how religious institutions and religious thought may simultaneously serve as a source of domination and progressive social change.* (emphases added)[7]

So on the one hand, the adjective "critical," at least as currently used in our field, implies not taking the participant viewpoint, or way of classifying and thereby organizing and understanding the world, for granted – therefore going so far as to study the very category religion itself, as an historically devised tool with practical uses and inevitable (though not always disclosed) limits. Yet, on the other, it means using our own group's commonsense nomenclature (i.e., religion vs. secular or good religion vs. bad religion) so as to make normative judgments about which sort of social change is progressive (as opposed to regressive, I suppose) and thus which form of religion can best promote the realization of our desired social world. Or, as stated in the close to their most recent editorial:

> Our goal at *Critical Research on Religion* is not to trash or promote religion but to build political alliances based on commonly agreed upon values regardless of where one positions oneself within, alongside, or in opposition to the trajectory between the secular and the religious. (Goldstein et al. 2017: 8)

While the former is clearly meta-theoretical in focus, the latter reminds me of Kurt Rudolph's earlier but still classic statement of the role of ideology critique in the history of religions: "the practice of critiquing tradition would have an

---

7 See http://www.criticaltheoryofreligion.org/crr/ (accessed July 7, 2017). Although my work is influenced by a Marxist literary critical tradition (e.g., Raymond Williams and Terry Eagleton's work), for my own thoughts on how this sort of so-called critical (but, I'd suggest, theologically normative) approach to, for example, biblical studies fails to meet the requirements of what I understand as the academic study of religion, see chapter 5, "How to Give Up the Bible and Learn to Love it Again," in McCutcheon 2015.

enlightening and emancipating effect on the self-understanding of contemporary religions, which are still in part rigidly orthodox and dogmatic." For, as he goes on:

> The history of religions should pursue and attempt to validate historically Marx's notion of religions as, on the one hand, "the opium of the people," and on the other, "the protest against real distress." (75)[8]

Such an approach, then, seeks to identify the illusory from real elements of religion so as to distinguish how they might work against dominance in support of solving the so-called real distresses of modern life.

It should be obvious, I would hope, that these are rather different uses of this one qualifier – and not just different but, to my way of thinking, mutually exclusive. It might therefore be more helpful if accounts of a so-called critical approach opened by saying, "*This* critical approach … ," or, as the UK group rightly phrases it, "'critical religion' *as we pursue it* … ," as opposed to suggesting, as we see in the latter case above, that a writer is defining what counts as defining *a* critical approach (suggesting, to me, not one among many but a rather more universal aspiration consistent with the journal's emancipatory agenda). For, from the point of view of the former (interested, as it is, in the conceptual and socio-political utility of the category religion) the latter (inasmuch as it is concerned with making normative judgments about religions) *is but one more object of study*.

I therefore read the UK-based tradition as being in line with what my own colleague, Steven Ramey, wrote in his introduction to a published collection of annual lectures delivered at Alabama:

> [C]ritical study … extends beyond an effort to replace one particular ideology with another. Too often, scholarship in religious studies … serves to challenge assumptions in order to replace them with assumptions that scholars deem preferable, such as generating appreciation of other religions [or, we might add, identifying and amplifying what we consider to be their supposedly positive traits] in order to replace exclusivist commitments with pluralist ones. Fully enacting critical study should encourage people to question a range of ideologies and assumptions, their own, those of the authors they read, those of politicians, and those of professors. (2015: 9)

While there are what seems to me to be a surprising (or, rather, disappointing) number of scholars who understand the word critique to function as part of a continuum that runs from praise and advocacy to criticism (and thereby used not in the sense of literary criticism but, instead, in the sense of finding fault in order to

---

8 It should be pointed out that Wiebe has characterized my work as being in agreement with Rudolph (Wiebe 2005, e.g., n. 20) – a position with which I disagree; for my reply to Wiebe, see McCutcheon 2015: 154–155.

improve),⁹ the tradition to which Ramey (as well as the UK association) refers – a tradition with which I identify as well – is one that is, in the words of Cécile Laborde, "not [concerned with] the critique of the beliefs or practices of self-described religious individuals or groups but rather the critique of the concept of religion as a scholarly category."¹⁰ Thus, as I have argued elsewhere, as I envision it the scholar of religion *qua* social critic (unlike a film critic who rates films so that moviegoers can pick which to watch) implies working at a distance from the situations under analysis, historicizing the items he or she may study, and thereby endeavoring to examine their conditions, workings, and effects – doing so regardless whether the scholar feels anything from (what Bruce Lincoln characterized as) sentiments of affinity to estrangement toward the situations or people under examination. Such a stance satisfies what I take to be the requirements of a non-confessional approach to the study of religion, one that is in keeping not only with the publicly funded nature of the field but also with the widely adopted canons of the Human Sciences (much as we'd hope, I would imagine that a Political Science course studies the mechanisms of party politics and avoids deploying normative judgments about which of their politics is progressive and thus preferable). It should be clear that, whether or not they find use in my work for their purposes, there are those of us who carry out our research and teaching at a considerable distance from the sort of critical approach advocated by the Sage journal.¹¹

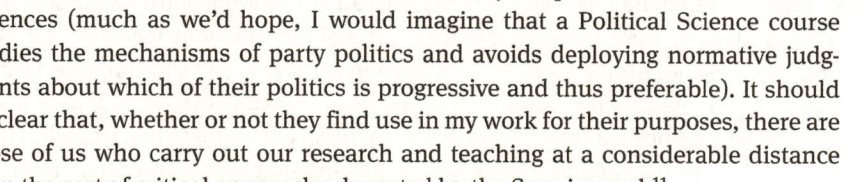

---

9 See the podcast on critics vs. caretakers (a terminology associated with myself but which I borrowed from a 1989 Burton Mack essay [published in 2001]), posted at the Religious Studies Project, for examples of such a, I'd say, peculiar (and, in fact, dismissive) understanding of the notion of critique: http://www.religiousstudiesproject.com/podcast/podcast-should-scholars-of-religion-be-critics-or-caretakers/ (accessed July 7, 2017; my own reply, which draws attention to this at its start, begins at the 18:15 point).
10 See the blog post, "Three Approaches to the Study of Religion," at http://blogs.ssrc.org/tif/2014/02/05/three-approaches-to-the-study-of-religion/ (accessed July 7, 2017). Placing Daniel Dubuisson in this tradition along with the previously named Fitzgerald and Goldenberg, the author sides with Winnifred F. Sullivan's approach and names this disaggregating, rather than critiquing (let alone upholding or defending) religion.
11 Stirling University's current Critical Religion Research Group (which has inherited earlier work carried out by the above-named association, and which I also understand as an attempt to reorganize and rebrand after the study of religion's support among the senior administration came into question in the summer and fall of 2015, resulting in some faculty departures and then a slow recovery and reinvention of the program) now attempts to bridge what I see as mutually exclusive, or in the least competing, alternatives; for example, see http://www.criticalreligion.stir.ac.uk/what-is-critical-religion/ (accessed July 8, 2017). Concerning the reorganization of the study of religion at Stirling, see the critical statement of the British Association for the Study of Religion (dated Sept. 3, 2015) that is posted at https://basr.ac.uk/2015/09/03/statement-of-support-proposed-closure-of-the-religion-department-at-the-university-of-stirling/ (accessed

That this distance exists also seems to be evident to the journal's editors. Writing in one of their many editorials that addresses (and, as it seems to me, tries to bridge) this divide, Goldstein, Boyarin, and Roland Boer begin their journal's second volume with this:

> In the first year of publication of *Critical Research on Religion* (CRR), we have become urgently aware of a significant difference of opinion about what it means to approach religion critically. The dispute turns on whether those writing and doing research from "within" a given religious discourse can be critical. Some of our colleagues apparently presume that only those following secular academic approaches are critical. We disagree, but we have also realized that there is more we need to say, especially since this issue affects our editorial choices. (2014: 3)[12]

Basing their argument on the fact that all approaches have normative dimensions, they argue that at least sharing social science methods helps us to see otherwise different approaches as having common cause (making both social scientific work and what they term critical theology equally relevant for their journal); and, besides, not unlike theology's interest in achieving a world characterized by justice and equality, they observe that this is also a goal shared by feminist and queer studies – both of which have already gained a legitimate place in what they characterize as the secular university (suggesting that so-called critical theology may not be so out of place after all). And, as an aside, that studying gender or

---

July 12, 2017) and that of the North American Association for the Study of Religion, posted the following day at https://naasr.com/2015/09/04/in-support-of-basr-and-the-study-of-religion-at-stirling/ (accessed July 12, 2017). Although the impact of such statements is often minimal to negligent, my own message to the principal of the university, Gerry McCormac, which was sent on Aug. 22, 2015, read as follows:

> I've no idea who has taken to writing you directly about the recently announced news of your school terminating its degree programs in the academic study of religion, but I decided to, given that this news is as surprising as it is unfortunate. I'm sure you've heard your share of arguments for why this shouldn't happen and, given that I obviously don't know the ins and outs of what's happening on the ground there, I won't pretend to have persuasive reasons for reversing this decision; instead, I just want to make sure that you know that people internationally are watching this and are rather dismayed, to say the least, that a major university can end its students' ability to engage in the academic study of religion. A truly unfortunate decision.

12 The key here is, of course, how "critical" is defined. If it means subjecting participant claims to naturalistic analysis and theorizing, so as to determine the possible mundane cause of experiences claimed to be religious, then a bright line will separate so-called insider from outsider claims. But if "critical" means criticizing views and modes of social organization with which we disagree so as to establish an order conducive to our interests, then more than likely anyone who shares those interests will be seen as making a legitimate contribution to their realization.

sexuality so as to realize the social change that is termed justice is hardly the only way to practice; a feminist or queer approach cannot go unnoticed.

Pressing this editorial's defense of the editors' broad sense of "critical," the members Culture on the Edge, a social theory research initiative in which I participate, penned a collective reply, which was published two issues later (Martin et al. 2014), specifically challenging the position that Goldstein, Boer, King, and Boyarin then elaborated even more the following year, in yet another editorial:

> Rather than pitting the secular against the religious, we seek a more synthetic approach. In each religious tradition, there is an invaluable content, which through criticism calls for redemption. Likewise, in every secular ideology, there are religious aspects, which need to be discerned. (2015: 11)[13]

Members of the Culture on the Edge research collaborative had noted that:

> understanding the notion of critique to imply either undermining or reforming something surely limits the role of the critic to a rather traditional debate – one in which the scholar is here either to correct those whom he or she may study … or, conversely, in which the scholar's aim is to enhance, nurture, or improve the object of study … For both of these understandings of critique carry with them an obviously normative streak and thereby fail to entertain that an alternative route could entail a form of critique somewhat akin to the notion of historicization, denoting a scholarly attitude in which our work rigorously examines situation and consequence, taking seriously the human and the happenstance, examining the contingent and the always interested basis of claims of identity and place.

---

13 See also Goldstein et al. 2016, where, among other items, Facebook comments of my own are used as the basis to offer yet another defense of their sense of "critical." They argue there: "As it stands, the approach of critical religion [as advocated, they claim, by myself and by Martin, the latter who is now affiliated with their center] is solely deconstructive and not constructive; it does not build anything" (4). To my way of thinking, this distinction between so-called deconstructive and constructive scholarship is a rather tired and, to be frank, sloppy rhetorical attempt to dismiss the former. The main difference between our approaches, that they fail to name, is, again, as I see it, that their approach (not unlike Eliade's New Humanism) is not bridled by disciplinary and professional limits, for it wishes to fix society, in competition with all other interests working to do likewise but in drastically different ways. My own view, as argued in a variety of places (e.g., see McCutcheon 2016 chapter 8 and 2018 chapter 8), maintains that *qua* scholar of religion, my goal is to work within my professional expertise and the limits of the field instead of committing the fallacy of misplaced authority by assuming that a doctorate in the academic study of religion qualifies me to diagnose society's ills. Only if one subscribes to what I also argue to be a highly suspect theory of religion – thereby seeing it as a uniquely and deeply meaningful domain of the human – could one assume that the scholar of religion was in a position to engage in such emancipatory work.

As elaborated in the introduction to the published transcript of the group's conversation on the journal's use of "critical:"

> In this case, the scholar cares little about adopting either an insider's or an outsider's point of view (if we opt for those often-used names) and has no dog in the fight over whether to pull the rug out from under the item being studied or to nurture it so that it lives another day in some purer, authentic, or revised manner. This suggests that scholars can examine not why religion is either right or wrong, valid or invalid, thereby avoiding questions of how to improve it or dispense with it; instead, they can work to see how those elements of culture named religion function with regard to other segments of the larger cultural world, in order to make possible and credible the various regimes of truth that are presupposed in the traditional tennis match of inside vs. outside and reformer vs. critic. (Martin et al. 2014: 300)

What should be evident, but sometimes (as in the case of the journal, it seems) sadly is not, is that dialectically *synthesizing* such opposed alternatives is far different from *historicizing* the conditions that contribute to, and the social worlds that result from, using such conceptual pairs as religious/secular (however they are defined). To rephrase, while one approach assumes the existence of "invaluable content" (judged according to what scale?), the other wishes to examine the interests that either motivate such a judgment or which this judgment legitimizes.

Now, this is not the place to repeat what I've argued in detail on this very topic elsewhere in print (e.g., see the opening and concluding chapters to McCutcheon 2003 and also McCutcheon 2005 and, most importantly, perhaps, Arnal and McCutcheon 2013 chapter 7); instead, suffice it to say that what I consider to be a critical approach would not be one that so easily adopted local social interests (even if, in other parts of our lives, we share them) and thereby presumed that certain political arrangements are best understood as progressive or that certain social relations are equal or just. Rather, taking seriously that the distance between two posited extremes, such as just/unjust or progressive/regressive, provides the space in which those activities that we commonly collect together as culture take place (quoting Burton Mack, this is elaborated in McCutcheon 2003: 106–107 as well as in Hughes and McCutcheon forthcoming) suggests that people *qua* scholars are rather more hesitant or modest when it comes to such value judgments. This is inasmuch as they understand their possibly arbitrary, ad hoc, situationally specific, and self-interested nature (let alone reserving an interest to employ a hermeneutic of suspicion when it comes to agents talking about their own worlds, meanings, and motives). To not recognize this might lead to an unregulated economy of criticism, since pretty much everyone likely has their own view on "the good" and how to realize it, let alone having an opinion on the value (as opposed to the function) of religion. For example, in yet another editorial, this is all too apparent, for the editors are here intent on policing the limits of critique:

> Despite emphasizing in previous editorials that critique means to discern both the positive and the negative based on sets of values, we have nevertheless received some manuscripts whose primary aim is to trash religion without considering its positive role … . (Goldstein et al. 2017: 3)

With all this in mind, we see here a rather nice illustration of the distance between these two critical options in the current field (one that is sometimes now called not just the academic study of religion but also the critical study of religion, in fact). While the UK's association seeks to examine the discursive enabling conditions of modernity – aptly summarized in Fitzgerald's definition of critical as the "historical deconstruction of 'religion' and related categories" (2015: 303–304) – the admirably dogged efforts of the journal's editors to redefine critical, doing so in a way that allows their emancipatory and politically engaged work to take place within the space of the academy, is what I would describe as an endeavor firmly lodged within, and thus constitutive of, the project of modernity. Its efforts to synthesize theology and so-called secular scholarship (as opposed to redescribing the former as but one type of rhetoric) presupposes and extends modernity's discursive parameters, aiming to achieve practical outcomes *that the UK's group has tried to historicize*. Or, to rephrase, when many of us use the term "critical thinking," as in the skills that we hope to help students in the Humanities to develop, I don't think that we mean to imply that we aim for them to heroically emancipate their fellows from oppressive socio-political conditions. While we certainly recognize that a student may try to put these tools to that particular use, of course (in support of who knows which practical goals), it strikes me that we mostly assume a far narrower and more specific use for the qualifier, i.e., teaching skills that identify assumptions and investments, that scrutinize the production of meaning in the light of changeable historical conditions and situations, and that even work to situate scholars themselves, inasmuch as they are social actors no less than the people whom they may study. After all, it is easily recognized, to the "critically minded" in the tradition that I have in mind, that the justice or the equality that one student seeks to realize can exist at a considerable distance from those being normalized by another.[14] Whether use of those skills amounts to progressive change (whatever that may actually signify) is a matter that, I contend, is best left to scholars to pursue when they're off the clock, as we say, and while wearing any one of the many other hats that agents in complex and diversified, hierarchical societies now regularly don.

---

14 See Kavka and McCutcheon 2017 for an illustration of the problematic manner in which such undefined terms as justice are sometimes used in our field.

With this lengthy aside concerning the varied uses to which scholars of religion now put this word critical – some of which, it should be clear, I read as being rather suspect – let's return to critical realism; although, as will soon be evident, I am not in agreement with Schilbrack on some key issues in the field, it seems to me that we might agree that the supposedly critical turn in our field is *not* an emancipatory one but one that instead simply comes with a degree of distance and thus alienation from any situation under examination – and thereby a so-called critical distance that provides for scholars an opportunity to think and talk about a claim, practice, or institution in ways other than those of the invested agents who are themselves immersed in it.[15] This does not imply some old and now indefensible sense of objectivity, of course, but merely contends that the ground can be shifted from "for and against" debates, and thus the search for better or worse ways of being religious or even being human, to an alternative understanding of the field's methods and contributions. In fact, Craig Martin has nicely described the result of just such a shift when he states that:

> [w]ithout an analytically useful, non-normative concept of religion, we should reconceive religious studies as the study of the rhetorical games and institutional politics taking place in those forms of culture that falls under the folk taxon "religion," as well as the concept of religion itself as a site of contestation – much as race studies today focuses not on racial essences but rather on the social construction and performance of race. The academic study of religion need not require the word "religion" to have a referent. (2015: 300)

But it is at the point at which Martin mentions "those forms of culture that falls under the folk taxon 'religion'" that Schilbrack's appeal to the critical realist option re-enters the conversation. While I'd speculate that he would agree with some of what Martin wrote in his "Theses on the Critique of 'Religion,'" he may be unwilling to reinvent the field so entirely, given that he retains confidence that what Martin characterizes as an "unsophisticated colloquialism" still has sufficient analytic utility for scholars to keep using it.[16] We would therefore do well to turn to Schilbrack's understanding the deflationary critiques of "religion" (how he refers to those who wish to do away with the concept) and what he characterizes as his reformist proposal.

---

15 I admit that I am somewhat tentative in proposing that we share this position since the critical realist school of thought could easily be described as seeking social change and, perhaps, emancipation, by positing a real, external world that we can describe in better or worse ways.
16 To elaborate, in his thirteenth thesis, Martin writes, "Scholars of 'religion' have failed to provide a definition that meets both of these conditions [i.e., using it as a second-order term with some analytic purchase or benefit], likely for *a priori* reasons. Until a useful definition is provided, we shouldn't use it except as an unsophisticated colloquialism, much as a psychologist might use the term 'crazy'" (Martin 2015: 300).

Using the sort of precision that one might expect from those trained in philosophy, Schilbrack develops a typology of levels to the critique of "religion," all in order to set the table for his proposed alternative – a proposal that places him into what he terms the "retentionist" camp (as opposed to being what he terms an "abolitionist").[17] Now, as stated from the outset, I welcome his interest in this area; in fact, keeping in mind the specificity of the various levels into which he helpfully disaggregates this critique, I would suggest that the differences within this group of critics might be worth exploring (differences, I realize, that may only be apparent to me inasmuch as I find myself to be among the group he studies).[18] For – if participant disclosures are worth anything – I admit that, while recognizing my work in some of his descriptions, I nonetheless fail to recognize myself in others, such as what he names as the second level to the critique of "religion," i.e., the claim that the category *distorts* the world it seeks to describe.[19] Significantly, though it is cited at other points as examples of critics of "religion," my own work is not cited as an example at that point in his article; instead, Schilbrack includes only S. N. Balagangadhara, Fitzgerald, and Asad as representatives of this position. I distance myself from this aspect of the critique (though, indeed, Schilbrack is correct that others do make this claim) because, if we take the social constructionist position seriously, we'd likely not use such terms as "distorts," and neither would we claim that any category was "flawed" or more usefully descriptive than others, inasmuch as such a scholar does not presume that an authoritative, proper, or innocently natural and thus correct or real world simply underlies the socially derived categories used to name it. To rephrase, unless one reserves an undisclosed realism (or a realism that is overtly obvious, as in Schilbrack's case), the social constructionist critique lacks an authoritative standard against which one can measure the so-called deviation of the supposed distortion. My work, at least as I understand it, has not been concerned with developing a better or more accurate way to name the

---

17 As described by Schilbrack, the three, interrelated levels to the critique of "religion," as commonly laid out, are as follows: 1. the category religion is a social construction because it can be shown to be a recent invention; 2. this social construction is flawed because it distorts that which it ostensibly seeks to describe; and 3. this social construction distorts because it is ideologically motivated, such as the imperialist ambitions that are argued to drive its early modern use (2010: 1113–1115).
18 On past occasions, I have suggested that a doctoral dissertation might be an ideal place to explore not only the differences within this group of scholars but also the possible reasons for why this critique arose when and where it did. This echoes comments added by Arnal into our co-authored preface (2003: xiii).
19 Because one can think that the category either arose or had utility in moments of contact (i.e., colonialism) – what Schilbrack names as the third level of the critique – without assuming that it distorts the world, the seeming progression through his three levels is not necessarily accurate.

actions formerly known as religious.²⁰ Instead, it has stressed the utility of the cognitive and social demarcations made possible by the category religion, however it is defined, and has therefore suggested that we consider that such a portioning of the social world comes with practical effects and promotes certain interests – interests that, as I have gone on to argue, it is best the scholar of religion not simply adopt as self-evident, correct, or innocently transparent.²¹

To clarify this point, let me quote at length from an earlier article published over a decade ago, where I argued as follows:

> Take, for instance, [Ivan] Strenski's example of how the *Los Angeles Times* "religion" section failed to list Roman Catholic churches [see Strenski 1998: 113]. Far from demonstrating, as he concludes, that the newspaper's use of the term is incorrect, insufficient, or uninteresting, the manner of its use – or, in this instance, its lack of use – of "religion" tells us a great deal about how this newspaper and its editors (not to mention the wider society which turns mere stuff into useful information by means of such categories and such periodicals) make their worlds intelligible by means of deployed classifications. Only if we assume religion to be comprised of an obvious family with stable characteristics would we conclude, along with Strenski, that "[w]e would learn little by using the *Los Angeles Times* list to guide our thinking about the definition of religion, and, indeed, because of the exclusion of Roman Catholics, we even would have been badly misled in our efforts to do so" (1998: 113). I couldn't disagree more; studying any group's use of its classification systems – rather than either contesting an indigenous system or using it as a prototype to guide scholarly thinking on the matter – tells us a great deal. Accordingly, in arguing against those who wish to "purge 'religion' from our conceptual vocabularies," Strenski seems to miss the point that his supposedly dangerous interlocutors are not trying to purge the category from indigenous vocabularies but, instead, trying to prompt their colleagues to become scholars of classification systems and not merely participants in local classification

---

20 Elsewhere, Schilbrack has made plain that the loss of an external referent/world from our approaches – a move that risks not only undermining our ability to claim one theory is more accurate than another but also the ability to explain what is going on in the world – is a cost that he is unwilling to pay (2017b: 173; on its face, this seems at odds with his more recent claim to use a stipulative definition "whose value cannot be measured by comparing it to that which it defines, but only by pragmatic criteria of what it lets us do" [2017a: 2]). Recognizing these costs, my work has therefore moved from an earlier notion of explanation as reducing something to its more basic or rudimentary natural causes to redescription (understood as the way in which scholars signify some action or claim in light of a social theory and set of interests that they bring to their work). See note 33 also.

21 Within my own work there is, of course, development and change (possibly even contradiction), and far be it from me to portray my oeuvre as uniquely uniform or homogenous. The writer was and continues to be, of course, an historical agent. Again, if my own self-representations are worth adding to the record, I would claim that an earlier interest (evident in *Manufacturing Religion* [1997]) in championing naturalistic theories of religion developed (most apparently, perhaps in essays collected in *The Discipline of Religion* [2003]) into an interest in the wider political ramifications of the discourse on religion – however it is defined.

systems. Therefore, unlike Karl Barth, whom he seems to group together with all the other misguided despisers of "religion" (1998: 114–116), the members of the so-called cabal wish merely to study the history and contemporary use of "religion" and its role in helping to make possible certain groups' conceptual and social systems. The writers and readers of the *L.A. Times* certainly constitute one such group; scholars qualify as another. (2004: 176)

That one way of characterizing the world may conflict or undermine another (such as Strenski's disagreement with the newspaper) goes without saying, of course, but the claim of distortion (not unlike the claim that some politics are progressive) only amounts to a rhetorical claim in defense of the view for which one party happens to have sympathies (for "distortion" presupposes the primacy of an original standard and the illegitimacy of its various deviations and distortions). That not all critics of "religion" would agree in this more nuanced clarification is evident from Schilbrack's citations (in support of what he terms the second level to the critique), but this significant difference among us, at least as I understand it, points to the dangers of simply assuming that one can unproblematically collect together any group, the critics of "religion" included, as a uniform school of thought against whose position one can mount an effective defense.[22]

That clarification having been offered, I agree with Schilbrack – who, I should note, himself agrees that at least "*the concept* of 'religion' is socially constructed" (2010: 1117; emphasis added)[23] – in characterizing it as "a shame" that critics do not elaborate more when they make such claims as saying that "there is no such thing as religion in the real world." Finding trouble with such claims is, I find, a common critique of the social constructionist position for, or so some respondents note, a quick look around the world makes evident that there are all sorts of religions, let alone religious people and religious objects. (Or, as the realist Dr. Johnson is said to have replied to the idealist Bishop Berkeley, "I refute you thus.") Apparently, just a quick perusal through the *L.A. Times* makes this

---

[22] Having said this, I should also add that I appreciate that differences among critics are indeed noted by Schilbrack in a subsequent paper on the topic, aimed largely at understanding Tim Fitzgerald's critique of the category (see Schilbrack 2012: n. 20). Importantly, these are differences that Fitzgerald himself also recognizes, for elsewhere he has recently noted, "Russ McCutcheon and Craig Martin are important critical voices, and they are both writers I respect. We do share significant solidarities, especially when facing the entrenched, uncritical practices that still dominate religious studies and other areas of the humanities. However, this does not commit us to being members of a club, and it does not commit us to agreeing on everything" (2016: 308).
[23] We will return to this point, of course, for it is worth noting that recognizing that the *concept* is socially constructed does not necessitate that one agree that the things so named are themselves socially constructed; that is, his insertion of the word "concept" here is crucial to his argument.

all too apparent. Speaking only for myself, of course, the claim that there is "no such thing as religion in the real world" is a provocation, an exaggeration in the service of knowledge (as J. Z. Smith once described a comparison [1990: 52]), and not, I would contend, a false or misleading way to make a point (as Schilbrack himself concludes [2010: 1120]); it is instead meant to suggest the (at least for some in our field) subtle point that the category religion – or, to put the finer edge on it that I usually do, *the discourse on religion*, which signifies more than just words by also including a host of other interconnected judgments, practices, and institutions[24] – *is not passively descriptive but actively constitutive*.[25] As a helpful example, I could cite the concluding essay in Smith's *Relating Religion* (2004) in which he demonstrates, in careful detail, how certain practices can come to be understood by the U.S. Supreme Court *as* religious (or not), thereby enabling the court to sanction or suspend certain governmental actions directed against citizens (thereby, I would hope, making explicit and thus obvious the practical effects of discourses). Or instead, let's consider how groups for whom there exists no local equivalent to the category religion strategically figure out how to employ and thereby take full advantage of the category (by selecting and grouping what hitherto had been seen locally as a diverse collection of claims, acts, and institutions) once they interact with powerful groups for whom the category religion is a privileged element of their own folk social taxonomy. (I think here of Josephson's study of the invention of "religion" in Japan, and thus the invention of an aspect of local society that could not be understood *as* religious – both by those at home

---

24 Schilbrack seems to suggest that critiques of "religion" are all about a word that is either spoken or written, such as when he suggests that it is a significant move to go beyond just the word to consider that the category is performed, thereby transforming bodies (2010: 1120). Again, speaking for myself, I find this to be precisely what some of us have been talking about all along; so, as noted in this chapter, at least my own preference for discussions on *the discourse on religion* and thus the interconnections between claims, actions, and institutions, makes Schilbrack's argument that religion is not just a concept but also about inhabited worlds something less than novel. For studying the creation and maintenance of that particular habitation is what studying the modern discourse on religion is all about.

25 If pressed, I would argue that no description is descriptive but always (appealing to J. Z. Smith here) is involved in translating from one system to another, making all description redescriptions (in a mundane sense of the latter term). This position has implications for yet another distinction Schilbrack later introduces (2012: 1122), between *identifying* a practice as opposed to *interpreting* it. Should we trouble the notion of value-neutral demarcations (inasmuch as any seemingly innocent description, at the very least, requires values, assumptions, and judgments – none of which, I have contended on various past occasions, are native, contra to Schilbrack's understanding of this stage of our work ["it is true that one must identify a practice using native terms ..." (2010: 1122)] that enable us to ignore a great deal in the world so as to pay attention to any one thing long enough to say something about, say, its color or mass or age, etc.), then this distinction holds little to no water.

and, more importantly perhaps, by those abroad, such as those in Europe and North America [2012].) We therefore miss the point of this critique, I'd contend, if we fail to examine *the claims and practice, articulated within (or against) authoritative institutional settings, that allow specific elements of our modern world to be signified so as to enjoy the status that, for good or ill, comes with being classified as religious*. Had Schilbrack continued his quotation of my citation of the late Gary Lease's comment about there being no religion (cited by Schilbrack in 2010: 1117), he would have made this point evident to his readers; for, after writing that a history of religions was not possible "for the simple reason that there is no religion," Lease immediately went on to write, "rather such a history can only trace how and why a culture or epoch allows certain experiences to count as 'religion' while excluding others" (Lease 1994: 472; cited in McCutcheon 1998: 61). Moreover, as already indicated, though constituted by means of a variety of social practices, these classifications have consequence and effect, to be sure – just ask the members of the group known as Santeria who, because of the Supreme Court's judgment, could once again engage in practices that the local town council had tried to outlaw (one of the two cases described by Smith in the above-cited essay).[26]

But with the notion of the so-called real world effects of discourses in mind, a further clarification is needed with regard to Schilbrack's use of Searle's distinction between socially dependent as opposed to socially independent facts.[27] Schilbrack draws upon this distinction in the following key paragraph of his essay:

> But to show that a concept is a social construction says nothing about whether or not that concept identifies something real. The concept of "molecule" and "magnetic field" are socially constructed, but this alone does not show that the entities so labeled are chimerical. Or, to take cultural examples, "gender" and "sexism" and even "colonialism" and "imperialism" are social constructions, but nevertheless indicate social realities that exist in the world. This view is what makes critical realism a form of realism. (2010: 1121)[28]

---

26 I am referring here to Church of the Lukumi Babalu Aye, Inc. v. Hialeah, 508 U.S. 520 (1993), in which the town council, upon hearing about what many would simply term chicken sacrifices, quickly enacted a series of ordinances to make these practices illegal. The city's actions were judged to be unconstitutional by the court (in a unanimous decision).
27 Aside: much like "society," "economy," and "the nation-state" – not to mention "religion" – I'm quite happy to call both "laptop" and "chair" analytically or heuristically useful everyday fictions as well – making evident my trouble with the notion of either natural or socially independent facts; see Schilbrack 2010: 1120, n. 18.
28 The preceding lines in the paragraph from which this quote derives, in which he argues that a social constructionist approach is important "because it introduces reflexivity into one's study, [allowing] scholars of religion [to] raise questions of who gets to define what religion is and what purposes their definitions serve" prompts Schilbrack to conclude that this is "what makes a critical realism critical."

As I read him – and here we return to the crucial role played by his strategic (because limited) admission that *concepts* are socially constructed – concepts are socially constructed (because we come up with the words and their definitions), but entities are not. Or, to approach this from another direction, the concepts of molecule and magnetic field are apparently not what he calls "cultural examples," suggesting that we see here the once common but, at least to some, now troublesome distinction between cultural and natural or ideal and material – a distinction troublesome for the same reason that Searle's distinction among facts is troubling, for I am unaware of how to test or confirm the speculative claim that some facts exist independently of social groups and culture.

Simply put, Schilbrack's apparent confidence in the observer-independent reality of some things is where the problem lies. Whether that proverbial tree, of which we're not aware, actually makes a noise while falling in the forest is, to my way of thinking, a question that makes no sense, for I have no idea how to answer it; to do so requires me to engage in a mind game in which *I imagine* an independent observer who, floating outside of bodies (and thus, somehow, free of the inevitably embodied and thereby situated person *who conjured that observer into existence in the first place*), can witness that tree topple, despite my being unaware of it. To rephrase: both the observer in this scenario and the toppling tree are conjured into existence by my imagination, all in an effort to identify or confirm something that supposedly exists independently of that very same imagination. I would hope that the analogous problems with discussing the supposed entities named as molecules or magnetic fields, let alone colonialism and imperialism, are all too apparent. That is, if we start with the presumption, as it seems Schilback does, that words are names that we give to pre-existent things, then we're stuck playing the speculative game of imagining molecules – or whatever you want to call the real entities – interacting, forming compounds, and patiently awaiting us to arrive with their labels, i.e., we're now so confident in our use of, for instance, the category germ to name something in the world that we just assume that, pre-Pasteur, they were there, much like that unwatched tree in the forest.[29]

Now, this does not mean that I don't think there are germs – I wash my hands or cover my mouth when I cough, just like everyone else. And it doesn't mean that I don't think that germs cause … – but wait; the key in those two sentences, that we usually overlook, was the "I think" part, i.e., as a scholar interested in historical

---

[29] See Touna 2017 for what I read as a persuasive example of how this problematic position is applied to what might otherwise be understood as anachronistic identifications of religion in the ancient world; presumably, given his realist inclinations, this is a different position than the one argued in Schilbrack forthcoming.

specificity, I feel compelled to acknowledge that "germ" is *my* concept, defined in a particular manner and shared with a great many people today, of course, having been taught it by others and which I and many other people use daily *to make sense of our world and steer our way through it* while avoiding getting either the things we know (and devalue) as sniffles or food poisoning, as best we can. That devotees bathing in or drinking water at the Ganges seem unconcerned with how contaminated it is with both industrial and human waste – at least as others of us would certainly not hesitate to characterize it – tells us all we need to know about the supposed reality of germs. For should such people get sick from it (a causal judgment we'd undoubtedly make), they may in fact signify their bodily condition as being something other than sickness or they might attribute its cause to something other than their time spent in the holy water. So while I, and others, quite successfully employ "germ" as part of our folk taxonomy, routinely using it in concert with our local (but, yes, perhaps widely shared) assumptions of health and norms of human longevity, we ought not to assume too easily or quickly that this is but a name that we give to stable and pre-existent, real entities.[30] While I'm not willing to throw caution to the wind and, say, start licking doorknobs in public, I'm also not so confident in the world that I happen to occupy as to assume that my early 21st-century concepts and interests are in a one-to-one fit with an actual reality on the ground; after all, many of our predecessors were indeed just that confident and look at how outdated, wrong-headed, or just plain old silly we now see many of their taken-for-granted worlds to have been. In fact, if asked, *this* is precisely how I would redefine *critical realism*, so as to name an attitude that assumes (i) the socially created and thus situated nature of reality but which (ii) holds open the very real possibility that other social actors, talking about the world in different ways, with different interests, can impact how we talk about and thereby constitute our own world. According to such a position, we use concepts tentatively, as if they work, aware that, as historical creations with a specific manufacturing history and purpose, they are bound to fail in the situations of the unanticipated future. While some categories are indeed discarded entirely and forgotten, the gradual redefinition of religion and Other on the colonial frontier (as so nicely chronicled by Chidester [1996]) constitutes an example of the fine-tuning necessary if we are to retain them, while contemporary contests

---

30 Elsewhere, I phrased the problem of normalizing the familiar as follows: "I wonder what scholars here would make of a book originating from, say, a contemporary Polynesian author and arguing that mana was a natural part of the pan-human cognition and not simply a local term that is merely of ethnographic curiosity to us – a book that explained the mana-like experiences that you and I have, despite our lacking the word in our local and thus understandably limited vocabulary?" (2010: 1187; on the discourse on mana, see Meylan 2017).

over the binary nature of identity and attendant redefinitions of gender count as another (see Brubaker 2016).[31]

So, instead of starting from our god's eye view, where we somehow just know that such entities are (or, like chimera, are not) out there prior to us arriving on the scene – and rather than employing either Schilbrack's implied the cultural/ natural distinction or Searle's division between types of facts – we might take seriously the reflexivity that Schilbrack values (as noted above) and begin our studies always with a situated social actor making a claim, content not to speculate on the prior reality or meaning of the situation. For understanding such agents to be, along with many others, co-constituting their worlds – and not from scratch, of course, since none of us likely invented tying shoelaces from whole cloth (for we are *social* actors, after all) – brackets metaphysical speculations and focuses our attention on people doing things.[32] And one of those things, at least for some of those people – among who most of us live and carry out our work as scholars – is talking *as if* there are such things in the world as religions, acting *as if* there are such things in the world as religions, and organizing *as if* there are such things in the world as religions. Whether religions really are there, regardless our involvement, is a question of no use to ask for, as noted earlier, to answer it requires me to imagine a pilotless, self-made drone floating above my own imagination.

At this point, however, I think that I should stop, for a moment, to observe that all of the above constitutes words, used in the light of the rules and structures that you and I were taught (and which are reproduced in the using of them) – otherwise, you would not be looking over the lines and reading them as meaningful. I therefore don't presume any of these words *refer to any real things* – they might, of course, but I have no idea – in fact, if they do, it's only an idea of mine, for all I know. But, inasmuch as we use these words, in concert with ways of acting and organizing, we make worlds meaningful and real – if by real we now mean situations that have effect and consequence that we, as members of that constituted place, must navigate and with which we have no choice but to contend. Among those consequences are sometimes life and death, of course;

---

31 This is not to be confused with Vaihinger's "as if" philosophy (1924), but there may be some unanticipated overlap, notably the pragmatism (rather than truthfulness) that likely governs our use of categories.

32 And yes, I do indeed understand "person" to be no less of a situated category; anyone familiar with, for instance, either the history of slavery and civil rights in the U.S. (in which African-Americans of an earlier era were considered only 3/5 of a person) or current pro-choice and anti-abortion debates over the status of a fetus would have to acknowledge that. It is therefore a heuristically useful fiction, as Schilbrack quoted me earlier, that, held lightly, allows scholars to demarcate an aspect of our world that they find curious. However, held tightly, it comprises an effective rhetorical lever to dedicate resources to allies and withhold them from adversaries.

but the fact that some people seem to fearlessly or willingly face death – I have in mind the graphic example I selected for discussion in my first book, the case of so-called South Vietnamese self-immolations (1997: chapter 6) – doing so in a manner that many others of us see as ill-advised, counter-intuitive or, perhaps, even crazy, suggests to me that the supposedly natural and diametrically opposed distinction between these two states is also not so natural.

To bring this all home: consider an otherwise insignificant line from Schilbrack's 2010 article, the first, as far as I am aware, of his many pieces on critics of "religion:"

> To apply this distinction [between identifying vs. interpreting] to a religious example: one might identify what certain participants are doing using their own terms, say, as honoring the ancestors. If one then wants to redescribe what they are doing in one's own terms, in terms that the practitioners do not know, then one is redescribing or interpreting that practice. One is arguing that "honoring the ancestors" is a form of religion. (2010: 1122)

Something interesting (and surprisingly uncritical) has just happened here. After using a mountain-climbing illustration to exemplify what he means by redescription[33] – what I gather is a nonreligious example – Schilbrack seems effortlessly to shift to "a religious example" (despite acknowledging, seemingly in agreement with my epigraph from Martin, "that the concept 'religion' is not innocent" [2010: 1134]). However, I am left wondering what has just happened in his text: is honoring ancestors obviously religious or has he himself – as he later suggests is happening when scholars make such a move – just constituted the things that he's grouped together as honoring ancestors (his first grouping and interpreting act) *as* religious (his second) inasmuch as he presumably thinks that such a

---

33 Earlier, I mentioned a mundane use of the notion of redescription (see n. 25) – Schilbrack's examples here illustrate this rather nicely, for by redescription he seems only to mean a paraphrase or what we might otherwise term an alternate description, such as his just-mentioned mountaineering example: "When you climbed K2, you climbed the second tallest mountain in the world." As I read Smith, who, at least in our field, is likely most associated with the notion of redescription (e.g., 2004: 29, quoting from Smith 2000: 239), the term can do rather more work for us as scholars. For instance, in Smith's work, redescription signifies the comparative operation of re-examining our initial account of exemplum A in the light of a subsequent account of exemplum B, with a view toward eventually rectifying the means by which we initially placed them alongside each other (i.e., of what are they both examples) – such as reconsidering how two narratives are both instances of myth only once we have compared them by means of our category, "myth," and found unanticipated similarities or differences between them. As he then elaborates on this more technical sense of the term: definition, classification, comparison, and explanation "have in common that they are all varying modes of redescription" (2004: 58 n. 110). In my own work, I have adapted Smith's usage and often meant by redescription the act of considering the similarities or differences of objects in the light of a nonindigenous social theory.

collection of claims, actions, and institutions are distinguishable in one or more key ways from mountaineering? And this is, I think, the difference between our approaches – for the ease with which the so-called religious example comes to mind suggests that, for Schilbrack, there is indeed something in the entity (to continue to employ his term) that should properly be understood as religious, regardless the social history or limitations of that designation – since we all seem to know that honoring the ancestors, which just seems to be an update of what an earlier generation of scholars characterized as ancestor worship, is just part of what religion is. That some of our intellectual predecessors might have had no difficulty understanding ancestor veneration as *not* being religious but, instead, pagan or even sinful, for example, throws a wrench into things, however.

Another place where we can illustrate some of the problems of his approach is Schilbrack's more recent article, "A Realist Social Ontology of Religion" (2017). Defining religion (in a stipulative manner, an approach to definition also evident in his earlier, 2013 article) as "forms of life predicated on a belief in the existence of superhuman beings" (166), Schilbrack then elaborates that "a realist account of 'religion' is an account that holds that there are forms of life predicated on a belief in the existence of superhuman beings 'out there' in the world, not brought into being by the use of the term." This is a perplexing move, I admit, for on the surface it seems to make great sense – there are people who believe in the existence of gods and other beings and who therefore organize their lives around those beliefs, so religion must exist independent of whatever we end up calling it. Or, as he argues a little later, the structures are there before we name them and so, regardless what we call it, the religiously structured society exists (see 2017: 167) – sufficient warrant to continue using the term despite the long shadow we now know it to cast. But, again, to come to this seemingly commonsense conclusion, we must miss Schilbrack's own role as the seeming disinterested observer floating above the scene, in setting the stage (or, others might say, stacking the deck) to make such an apparently commonsense, realist observation possible. First off, *he stipulates this definition*; of all the things in the world that might occupy our attention, we have this particular one framed for us as worth looking at (i.e., the belief in superhuman beings, however wide or narrowly one applies that term). So, had belief not been an element of his stipulation, then we would have paid attention to who knows what in the world *as* religion; but, second and more importantly, had this one observer not been moved to stipulate that something in the world should be named as religion in the first place, then I'm not convinced these apparent beliefs in superhuman beings, however defined, would have struck us as inherently interesting and thus deserving of our focus let alone a name of their own. So, as already noted above, his own constitutive role in all this seems not to be apparent to Schilbrack, perhaps because he is so immersed in a particular social world that, like many others, he cannot help but see certain beliefs as obviously distinct and thus curious. But (thirdly) there's more; for, as correctly identified by Martin (2017: 7–9), Schilbrack assumes that these beliefs are causal, i.e., the ways of living one's life are *predicated* on them, after all (i.e., founded or based upon, established or caused by). This classically idealist approach still permeates much of the field (lending substance to Martin's charge, aimed not just at Schilbrack, that a form of neo-perennialism has returned – or never left – the field [see Schilbrack 2017a for his reply to Martin]).[34] It would not be difficult to set off from an entirely different starting point, such as one that took these supposed interior states popularly known as beliefs to be secondary effects of prior social situations and material conditions, such that a stipulative definition of religion could not begin with the believing mind of one or more devotees but, instead, with the economic conditions in which such people live and interact with one another. Now, should we wish to argue that religion somehow naturally exists apart from whatever we happen to name it, then this materialist starting point is likely undesirable, since it admits, from the outset, that what someone else might call religion is actually epiphenomenal and should instead be studied as, at least in this arbitrary example, an economic effect. Simply put, retaining the term religion and using it to name a subset of human claims, practices, and institutions that are best or properly grouped together as necessarily related (e.g., seeing what a group does at the birth of a baby, at the coming of age of an adolescent, when marking an authorized pair-bonding, and at a member's death as all necessarily related inasmuch as they are all, say, Christian or Hindu rituals) is a position that is not inevitable, necessary, or naturally held. One can hold it, of course, but then one must demonstrate the reason(s) why we, as scholars, ought to retain the particular indigenous classificatory system that some people in the world happen to use (a group from which many of us result, to be sure) to organize their world, inasmuch as we can no longer just claim that the structures are just self-evidently out there, waiting to be named by us once we arrive on the scene.[35] For one can assume that all human beings have a gender,

---

34 Stephen Bush and Jason Blum are the other two writers whose work exemplifies the neo-perennialist tradition, at least as Martin argues. Their own replies appear along with Schilbrack's, along with Martin's rejoinder.

35 To clarify: I have trouble imagining social structure to be out there without the observer who first goes looking for them – if for no other reason that there are (adopting a realist position) likely a host of structures, so which will stand out as worth examining is dependent on the observer's interests and choices? Will we study gender or politics, sexuality, nationality, or generational issues? Again, I would argue that the interests and choices of the observer operationalizes the structure into existence; while assumed to exist independently of the observer, for the purposes of research, one cannot forget that this is the observer's assumption.

and one can productively employ that same category to do all sorts of work on how it is that we think human beings identify themselves and negotiate resources and authority, thereby learning all sorts of things we can apply to other identifications, but I'm not convinced that readers of this chapter are self-consciously sitting there believing that they have a gender while reading this book. Instead, as I've argued on other occasions, this identity is more than likely operationalized in the social moment, in discrete settings, when (for example) an unanticipated situation arises, such as someone challenging how you carry yourself "as a gentleman" or "as a lady." It is in this exchange – between participant and nonparticipant – that the identification comes into existence and, yes, has effect. (I nod, here, of course, to the notion of interpellation and the work of Louis Althusser.)

So, in reply to his claim that "[t]hough the invention of the concept of 'religion' is recent, the claim that there really is religion in a culture that lacks the concept is analogous to the claim that there really is money, property, royalty, or sports in a culture that lacks those concepts" (2017: 167), we can say: *Yes, indeed* – but not for the reasons he concludes. Instead, we can reply that the analogy exists at the level of observer description and interpretation – which is dependent on nonparticipant classificatory acts, based on the observer's own interests and assumptions, not to mention his or her own folk taxonomies, projected onto the world *as if* they are universal. In fact, the Latin-based concept "culture," which Schilbrack deploys as if it is a descriptive term, could also be argued to be something conjured into existence in the notebook of the ethnographer (as anthropologists over a generation ago considered), making it but one more of our own folk categories to be added to the list, along with religion, money, sports, etc.

Before I close – for I fear that this investigation of the various ways in which the qualifier critical is today understood by scholars of religion has gone on far longer than I had anticipated – let me offer one final difficulty I have with Schilbrack's defense of the category: "there are no terms whose history or implications are free of politics," he acknowledges in his conclusion. He goes on:

> None of our thinking is without ideological baggage. None of our perspectives are neutral. There is no way to study what we now call religious rituals, stories, experiences, institutions, and so on, without the acts of classification that make possible value judgments between cultures. This is why I argue for retaining the word "religion," though now conscious of the shadows it casts. (2010: 1135)

This strikes me as an odd leg on which to leave the reader standing; while I differ, as noted earlier, from some who make claims concerning what Schilbrack calls the second and third level of the critique, I nonetheless am interested in how use of the category, variously defined, helps to constitute specific sorts of worlds in modernity, having argued on many past occasions that our task, as scholars of religion, ought to be studying the techniques of such constitution rather than taking their products for granted and thereby normalizing the outcomes and possibly obscuring the processes (what I take Martin to be advocating in the epigraph to this chapter). That, for me, is the work of historicization. But that does not seem to be Schilbrack's conclusion; thinking back to where his 2010 essay has taken its reader, what with his distinction of description from interpretation and socially dependent vs. independent facts (both an important basis for him to make the claim that, as a critical realist, he's interested in "distinguish[ing] between people's beliefs about reality and reality itself" [2014: 167]),[36] he seems to accept that, regardless what we call them, there are such things in the world as religious rituals, stories etc. (though, not unlike "religion," "ritual" and "story" are, of course, words that name items we've grouped together as constituting a class); that is, given that they've become widespread objects of discourse, we seem to have no choice but to continue to study them *as* religious rituals, stories, etc. Or, to appeal again to J. Z. Smith, rectifying our initial understanding of such practices and narratives by redescribing the ostensibly religious by purposefully comparing it to something novel, something nonreligious (and thereby seeing them both as interesting instances of, say, social formation [as I had once before argued (1998)]) seems not to be an option. But it is not at all clear why. Although I will not even inquire as to which other categories he would continue to use in scholarship despite our current awareness of the (in his words) shadows they cast, such an inquiry would be a helpful thought puzzle to tease out Schilbrack's possible reasons for why retaining this particular troubled qualifier is warranted. For some scholars, I suspect, it is because the discourse on religion has been so successful that they cannot unthink their shared assumption that some parts of the human are transcendental and thus deeply meaningful (a classic understanding of religion that we see throughout what some term the liberal humanist tradition that informs much of the discussion on the topic of religion – whether within or outside of the academy). I'm not sure if this is his reason and I'm not clear if he would just advise us to continue its use while we hold our nose, or just how long those shadows must be before we retire the concept (as I recall Willi Braun once saying we ought to be willing to do with some of our categories, from time to time [e.g., 2008: 487]). I have a sense that although Schilbrack is sympathetic to some of the goals of those who seek to historicize this category, along with the discourse that operates around and through it, and while he also appears to be interested in examining the role it has played in helping to make this modern world of ours a persuasive possibility, he seems oddly ambivalent about the critique inasmuch as

---

36 Schilbrack is here quoting from Christian Smith 2010: 127.

he wishes not to relinquish commonsense assumptions about a tangible exterior world. His most recent article in what seems to be a series, a detailed attempt to re-read J. Z. Smith's work as supportive of a critical realist approach, makes this evident (Schilbrack 2017b). But despite differing on much, we seem to enjoy talking to each other (possibly for pragmatic reasons), so I'm hopeful that we can hammer out a common project in the near future that, although it will likely not resolve our differences, may at least highlight the points where they overlap. Then, we might decide that there are times to disregard the differences in the service of the common sled we can pull, at least for a ways.[37]

References

Arnal, William E. and Russell T. McCutcheon (2013). *The Sacred is the Profane: The Political Nature of Religion*. New York, NY: Oxford University Press.

Braun, Willi (2008). Introducing religion. In Willi Braun and Russell T. McCutcheon (eds.), *Introducing Religion: Essays in Honor of Jonathan Z. Smith*, 480–498. New York, NY and London, UK: Routledge.

Brubaker, Rogers (2016). *Trans: Gender and Race in an Age of Unsettled Identities*. Princeton, NJ: Princeton University Press.

Chidester, David (1996). *Savage Systems: Colonialism and Comparative Religion in Southern Africa*. Charlottesville, VA: University of Virginia Press.

Fitzgerald, Timothy (ed.) (2007). *Religion and the Secular: Historical and Colonial Formations*. New York, NY and London, UK: Routledge.

— (2015). Critical religion and critical research on religion: Religion and politics as modern fictions. *Critical Research on Religion* 3 (3): 303–319.

— (2016). Critical religion and critical research on religion: A response to the April 2016 editorial. *Critical Research on Religion* 4 (3): 307–313.

Goldstein, Warren S., Roland Boer, Rebekka King, and Jonathan Boyarin (2015). Editorial: How can mainstream approaches become more critical? *Critical Research on Religion* 3 (1): 3–12.

Goldstein, Warren S., Jonathan Boyarin, and Roland Boer (2014). Editorial: Can a religious approach be critical? *Critical Research on Religion* 2 (1): 3–5.

Goldstein, Warren S., Rebekka King, and Jonathan Boyarin (2016). Editorial: Critical theory of religion vs. critical religion. *Critical Research on Religion* 4 (1): 3–7.

— (2017). Editorial: On a balanced critique (or on the limits of critique). *Critical Research on Religion* 5 (1): 3–8.

Hughes, Aaron W. and Russell T. McCutcheon (forthcoming). The gatekeeping rhetoric of collegiality in the study of religion. In Leslie Dorrough Smith (ed.), *The Architecture of the Academy: Processes, Institutions, and Power in the Academic Study of Religion*. Sheffield, UK: Equinox Publishers.

---

[37] My thanks to Craig Martin for his helpful comments on an earlier draft of this chapter.

Josephson, Jason Ānanda (2012). *The Invention of Religion in Japan*. Chicago, IL: University of Chicago Press.
Kavka, Martin and Russell T. McCutcheon (2017). Justice, that fraught idea: A response to "The normal and abnormal." *Journal of the American Academy of Religion* 85 (1): 244–254.
Lease, Gary (1994). The history of "religious" consciousness and the diffusion of culture: Strategies for surviving dissolution. *Historical Reflections/Reflexions Historiques* 20 (3): 453–479.
Mack, Burton (2001). Caretakers and critics: On the social role of scholars who study religion. *Bulletin of the Council of Societies for the Study of Religion* 30 (2): 32–38.
Martin, Craig et al. (2014). Keeping "critical" critical: A conversation from Culture on the Edge. *Critical Research on Religion* 2 (3): 299–312.
— (2015). Theses on the critique of "Religion." *Critical Research on Religion* 3 (3): 297–302.
— (2017). "Yes,... but...": The neo-perennialists. *Method & Theory in the Study of Religion* 1–14. DOI: 10.1163/15700682-12341396.
McCutcheon, Russell T. (1997). *Manufacturing Religion: The Discourse on Sui Generis Religion and the Politics of Nostalgia*. New York, NY and London, UK: Oxford University Press.
— (1998). Redescribing "religion" as social formation: Toward a social theory of religion. In Thomas A. Idinopulos and Brian C. Wilson (eds.), *What is Religion? Origins, Definitions, and Explanations*, 51–71. Leiden, NL: Brill.
— (2003). *The Discipline of Religion: Structure, Meaning, Rhetoric*. New York, NY and London, UK: Routledge.
— (2004). Religion, ire, and dangerous things. *Journal of the American Academy of Religion* 72 (1): 173–193.
— (2005). *Religion and the Domestication of Dissent, Or How To Live in a Less Than Perfect Nation*. New York, NY and London, UK: Routledge.
— (2010) Will your cognitive anchor hold in the storms of culture? *Journal of the American Academy of Religion* 78 (4): 1182–1193.
— (2012). Introduction. In Craig Martin and Russell T. McCutcheon (eds.), *Religious Experience: A Reader*, 1–16. New York, NY and London, UK: Routledge.
— (2015). *A Modest Proposal on Method: Essaying the Study of Religion*. Leiden, NL: Brill.
Meylan, Nicolas (2017). *Mana: A History of a Western Category*. Leiden, NL: Brill.
Ramey, Steven W. (ed.) (2015). *Writing Religion: The Case for the Critical Study of Religion*. Tuscaloosa, AL: University of Alabama Press.
Rudolph, Kurt (1985). *Historical Fundamentals and the Study of Religions*. Joseph M. Kitagawa (intro). New York, NY and London, UK: Macmillan.
Schilbrack, Kevin (2010). Religions: Are there any? *Journal of the American Academy of Religion* 78 (4): 1112–1138.
— (2012). The social construction of "religion" and its limits: A critical reading of Timothy Fitzgerald. *Method & Theory in the Study of Religion* 24 (1): 97–117.
— (2013). What *isn't* religion? *Journal of Religion* 93 (3): 291–318.
— (2014a). Do people have religious experiences? Paper presented as part of "Collaborations: Directions in the Study of Religion," Lehigh University, Oct. 28, 2014.
— (2014b). Embodied critical realism. *Journal of Religious Ethics* 42 (1): 167–179.
— (2014c). *Philosophy and the Study of Religions: A Manifesto*. Chichester, UK: Wiley.
— (2017a). The place of subjectivity in the academic study of religion: A response to Craig Martin. *Method & Theory in the Study of Religion* (posted online; DOI: 10.1163/15700682-12341397).

- (2017b). A realist social ontology of religion. *Religion* 47 (2): 161–178.
- (forthcoming). Imagining religion in antiquity: A how to. In Nicholas P. Roubekas (ed.), *Theorizing "Religion" in Antiquity*. Sheffield, UK: Equinox.

Smith, Christian (2010). *What Is a Person? Rethinking Humanities, Social Life, and the Moral Good from the Person Up*. Chicago, IL: University of Chicago Press.

Smith, Jonathan Z. (1990). *Drudgery Divine: On the Comparison of Early Christianities and the Religions of Late Antiquity*. Chicago, IL: University of Chicago Press.

- (2000). Epilogue: The "end" of comparison: Rectification and redescription. In Kimberley Patton and Benjamin Ray (eds.), *A Magic Still Dwells: Comparative Religion in the Postmodern Age*, 237–241. Berkeley: University of California Press.
- (2004). *Relating Religion: Essays in the Study of Religion*. Chicago, IL: University of Chicago Press.

Stack, Trevor, Naomi R. Goldenberg, and Tim Fitzgerald (eds.) (2015). *Religion as a Category of Governance and Sovereignty*. Leiden, NL: Brill.

Strenski, Ivan (1998). On "religion" and its despisers. In Thomas A. Idinopulos and Brian C. Wilson (eds.), *What is Religion? Origins, Definitions, and Explanations*, 113–132. Leiden, NL: E. J. Brill.

Touna, Vaia (2017). *Fabrications of the Greek Past: Religion, Tradition, and the Making of Modern Identities*. Leiden, NL: Brill.

Vaihinger, Hans (1924) [1911]. *The Philosophy of 'As if': A System of the Theoretical, Practical and Religious Fictions of Mankind*. New York, NY: Harcourt Brace.

Wiebe, Donald (2005). The politics of wishful thinking? Disentangling the role of the scholar-scientist from that of the public intellectual in the modern academic study of religion. *Temenos* 41 (1): 7–38

7 Historicizing the Elephant in the Room

> [N]o one ever theorizes for the first time, much as no one claims originality while narrating a myth, although in both cases one's relation to predecessors – and contemporaries – is always more fraught than one knows or admits.
> (*Lincoln 2012: 53*)

Given what I have written in the past – such as my critique of Jacob Neusner's thoughts on the, in his words, "special promise of the academic study of religion … to nurture this country's resources for tolerance for difference, our capacity to learn from each other, and to respect each other" (McCutcheon 2001: 155–177) – I admit that I was surprised when, in early 2014, I received an invitation to respond to a panel that fall at the annual meeting of the American Academy of Religion (AAR) that was sponsored by its "Interreligious and Interfaith Studies" group. Their statement of purpose – to "create a space for critical interdisciplinary engagement with interfaith and interreligious studies, which examines the many modes of resvponse to the reality of religious pluralism" – caused me to pause before responding. I am on the record arguing that such *engagement* (not an insignificant word) is not akin to the academic study of religion, inasmuch as it champions one of many positions along a complex theological spectrum; not every religious position wishes to be in a "conversation" with others, so why should scholars play favorites by advocating for one over the others?[1] After all, despite what the group asserts, for many people (both historically and yet today), there is no "reality of religious pluralism" but, instead, there are merely "the faithful" as opposed to "the damned" (or whatever nomenclature each group uses to distinguish the favored us from the illegitimate

---

[1] For a critique of the manner in which scholars often are involved in constituting a specific, orthodox subject to the exclusion of others, see the already-cited Ramey 2015: 223–237.

Note: The following chapter, originally written in celebration of the career of Bruce Lincoln, is destined for a *Festschrift* in his honor (published by Oxford University Press) but also appears in this volume. Lincoln's work – which I have considered in print on past occasions – has been deeply influential of my thinking, almost from the very start of my career, though his work also exhibits differences from my own preoccupation with discourse and classification. Such differences notwithstanding, and as noted elsewhere, I likely owe much to him since, unbeknownst to me at the time, he was Oxford University Press's sole outside reviewer for what eventually became my first book – a book strongly criticized by some once it was published, which makes evident the very different fate I may have had if the publisher had invited someone else to assess it for them. So, in appreciation, it seemed to me that an essay offering a novel attempt to historicize an old, taken for granted tale that's still used throughout the field – thereby saying something strange about the familiar – would make for a fitting testament to the role his work plays in my own.

them). Moreover, the idealist rhetoric of faith that we find here is itself a modern, liberal humanist technique that depoliticizes certain social settings by individualizing and spiritualizing them, making the category faith (no less than the category belief [on the politics of the discourse on belief, see Lopez 1998: 33]) evidence of a practical struggle; it is therefore used as a way for social actors to circle the wagons in order to create the impression of a delimited, immaterial unity, precisely when there is something to be gained by disregarding various publicly observable differences.²

Given such a starting point – one indebted to a variety of scholars, none more so than Bruce Lincoln – I wasn't sure what I had to contribute to this panel; but, in another lesson learned from Lincoln, invitations to speak with one another *as scholars* entail serious professional responsibilities, and so declining was not something to be done lightly.

Re-reading the invitation, I found the proposal intriguing; the panel was to be concerned with investigating the "limits of interreligious dialogue activities" to identify the "power relations that underlie these activities." This struck me as a fresh approach, since it seemed to entertain the positionality and historicity, and thus inevitable limits and unstated interests, of discourses on the one and the many. Because any act of identification requires an Other, and thus a limit (no matter how large we claim the so-called big tent to be), more closely examining that canvas's edges might prove illuminating, especially when its occupants, much like those skilled cartographers in Borges' well-known fable (Borges 1999: 325), seem to think its borders are coterminous with reality – something I often find to be the case in interreligious dialogue.³

So the aim to examine these limits and interests seemed an innovative project, especially when carried out within the AAR, given that the organization's now well-established phrasing of "religious studies *and* theology" signals an unarticulated acceptance of a particular type of theology to the exclusion of many others – an exclusion never made explicit, of course, and thus never defended. Like the undisclosed boundaries of the big tent, if it *were* to be examined, if the normative theological and political engines that drive determinations concerning what investments appear on the program of its conference, or in the pages of its journal, were to be made public, thereby becoming an item of debate, then the illusion that this scholarly, nonprofit organization is, in large part, something other than a liberal theological interest group would be dispelled.

---

2 For example, see the last chapter of McCutcheon 2003 and also McCutcheon 2005; this is also a position argued forcefully throughout Martin 2014.
3 As for what might be past those edges? "There be monsters" said the old map makers – "There be terrorists and fanatics" might be an apt modern translation.

So I accepted.

Now, something became apparent to me while looking over the pre-circulated materials for the session and investigating the prior works of the panel's other members. Contrary to what the proposal characterized as three separate disciplinary strands that might be profitably consolidated – i.e., theology, conflict and/or peace studies, and sociology – I saw, in one co-written paper (Koch and Lehmann 2014), an attempt at developing a social theory of the motivations for engaging in this sort of activity (thus a social theory of interreligious dialogue), along with an analysis of the techniques used to create the impression of similarity. The two other papers were instances of data that the panel's two social theorists could use as test cases to explore their theory's explanatory power. For instance, their hypothesis that, in order to be useful in interreligious dialogue activities, the category of religion must be constructed in "a particularly ambiguous way" (an ambiguity presumably evidenced in grounding it in the above-mentioned individual faith, belief, or non-empirical experience, as so many do) equally applies, I think, to two notions frequently used in the session's other papers: "ultimate reality" and "peace." For example, I think here of one of the participants, Leonard Swidler (2014b),[4] and his paper's definition of religion as "an explanation of the *ultimate* meaning of life" (emphasis in the original), drawing as it does on the category "ultimate" – what I would characterize as a usefully vague rhetorical term (akin to "n+1" in mathematics, as I've noted on previous occasions, where n can be assigned any value, in order to trump competing claims); I'm unsure what can be denoted by a signifier that purportedly identifies the final terminus and thus end of all forms of signification.[5] This useful ambiguity is also evidenced in a book by the other panelist: Mohammed Abu-Nimer's *Nonviolence and Peace Building in Islam* (2003)[6]; I have in mind its undefined (at least as far as I could tell) notion of peace; for, despite a 1992 UN secretary-general report's assertion that "[t]he concept of peace is easy to grasp,"[7] I would think that it, too, is a purely rhetorical term that, today, often names (in yet another undisclosed, and thus strategically useful, way) the stable and thus predictable

---

4 Much of this conference paper's arguments are also found in Swidler 2014a.
5 Here I purposefully echo Robert Sharf's phrasing in his critique of the category experience (1998: 113).
6 Given that there was no pre-circulated paper by this panelist, as preparation I had little choice but to read some of his previously published work on the topic of the panel.
7 "An Agenda for Peace: Preventive Diplomacy, Peacemaking and Peace-Keeping" (17 June 1992); Report of the Secretary-General pursuant to the statement adopted by the Summit Meeting of the Security Council on 31 January 1992. Posted at http://journals.sagepub.com/doi/pdf/10.1177/004711789201100302 http://www.un-documents.net/a47-277.htm (accessed Jan 29, 2018).

socio-political conditions deemed by those who own the means of production as being favorable to their long-term investment and profit.

As but a quick example of its rhetorical, rather than analytic, utility, consider British Prime Minister Neville Chamberlain's infamous Sept. 30, 1938 proclamation concerning "Peace for our time" (a phrase echoing the words of his political predecessor, Benjamin Disraeli)[8]; however, depending on who you are, and what your interests may be, this claim could be heard as not being about peace at all, whatever that may in fact be, but, instead, as a way to sell what others soon termed acquiescence or appeasement. For instance, would one call it peace if one were a Czechoslovakian of non-German descent who, in late 1938, awoke suddenly to find oneself now living in the newly invented Sudentenland thanks to the Munich Agreement of Sept. 20, 1938? That both Swidler and Abu-Nimer not only anchor their work in such strategically ambiguous terms but also propose philosophically idealist approaches (inasmuch as the former, in his unpublished conference paper, asserts that "*how we conceive of reality determines how we will act*" [emphasis in the original] and the latter presumes that the social lives he studies are "rooted in Islamic *belief*" [2003: 6; emphasis added]) confirms for me that, as already mentioned, their approaches are best understood as data for scholars of identity formation, therefore indicating that, from the outset, that panel's topic – a possible consolidation of three different positions – was not possible since one of the three was not like the others whatsoever, inasmuch as it provided a method to study the other two.

If I am correct in thinking that not just on that panel but throughout much of our profession – making the panel, and thus this chapter's opening, but a useful e.g. – we often have two entirely different conversations going on simultaneously, operating at two distinct levels of discourse, then how might a research project that *theorizes*, rather than *engages in*, interreligious dialogue actually proceed? For the remainder of this chapter, I'd like to work through, in some degree of detail, one example of how we might rethink interreligious dialogue as an historical object of study, rather than a normative practice in which scholars of religion engage. I therefore propose that we consider a story well-known to religious pluralists: the tale of the blind men and the elephant. It is a popular (i.e., useful) story because (Koch and Lehmann's hypothesis seriously) of the way in which ambiguity is its driving theme. After all, other than the omniscient narrator, who

---

8 Chamberlain's speech, on the steps of 10 Downing Street, was as follows: "My good friends, for the second time in our history, a British Prime Minister has returned from Germany bringing peace with honour. I believe it is peace for our time ... Go home and get a nice quiet sleep." The reference was to Disraeli's return, in 1878, from the Congress of Berlin, which determined Balkan national boundaries after the Russo-Turkish War (1877–1878).

is the listener's/reader's guide, no one can see what they're touching. But this feature of the tale – a narrator's privileged gaze and its blind protagonists – is the very thing worth reconsidering, for while the content of the story is anchored (if that is even the correct metaphor) in utter vagueness, its narrative structure is quite confident and thus, I'd say, naïvely realist. The reader, like the narrator, sees the elephant all along, knows with whom to identify, therefore making the tale not about plurality or many-sidedness at all, but, instead, all about unimpeded, universal vision. In fact, this sleight of hand is, I would argue, the source of the tale's enduring appeal; for a story whose plot is ostensibly about uncertain, even limitless, difference actually turns out, when read on the structural level, to be all about authorized, unimpeded certainty. What's more, not unlike claims concerning ultimate reality being somehow different from whatever reality one's interlocutor might describe (recalling the topic of Swidler's conference paper), the enduring nature of this tale is also a result of how it can be used by virtually anyone to bolster claims concerning whatever bigger, unified whole they wish to find lurking behind any happenstance situation. For instance, search the tale online and you'll come across its widespread use not only in world religion textbooks but also in everything from articles on the U.S. trade deficit to parenting advice and even "the" Quaker view toward homosexuality.

And it is the varieties of the tale, and the many uses to which it can be put, rather that its attempt to resolve difference into uniformity, that I find rather interesting – something usually overlooked by those who put the tale to work in the service of this or that grand scheme. For this reason, historicizing this fable – as but one possible example of studying the labor that goes into promoting seemingly unified affinities – seems a good place to consider how we, as scholars, might more productively talk about the management of difference and identity that, at least in our field, goes by the name of interreligious dialogue.[9]

But before trying to identify this variety, let's start with the common way in which the tale is understood today. It is usually said to derive from a Pāli text known as the Udāna, a collection of what are often termed "solemn utterances" or "inspired sayings,"[10] arranged in eight chapters, each with ten discourses, all of which are part of the canon associated with what we today know as Theravada

---

9 In offering the following, I have in mind my earlier attempt to rethink how scholars of religion study the so-called problem of evil (see McCutcheon 2003: chapter 7) – a suggestion for how ways of grappling with anomaly can catch our scholarly attention but without ever taking the step toward the sort of normative position that characterizes much work on what Christian theologians refer to as theodicy. See also my attempt to reconsider how we approach discourses on spirituality (a chapter in McCutcheon 2018).
10 The term can more literally be translated as "breathing out" (see Anālayo 2008: 375).

Buddhism (a collection of oral tales thought to have been written down for the first time sometime just prior to the turn of the era). And so, in chapter 6, section 4, we read the following:

> So was there heard by me on one occasion when the Lord was staying at Sāvatthi, at Anāthapiṇḍika's Resort, in Jeta's Grove. And on that occasion, a good many recluses, brahmins, and wanderers of divers [sic] outlooks were residing in Sāvatthi, being of divers views, of divers persuasions, of divers inclinations, reliant upon the divers support for such a view. (Masefield 2007: 128)[11]

After detailing the disagreements among these specialists (a theme also present elsewhere in this collection of discourses [e.g., 6.5 and 6.6]), with some arguing that the world is eternal, others that it is non-eternal, some that it is infinite, and yet others that it is non-eternal, etc. – going so far as to tell readers that "[t]hey dwelled quarrelsome, disputatious, engaging in contention, needling one another with mouthed darts ..." – the narrator informs us that Gautma is eventually told of these disagreements by some monks who had overheard the dispute. After hearing their account, we are told that the Buddha replied:

> "Wanderers of other outlooks, monks, being blind, lacking vision, do not know what is to their benefit, do not know what is not to their benefit, do not know Dhamma, do not know that which is not Dhamma. And these, not knowing what is to their benefit, not knowing that which is not to their benefit, not knowing Dhamma, not knowing what is not Dhamma, dwell quarrelsome, disputatious, engaging in contenting, needling one another with mouthed darts ..."

At this point, the tale with which we are today so familiar begins when the narrator recounts the parable that Gautama is said to have told to his associates to illustrate the point:

> In a previous existence, monks, there was a certain king of this same Sāvatthi. Now that king, monks, summoned a certain man, saying: 'Look here, my man, now come you here! Have those of Sāvatthi such as have been blind from birth all congregate together!' That man, monks, gave his consent to that king saying: 'So be it, your majesty', collected those of Sāvatthi such as had been blind from birth, and then approached the king. And having approached, he said this to the king: 'Those of Sāvatthi such as have been blind from birth are congregated, your majesty'. 'Well, in that case, do I say, indicate the elephant to those who have been blind from birth!' That man, monks, gave his consent to that king saying, 'So be it, your majesty', and then indicated the elephant to those who had been blind from birth.

---

11 At this point, a disclaimer is necessary, for I am unable to add, as Lincoln himself so often does, that "all translations are original." I have done my homework as best I can, but my reliance on the skills of my own predecessors is evident in the following – such as depending on Peter Masefield's translation of the Udāna.

The Udāna's story-in-a-story then continues (Masefield 2007: 131):

> To some of those who had been blind from birth, he indicated the elephant's head saying: 'You have been blind from birth – an elephant is of such a nature'; to some of those who had been blind from birth, he indicated the elephant's ear saying: 'You who have been blind from birth – an elephant is of such a nature' …

And so on and so on. After the man then indicates to yet others the tusk, the trunk, the body, the leg, the back, and, finally, the tuft of the elephant's tail, the king approaches the blind and enquires from them what they have just experienced. Predictably, we learn that an elephant is just like a water pot, a winnowing basket, a peg, a plough-beam, a store room, a post, a mortar, a pestle, and a broom. And then? Well, much as with those quarrelsome specialists, "they beat one another with their fists, saying, 'The elephant is not of such a nature; the elephant is of such a nature,' as a result of which, monks, the king moreover became delighted in heart."[12]

Before proceeding to what, for some, might turn out to be an unfamiliar moral to this all too familiar tale, at least as it is found in the Pāli canon, let me jump ahead almost two millennia to a rather different starting point for those interested in telling a tale of this tale's origins and meaning. While few people today, let alone a century ago, are fluent in Pāli, or even know about the existence of such a thing as the Udāna, for the past century or two, many in the world have read English and it seems possible that the story of the blind men and the elephant became an item of discourse *not* because (as some today might conjecture) of its place in Theravada scriptures but, instead, because it was the subject of a once well-known mid-19th-century American poem, written by an affable after-dinner speaker and satirist who, in his day, was as popular as was Clement Clarke Moore (1779–1863; the author of the enduring 1823 poem that was originally entitled "A Visit from St. Nicholas" but which we know today simply by its first line, "T'was the night before Christmas"). The American humorist whom I have in mind was John Godfrey Saxe (1816–1887). He was born in northern Vermont and eventually became a lawyer, journalist, newspaper owner, candidate for the office of governor of Vermont (twice, in 1859 and then again in 1860), and a much-beloved and often-quoted writer whose work appeared regularly in such magazines as the *Knickerbocker* in New York (which ceased publication in 1865) as well as *Harper's* and *The Atlantic Monthly* and *Punch* in England (established in 1841). Saxe stood out, in his day, for being a "popular" poet whose verses (of all things) actually sold! – something which, the tongue-in-cheek *Atlantic Monthly* reviewer of his

---

12 For a short list of other texts in which references to this "maxim" appears, consult Jacobs, 1907: 3.

1866 collection, *The Masquerade and Other Poems*, called "a rather suspicious circumstance."[13] In fact, despite the remark later being attributed to the Prussian politician Otto von Bismarck (1815–1898), Saxe is thought by some to have been the person we ought to thank for likening legislatures to butcher shops when, on March 29, 1869, he wrote in the *Daily Cleveland Herald*, "Laws, like sausages, cease to inspire respect in proportion as we know how they are made."[14]

Although it is unclear exactly when it was first published, the earliest it seems that Saxe's poem "The Blindmen and the Elephant: A Hindoo Fable" appeared in print was in the *Boston Investigator* (a newspaper published in Boston, MA[15]) on Wednesday, Nov. 6, 1861 (Issue 29: 212). It also appeared in a variety of other newspapers that year and following[16] and was included in his *Clever Stories of Many Nations: Rendered in Rhyme* (Saxe 1865: 59–64) as well as in the 1868 and then also the 1876 editions of *The Poems of John Godfrey Saxe, complete in one volume*. The poem also appeared in subsequent posthumous collections (such as in *The Poetical Works*, published in 1889) and in such early anthologies as W. J. Linton's *Poetry of America* (Linton 1878: 150–152) – not to mention being a standard included in Cumnock's once well-known *School Speaker* (a primary reading exercise book) at the end of the 19th and start of the

---

13 The review then concludes: "If Mr. Saxe would only put forth a volume that should prove, in a mercantile sense, a failure, we think he would be surprised to find how happily he would hit certain critics who can now see little in his writings to justify their success. Let him join the fraternity of unappreciated geniuses, and he will find compensation – though not, perhaps, in the form of what some vulgar fellow has called 'solid pudding'" (Anon. "Review of John Godfrey Saxe, *The Masquerade and Other Poems*" [Boston: Ticknor and Fields], *The Atlantic Monthly* 18/105 [July 1866], 124). That Saxe is all but unknown today might prompt us to read this reviewer's comments as more prescient than witty.
14 http://quoteinvestigator.com/2010/07/08/laws-sausages/ (accessed Nov. 13, 2014).
15 The paper, founded in 1831 by Abner Kneeland (then a lecturer for the First Society of Free Enquirers and later convicted of blasphemy for articles published in the paper), was devoted to freethinkers and, because its costs were subsidized, was widely read by the city's poor. The paper merged with the *Truth Seeker* in 1904. My appreciation goes to Barbara Dahlbach, collection coordinator for Social Sciences at the University of Alabama, for her assistance in tracing down the earliest known appearance of this poem via the 19th Century U.S Newspapers database.
16 Early examples of Saxe's "The Blind Men and the Elephant," in various versions, are also known to have been published in: *Daily Milwaukee Press and News* (Milwaukee, WI) Nov. 20, 1861; *Daily Milwaukee Press and News* (Milwaukee, WI) 1861: 2016/2; *Manchester Times* (Manchester, UK) Saturday, Jan. 25, 1862: 133; *Freedom's Champion* (Atchison, KS) June 22, 1865: Issue 20; *Daily Evening Bulletin* (San Francisco, CA) March 2, 1867: Issue 123; *Daily Evening Bulletin* (San Francisco, CA) Oct. 31, 1868: Issue 21; *Boston Daily Advertiser* (Boston, MA) Dec. 7, 1872: Issue 135; *Bangor Daily Whig & Courier* (Bangor, ME) Dec. 10, 1872: Issue 293; and *Daily Evening Bulletin* (San Francisco, CA) June 2, 1877: Issue 48.

20th centuries (Cumnock 1883: 87–89).[17] Whether Saxe became aware of this tale through an acquaintance with what were then surely the strange and novel tales from "the mystic east," or from various European editions of such then-designated Oriental sources as al-Ghazali (1058–1128 CE), who drew upon the tale (see his *Theology Revived*), the Persian poet Sana'i (d. approx. 1150 CE), or even the so-called Sufi master Jalal ud-din Rumi (1207–1273 CE), who also references the story (in his Persian poem, *Mathnawi*),[18] is unclear for the time being; but what seems not to be unclear is that it may have been through Saxe's poem, regardless its own sources, that the English reading world became aware of this still curiously useful tale.[19]

For those not acquainted with it, Saxe's poem, as published in 1861, reads as follows:

The Blind Men and the Elephant: A Hindoo Fable

It was six men of Indoostan
To learning much inclined,
Who went to see the elephant
(Though all of them were blind),
That each by observation
Might satisfy his mind.

The First approached the elephant,
And happening to fall
Against his broad and sturdy side,
At once began to bawl:
"God bless me! – but the elephant
Is very like a wall!"

---

17 See also the 1888 and 1904 editions.
18 A. J. Arberry's translation of section 71, "The Elephant in the Dark," reads as follows:

Some Hindus had brought an elephant for exhibition and placed it in a dark house. Crowds of people were going into that dark place to see the beast. Finding that ocular inspection was impossible, each visitor felt it with his palm in the darkness.
The palm of one fell on the trunk.
"This creature is like a water-spout," he said.
The hand of another lighted on the elephant's ear. To him the beat was evidently like a fan.
Another rubbed against its leg.
"I found the elephant's shape is like a pillar," he said.
Another laid his hand on its back.
"Certainly this elephant was like a throne," he said.

(Arberry 2006: 208; the moral of this version of the tale will be discussed below).
19 Although I have not been able to consult them, Saxe's papers reside at Middlebury College, where there may be further evidence concerning his first acquaintance with these tales.

The second, feeling of the tusk,
Cried: "Ho! – what have we here
So very round and smooth and sharp?
To me 'tis very queer:
The wonder of an elephant
Is very like a spear!"

The third approached the animal,
And happening to take
The squirming trunk within his hands,
Thus boldly up and spake:
"I see," quoth he, "the elephant
Is very like a snake!"

The fourth reached out his eager hand,
And felt about the knee;
"What most this wondrous beast is like
Is mighty plain," quoth he;
"'Tis clear enough the elephant
Is very like a tree!"

The fifth, who chanced to touch the ear,
Said: "E'en the blindest man
Can tell what this resembles most –
Deny the fact who can,
This marvel of an elephant
Is very like a fan!"

The sixth no sooner had begun
About the beast to grope,
Than, seizing on the swinging tail
That fell within his scope,
"I see," quoth he, "the elephant
Is very like a rope!"

And so these men of Indoostan
Disputed loud and long,
Each in his own opinion
Exceeding stiff and strong,
Though each was partly in the right,
And all were in the wrong!

MORAL.
So, oft in theologic wars
The disputants, I ween,
Rail on in utter ignorance
Of what each other mean,
And prate about an elephant
Not one of them has seen!

The moral of this poem should strike us, today, as rather familiar, I think; for, as with Saxe's poem, the tale is now used to suggest that beyond the necessarily limited viewpoints of social actors there lies a greater, non-empirical whole – represented by, at least to the poem's curious protagonists, the unseen pachyderm – of which their limited and flawed judgments are but a constitutive part; for, as the poem reads: "Though each was partly in the right ..." It is a moral not unlike a stanza in one of Saxe's early poems about the diversity of train passengers, "Rhyme of the Rail:"

> Men of different "stations"
>   In the eye of Fame
> Here are very quickly
>   Coming to the same.
> High and lowly people,
>   Birds of every feather,
> On a common level
>   Travelling together![20]

Case in point, consider Catherine Albanese who, opening the 1981 edition of her well-known textbook, *America: Religions and Religion*, concludes, after recounting the tale:

> [T]he moral of the story, of course, goes beyond the elephants to the secrets of the universe. Each individual tries to fathom these secrets from a place of personal darkness. Each describes the portion experienced, and none can speak about the whole ... Nobody will ever know the whole story because the vastness that surrounds us far exceeds our sense or our ability to understand. (1981: 1–2)[21]

That she does not entertain that "the whole" is hardly a descriptive term and may be doing just as much rhetorical work as the categories "peace" or "ultimate" is never entertained – as it never is by those who use the story in this manner.

But now to return to the moral of the tale as we find it in the Udāna; for unlike the familiarity of Saxe's conclusion, we find there something that might be rather unexpected – at least for those who favor using this story today. For Gautama's conclusion has nothing to do with apparent pluralism yet unforeseen complementarity; instead, that tale ends as follows (quoting once again from Masefield's 1994 translation [2007: 133]):

> In the very same way, monks, wanderers of other outlooks, being blind, lacking vision, do not know what is to their benefit, do not know what is not to their benefit, do not know

---

20 See Taft 1900: 26; full text available at http://hdl.handle.net/2027/loc.ark:/13960/t20c5r82p (accessed Oct. 28, 2014).
21 This passage is also quoted (but examined differently) in McCutcheon 1997: 110.

Dhamma, do not know that which is not Dhamma. And these, not knowing what is to their benefit, not knowing what is not to their benefit, not knowing Dhamma, not knowing that which is not Dhamma, dwell quarrelsome, disputatious, engaging in contention, needling one another with mouthed darts, saying: 'Dhamma is of such a nature; Dhamma is not of such a nature. Dhamma is not of such a nature; Dhamma is of such a nature.

Then the Lord, fathoming this matter, gave rise at that time to this Udāna.

At which point chapter 6, section 5, closes with the Buddha, via our omniscient narrator, of course, bringing his story of the king and his willing subjects back to those arguing recluses whom the monks had overheard disputing the nature of reality. "'Some brahmin recluses, would you believe, are attached to these. They contend divisively (as did) folk who were seers of a single limb [of the elephant].'" And so ends this version of the tale.

The moral?

While I'm unsure how best to phrase it, the text seems uninterested in a modern, theologically liberal, pluralist's punch line, for there is nothing comparable to Saxe's closing; instead, the tale simply illustrates that others *are wrong* – dead wrong, completely wrong, sadly ill-informed – and, in doing so, implies not just that there are manifold views but, more importantly, that the path taught by the Buddha, the Dhamma, *is the only correct one*. After all, it's only from this position that we, the listeners of the narrative, are privileged to know that there's actually an elephant (whatever all of this even signifies, for the correct Dhamma is never identified).

Apart from the curious distance between this modern religious pluralist's tale and an ancient story about how all others are terribly misguided, what may be just as fascinating is that Saxe's moralizing ending closely resembles al-Ghazali's own conclusion to his own far older version of the story – which reads:

> Now, each of these presented a true aspect when he related what he had gained from experiencing the elephant. None of them had strayed from the true description of the elephant. Yet, together, they fell short of fathoming the true appearance of the elephant.[22]

---

[22] The whole text in English (from M. S. Stern's edition of "The First Pillar: On the Nature of Repentance," in Book 31 of *Ihya' 'Ulum ad-Din*) reads:

> A group of blind men heard that a strange animal, called an elephant, had been brought to the town but none of them had seen its shape nor had they heard its name. They said: "We must inspect and know it by touch of which we are capable." So, they sought it out, and when they found it they groped about it. One of them grasped its leg, another its tusk and the third its ear. Then they said: "Now we know it." When they departed, the other blind men questioned them but the three differed in their answers. The one who felt the leg said: "The elephant is similar to a coarse cylinder outside although it appears to be softer than that." The one who had felt the tusk said: "It is not as he says. It is solid without any softness

This is comparable to Rumi's later variant, quoted earlier (see n. 25), which concludes:

> The sensual eye is just like the palm of the hand. The palm has not the means of covering the whole of the beast. The eye of the Sea is one thing and the foam another. Let the foam go, and gaze with the eye of the Sea. Day and night foam-flecks are flung from the sea: of amazing! You behold the foam but not the Sea. We are like boats dashing together; our eyes are darkened, yet we are in clear water. (Arberry 2006: 208)

All of this suggests that it might not be unreasonable to suggest that the American poet's inspiration was likely a long line of Muslim writers stretching back nine centuries before him, a lineage which itself came a thousand years or more after the tale might have first been written down in Pāli. Consider that the first Pāli-English dictionary was published by R. C. Childers in 1872,[23] almost a decade after Saxe's poem appeared in a U.S. newspaper (its earliest appearance, you recall, seems to have been in 1861), that the first Pāli texts were translated into English by Childers in Britain in 1869, and that what I gather to have been the first English translation of the Udāna (that being the translation of D. M. Strong[24]) was first published in 1902, nearly forty years *after* his poem. It all provides strong circumstantial evidence that this now-beloved tale, quoted so frequently today with the exotic but authorized provenance of its supposedly ancient Indian origins, has (not unlike the transmission of many of our so-called classics) a fraught and meandering history. It may have come to the attention of colonial-era English readers in the U.S. and Britain by means of a satirist somehow acquainted with translations of Arabic sources which themselves had already retooled the tale to suit interests far removed from whatever uses it might have once had.

My point? If we're wanting to study the "limits of interreligious dialogue activities," with an aim toward identifying the "power relations that underlie

---

> on it. It is smooth, not coarse. It is not at all stiff but rather it resembles a column." The third man, who had handled the ear, said: "By my life, it is soft and somewhat coarse. One of them is right but it is not like a column or a cylinder. It is rather, like broad, thick hide."
>
> Now, each of these presented a true aspect when he related what he had gained from experiencing the elephant. None of them had strayed from the true description of the elephant. Yet, together, they fell short of fathoming the true appearance of the elephant. Ponder this parable and learn from it. It is the pattern of most human controversies. If these words touch the revealed sciences and provoke ripples therein, this was not our intention (http://www.ghazali.org/works/repent-p1.htm; accessed Nov. 16, 2014).

23 Robert Caesar Childers. *A Dictionary of the Pali Language* (London, UK: Trübner & Co., 1872).
24 See Strong 2006. The text was translated into English several other times over the years, with Masefield's 1994 edition (used here) being the most recent, along with German (first done by Karl Seidenstücker in 1913) Italian, and Spanish. See Anālayo "Udāna," 375.

these activities," and doing so while following Koch and Lehmann's advice to keep a careful eye on the role played by semantic or situational ambiguity in helping to create a sense of affinity and thus unity among otherwise divergent social actors, then tackling a material history of the tale of the blind men and the elephant would be a pretty good place to start. Such a project would not be interested in some form of "engagement" or identification either with the story or its various tellers and neither would it be interested in establishing what the parable *really* or *rightly* means; instead, such an archeological project would be interested in the specific conditions and discrete situations that made it possible to mean something in the first place and thereby to be of rhetorical use to someone in a particular setting for particular (and changeable) purposes (recalling sound methodological advice from Lincoln's Thesis 4).[25] Moreover, it would be a project that would likely start not in northeastern India over 2,000 years ago, and then, like most histories, proceed forward, in irresistibly Hegelian fashion, to the present but, instead, it would begin with our knowledge today of Saxe's mid- to late-19th-century poem – for that is where the groping blind men and the passive elephant more than likely first entered *our imaginaire*. It would trace not just its printings, distribution, and reception on both sides of the Atlantic but also how changing tastes have led to a situation where Saxe, once "known to generations of schoolchildren" (J. G. S. and M. S. S. 1916: 338) has, unlike some of his contemporaries, become all but unknown today.[26] The project would then move from there to examine the ethos of his time[27] and to try to chase down what

---

25 "The same destabilizing and irreverent questions one might ask of any speech act ought to be posed of religious discourse. The first of these is 'Who speaks here?', i.e., what person, group, or institution is responsible for a text, whatever its putative or apparent author. Beyond that, 'To what audience? In what immediate and broader context? Through what system of mediations? With what interests?' And further, 'Of what would the speaker(s) persuade the audience? What are the consequences if this project of persuasion should happen to succeed? Who wins what, and how much? Who, conversely, loses?'" (Lincoln 1996: 225–226).

26 It is interesting that in 1916, J. G. S. and M. S. S. claim that Saxe's fame, twenty-five years after his death, had outlived many of his contemporaries ("Saxe – The Vermont Poet," 392).

27 For instance, as phrased by my colleague at Alabama Mike Altman in response to reading an earlier version of this chapter, "Saxe is writing in a time and place in which ideas about a universal or unified religion are all around. As Lydia Maria Child wrote in her *The Progress of Religious Ideas, Through Successive Ages* (1855): 'Unison of voice was the highest idea theology could attain to; but when religion can utter itself freely, worshippers sing a harmony of many different parts, and thus make a music more pleasing to the ear of God, and more according to the pattern by which he created the universe' (volume 3, 450). The search for a 'universal religion' can also be found in James Freeman Clarke's *Ten Great Religions* (1871), which began as essays in *The Atlantic* in 1868, Samuel Johnson's series *The Oriental Religions and Their Relation to Universal Religion* (1872, 1877, 1885), and Thomas Wentworth Higginson's 'The Sympathy of Religions' (written in 1855–6, delivered in 1870, published in the magazine *The Radical* in 1871). Saxe is thus part of a

circumstances might have prompted him to pen such a poem,[28] working our way backward, not forward, just as some of Saxe's more motivated and curious readers may have done themselves, through medieval Arabic and Jewish sources, all the way to a Pāli tale that came to be known more widely in English a generation after Saxe's poem. And we would carry out this work recognizing that it was the practical context of technological innovation and political dominance (whether in the medieval or the modern period), and not disembodied viewpoints, worldviews, or beliefs, that made knowledge of, and revisions to, this tale possible.

I find such a project compelling because it would follow two recommendations made by a second Chicago faculty member who has been influential of my work, Jonathan Z. Smith – one for developing a cross-cultural comparative study of scriptures[29] and the other outlined in an essay entitled "Scriptures and History" (originally delivered as part of a 1992 conference in Toronto on the work of Wilfred Cantwell Smith [see J. Z. Smith 1992]), where he observes that, with biblical studies' historical-critical method in mind,

> "J" or "Q" are not tenth century B.C. or first century A.D. Palestinian artifacts, they are artifacts of 19th and 20th century European thought. They stand towards the end rather than the beginning of the "history of the Bible over the past 20 centuries." [As an analogue I recall asking Mircea Eliade why his beloved 'primitives' (codeword, "archaic") had made no appearance in the first three volumes of his projected four volume *Historie des croyances et des idée religieuses*. "Because, Jonathan, they did not enter the history of the major religions until the 16th century." That is to say, the "archaic" is a discovery of the modern era. In light of this, I have often toyed with the idea of constructing a course about the west and its 'others' built around the chronology of when we became interested in them. It is a significantly different timeline than the one we are accustomed to – for example, the Sumerians not would [sic] appear until some 70 years ago.] (Smith 1992: 99–100)[30]

To rephrase: to hold that the story of the elephant is an "ancient Buddhist tale," as most do, overlooks that, were it not for Saxe and his poem about "six men of

---

larger stream of 'free religion' or 'free thought' among writers and intellectuals in the northeastern United States during the middle nineteenth century" (Personal correspondence, Feb. 22, 2016).
28 As with many other writers from this era, there are allusions to Arabic or Indian literature throughout his work, such as other poems included in his *Clever Stories of Many Nations* (1865), such as "The Caliph and the Cripple: An Arabian Tale" (67–75) or "The Pious Brahmin and His Neighbors: A Hindoo Fable" (77–83).
29 See the concluding comments in Smith (2009).
30 Of course it should be noted that Eliade himself would be the third Chicago professor important to my (not to mention Lincoln and Smith's own) work; but, unlike those AAR papers cited at the outset, in which two counted as data and only one qualified as method, when it comes to Eliade, Smith, and Lincoln, the scales tip the other way, inasmuch as the work of only one constitutes data while the latter two have offered to the modern field what I think to be its most important methodological lessons on how to carry out disciplined comparison and analysis.

Indoostan" – a classification shared with an earlier Arabic source that also tells us much about the later invention of Buddhism as a modern item of discourse – religious pluralists today might not be making good use of the vagaries of that story to build tactical coalitions that help to further a specific set of interests. In fact, were we not making such use of the story today, then we might have some difficulty attributing it to even earlier Jain sources – as many commentators still do – for, in correspondence with Paul Dundas (Reader in Sanskrit at the School of Literatures, Languages and Cultures, University of Edinburgh) I have confirmed that, despite such speculations, the tale does not occur in any Jain canonical text.[31] What's curious, then, is that this attribution (and thus presumed authenticity and thus authority of the tale) is likely possible only because modern readings of the text as a pluralist fable nicely fit with our understanding of the Jain doctrine of many-sidedness (i.e., Anekāntavāda) – a fit that results only when we anachronistically project the modern reading of the story backward in time, as if al-Ghazali's or Saxe's version overlapped with a pre-Buddhist, unsourced Jain use of the tale. In fact, to press this point even further, if this were our project, then we might have to reconsider how this very chapter is structured, beginning, as it does, with my own retelling the supposedly ancient, original tale, steeped as it is in "Oriental" authenticity, rather than beginning with Saxe, where this elephant may have first entered the scholar's study.

And so, to conclude, should we be serious in following Lincoln when he advises that we study truth claims and regimes of truth, rather than truth itself (see Thesis 13), and thereby investigate the limits, interests, and effects of discourses (in this case, that of religious pluralists). I would then imagine that this is the sort of project that we, as scholars of religion, ought to be tackling, adopting for ourselves the situated stance of the so-called blind men of that tale, each of whom is blissfully unaware of the supposed big picture, and thereby leaving

---

[31] As pointed out by Hugh Urban, upon reading an earlier version of this chapter, "there are references to the parable being used to support the doctrine of many-sidedness in later Jain philosophical texts [i.e., commentaries], such as Mallisena's 13th century text, 'Syadvadamanjari' ... ." According to the translation of this text by F. W. Thomas (Delhi: Motilal Banarsidass Publishers Pvt. Ltd., 1968), the story is briefly cited at 14.111 (in a chapter entitled "The Vedanta Theory of the Denotation of Terms" [page 87 of Thomas' translation]), where it is very briefly offered as an example of how all entities possess universal but also particular features – a use of the tale to be distinguished, I would argue, from the moral of both Saxe's and our own version today. And, at Thomas' 19.162, it is cited again (on page 125 of his translation) as an illustration this time of the error of "grabbing at superficialities" (i.e., what Thomas signals in the original as being more akin to "twig-grabbing" [125, n. 12]). Again, I would argue, that this is a rather different reading than that of the modern, since the tale as cited in the "Syadvadamanjari" does not appear to concern unity in diversity so much as the risk of overlooking larger conclusions by inappropriately focusing on minor or easily apparent ones.

to others the all-knowing speculations on the supposedly enduring elephant in the room. Then, instead of debating totalized universals, as do the so-called pluralists, those who historicize instead would be far more interested in studying how competing particulars are authorized to do specific jobs – for, no matter the differences between the two readings of this tale that I've offered here, both are no less concerned with asserting a particular; it's just that each authorizes it in a different manner (i.e., one highlights, in a rather imperial voice, "the divergence of views held by the ignorant" [as phrased by Jacobs (1907: 3)] while the other, in a no less imperial tone, asserts, "my Truth contains your truths"). Lacking the hubris of that king or the omniscience of both the character Gautama and the poem's narrator, we can at least study the means – case in point, this very tale itself – by which otherwise divergent social actors fabricate the impression of agreement and disagreement, the results being what Lincoln once so aptly termed sentiments of affinity and estrangement. In doing so, we will examine how and why people authorize some and what they do with those who undermine their goals (in fact, calling such competitors "quarrelsome and disputatious" might be one tactic that we adopt). Beginning such a project with but one of the many techniques used to carry out this work – i.e., a surprisingly recent tale of an vaguely perceived elephant that we pitch back into the authoritative but ambiguous mists of time – therefore seems to be a good place to start.[32]

References

Abu-Nimer, Mohammed (2003). *Nonviolence and Peace Building in Islam: Theory and Practice.* Gainesville, FL: University Press of Florida.
Albanese, Catherine (1981). *America: Religions and Religion.* Belmont, CA: Wadsworth.
Anālayo, Bhikkhu (2008). Udāna. In W. G. Weeraratne (ed.), *Encyclopedia of Buddhism*, Vol. 8: Fac. 2: 375–384. Ceylon: Ministry of Cultural Affairs, Sri Lanka.
Anonymous (1866). Review of John Godfrey Saxe, *The Masquerade and Other Poems* (Boston: Ticknor and Fields). *Atlantic Monthly* 18/105 (July): 123–125.
Arberry, Arthur J. (trans.) (2006) [1961]. *Tales from the Masnavi.* New York, NY and London, UK: Routledge.
Borges, Jorge Luis (1999). On exactitude in science. In Andrew Hurley (trans.), *Jorge Luis Borges: Collected Fictions*, 325. New York, NY: Penguin.
Childers, Robert Caesar (1872). *A Dictionary of the Pali Language.* London, UK: Trübner & Co.

---

32 My appreciation goes to Greg Johnson and Hugh Urban for comments on an earlier draft; also to Aaron Hughes, for the assistance with the Arabic sources and the identification of helpful English translations; as well as to Steve Berkwitz, for early conversations on the Udāna; and to as Willi Braun, William Arnal, Steven Ramey, Merinda Simmons, Vaia Touna, and Mike Altman for their own comments.

Cumnock, Robert McLean (1883). *Cumnock's School Speaker: Rhetorical Recitations for Boys and Girls*. Chicago, IL: A. C. McClurg & Co. (See also the 1888 and 1904 editions.)

Gómez, Luis O. (nd). The blind leading the blind: Reflections on a presumably Buddhist tale [Draft: Not for Quotation]" http://isites.harvard.edu/fs/docs/icb.topic267499.files/Gomez%20Blind%20Men%20Reflections.pdf (accessed Nov. 14, 2014).

Jacobs, G. A. (1907) [1900]. *A Handful of Popular Maxims Current in Sanskrit Literature*. 2nd ed. Bombay, IN: Tukârâm Jâvajî.

Koch, Anne and Karsten Lehmann (2014). Perspectives on sociology: Modeling pluralism from inward and outward. Paper presented at the Interreligious and Interfaith Studies Group of the American Academy of Religion (unpublished).

Lincoln, Bruce (1989). *Discourse and the Construction of Society: Comparative Studies in Myth, Ritual, and Classification*. 1st ed. New York, NY: Oxford University Press.

— (1996). Theses on method. *Method & Theory in the Study of Religion* 8 (3): 225–227.

— (2012). *Gods and Demons, Priests and Scholars: Critical Explorations in the History of Religions*. Chicago, IL: University of Chicago Press.

Linton, William James (1878). *Poetry of America: Selections from One Hundred American Poets, from 1776 to 1876. With an Introductory Review of Colonial Poetry and Some Specimens of Negro Melody*. London, UK: George Bell and Sons.

Lopez, Donald S. (1998). Belief. In Mark C. Taylor (ed.), *Critical Terms for Religious Studies*, 21–35. Chicago, IL: University of Chicago Press.

Martin, Craig (2014). *Capitalizing Religion: Ideology and the Opiate of the Bourgeoisie*. London, UK: Bloomsbury.

Masefield, Peter (trans.) (2007) [1994]. *The Udāna*. Lancaster, UK: The Pali Text Society.

McCutcheon, Russell T. (1997). *Manufacturing Religion: The Discourse on Sui Generis Religion and the Politics of Nostalgia*. New York, NY: Oxford University Press.

— (2001). *Critics Not Caretakers: Redescribing the Public Study of Religion*. Albany, NY: State University of New York Press.

— (2003). *The Discipline of Religion: Rhetoric, Structure, Meaning*. New York, NY and London, UK: Routledge.

— (2005). *Religion and the Domestication of Dissent, Or How to Live in a Less than Perfect Nation*. New York, NY and London, UK: Routledge.

— (2012). Introduction. In Craig Martin and Russell T. McCutcheon (eds.), *Religious Experience: A Reader*, 1–16. New York, NY: Routledge.

— (2015). The tremendous irony of it all. Blog post at: http://religion.ua.edu/blog/2015/10/the-tremendous-irony-of-it-all/ (accessed Nov. 5, 2015).

— (2018). *"Religion" in Theory and Practice: Demystifying the Field for Burgeoning Academics*. Sheffield, UK: Equinox Publishers.

Ramey, Steven W. (2015). Accidental favorites: The implicit in the study of religion. In Monica Miller (ed.), *Claiming Identity in the Study of Religion: Social and Rhetorical Techniques Examined*, 223–237. Sheffield, UK: Equinox Publishers.

S., J. G. and M. S. S. (1916). Saxe – the Vermont poet. *The Bookman: An Illustrated Magazine of Literature and Life* 43: 387–393. New York, NY: Dodd, Mead, and Co.

Saxe, John Godfrey (1865). *Clever Stories of Many Nations: Rendered in Rhyme by John Godfrey Saxe*. Boston, MA: Ticknor and Fields.

— (1868). *The Poems of John Godfrey Saxe, Complete in One Volume*. Boston, MA: Ticknor and Field.

– (1872). *Fables and Legends of Many Countries: Rendered in Rhyme*. Boston, MA: J. R. Osgood. Reprinted in 2010 by Kessinger Publishing.
– (1876). *The Poems of John Godfrey Saxe, Complete in One Volume*. Highgate Edition. Boston, MA: James R. Osgood and Company.
Sharf, Robert H. (1998). Experience. In Mark C. Taylor (ed.), *Critical Terms for Religious Studies*, 94–116. Chicago, IL: University of Chicago Press.
Smith, Jonathan Z. (1992). Scriptures and histories. *Method & Theory in the Study of Religion* 4 (1&2): 97–105.
– (2009). Religion and Bible. *Journal of Biblical Literature* 128 (1): 5–27.
Strong, Dawsonne Melancthon (trans.) (2006) [1902]. *The Udāna or the Solemn Utterances of the Buddha*. Whitefish, MT: Kessinger Publishing Co.
Swidler, Leonard (2014a). *Dialogue for Interreligious Understanding: Strategies for the Transformation of Culture-Making Institutions*. New York, NY: Palgrave Macmillan.
– (2014b). "Ultimate reality" reflects "real" reality. Paper presented at the Interreligious and Interfaith Studies Group of the American Academy of Religion (unpublished).
Taft, Russell W. (1900). *John Godfrey Saxe: A Biographical Sketch of Vermont's Lawyer, Journalist, Lecturer, and Rhymster*. Burlington, VT. (Privately printed; full text available at http://hdl.handle.net/2027/loc.ark:/13960/t20c5r82p.)
Thomas, F. W. (trans.) (1968). *Syād-vāda-manjarī*. Delhi, IN: Motilal Banarsidass Publishers Pvt. Ltd.

8 The Magic of the Melancholy: Shifting Gears in the Study of Religion

> It's delicate ... but potent.
> (*Don Draper*)

Jazz fans might know of the Canadian singer Holly Cole and maybe even her 1995 album of Tom Waits songs, "Temptation." In particular, I have in mind Cole's haunting version of his 1974 song, "(Looking for) The Heart of Saturday Night." It's bitter/sweet, for it makes me think of a home that I left long ago – one for which I may long but, because it doesn't exist anymore, it's a longing never to be satisfied.

And, at least according to its etymology, that's precisely what nostalgia is, isn't it? For it derives from two Greek terms that, once put together, might as well be translated as "homesickness." For whereas the word neuralgia is today used for a pain associated with a nerve, and myalgia is a pain in a muscle, nostalgia is a pain associated with a homecoming (Greek: *nostos*) – or, better put, a homecoming that is imagined, delayed, or even denied. So while the term could apply to a character such as Odysseus, who famously worked to return home amid obstacles, when applied to anything but a mythic hero, it is a word that's linked to an impossible task. While Odysseus successfully returned to Ithaca (after twenty years away), there will be no return to the place that this Holly Cole song conjures for me when I hear it, for no amount of cunning intelligence (that virtue known as *mētis* to the ancient Greeks [Deteinne and Vernant 1991]) can reverse time. As a child, I recall that after returning from more extended times away from

---

Note: Curiously, at least to me, I often seem to find my work criticized as not providing constructive alternatives to accompany its critique of the academic study of religion. While critique can rightfully stand on its own, if one wishes, contrary to this characterization, I tend to see all of my published work as offering practical and repeated alternatives, sometimes described in great detail, from the concluding chapter of my very first book, *Manufacturing Religion*, to the many essays I've written over the years on pedagogy and the various edited volumes and classroom resources that I've been involved with creating or helping to get into print (some of which have been explicitly directed toward early-career scholars). I see this (mis)representation of my work as a strategic caricature that undermines (by never seriously entertaining) the alternatives that I do offer; what would be far more helpful would be an argument, in some degree of detail, as to why these alternative approaches are not viable. And so, with that in mind, I've sometimes focused in specific detail on one site within the field and offered thoughts on how to rethink our approach to the topic – from how we, as scholars of religion, discuss the problem of evil to how we examine origins or discourses on spirituality, let alone how we use the category religion itself. This chapter, like the previous, follows in that tradition, this time inviting readers to reconsider what's going on when someone talks about being nostalgic.

home, such as going away to summer camp for a few weeks, I would go through the house looking for changes, finding the gaps and surprises that signified my absence (and which, upon finding them, signified my return). Here was an item that was moved or something that was new; but they were judgments based on an absent, imagined standard that allowed me to spot changes in which I hadn't participated – as if finding them somehow involved me in the change. But I hadn't been involved, of course; I had been away. And so finding the lamp that was now there and no longer here was a way to make the place mine all over again.

As with me making the rounds of the house as a child, we all try to bridge the gaps – which might be why a term such as *nostos* makes such a great marketing device, as was figured out by the owners of the Nostos Restaurant located in the U.S. (in Vienna, Virginia, to be precise – a city name that, like so many others in North America, carries its founders' own longing for a far off home).[1] For as they say on their website:

> "Nostos" is at the root of the word nostalgia and means a return to one's origins, a longing for a special time in our past. Through Nostos, we wish to share this past with you and stimulate your senses with a variety of traditional and new Greek dishes.[2]

Their hope seems to be that the gap between past and present, between traditional and new, between origins and the one who coaxes the time of the ancestors into existence here and now by retelling the origins tale, can be bridged when seated at their tables, eating their food, and no doubt listening to bouzouki music over their loudspeakers (sooner or later we'd expect to hear Mikis Theodorakis' well-known theme from "Zorba the Greek," no? For *that's* what Greek music is supposed to sound like, right?).

After all, who among us doesn't want to be like Dorothy Gale, tapping our heels together three times to extricate ourselves from some current predicament and just go back home? Apparently, there's no place like it.[3]

But there's a problem: to which of the many possible homes will we each return? For upon each return from camp it was apparent to me, even as a child, that home had changed yet again, and my idea of it was continually estranged from the actual place – minimally, yes, but my recognition of the differences meant

---

[1] Although originally known as Ayr Hill (named after a county in Scotland), in 1854 some of its new inhabitants, the Hendrick family, successfully moved to change the town's name to Vienna, after their own town in New York state. See the town's version of its own history posted at http://www.viennava.gov/index.aspx?nid=335 (accessed March 16, 2016).
[2] See http://www.nostosrestaurant.com/page/about-nostos-restaurant (accessed July 25, 2015).
[3] Although not the same approach, I think here of Salman Rushdie's wonderful meditation on the *Wizard of Oz* (2012).

it was estranged nonetheless. Even mythic Ithaca had changed when Odysseus finally returned – if it had been the same, then he would not have had to fend off (which is a nice way of saying "kill," I suppose) all the suitors who were by then vying for his wife, Penelope. And so, even for a hardcore realist who argues that an actual chronological past is real and tangible, which of all those memories, of all those different past homes, all competing for our attention today, will rise to the top and constitute some definitive sense of home? In my case, perhaps it will be that house on Weaver Road where I first lived and which my father built himself, the one that always smelled like sulfur (due to the well water), the one of which I have only vague and disparate childhood memories. Or perhaps it will be the one on Mitchell Street, to which we then moved and where, as a little boy, I first learned to write my own name and address (and yes, it was 321 Mitchell St., thank you very much). Or maybe it would be the small gas station on Davis Street, owned and operated by my parents, into which we moved in 1968 and where, from outside, I would tap lightly on the glass of the living room window, on dusky summer evenings, to be let in the back door, with my bicycle, fresh from some adventure with friends. And so which will remain standing once I've winnowed them all down (having already sorted the good from the bad moments, perhaps, highlighting the former and overlooking, even forgetting, the latter), inasmuch as it gets to stand in for the definitive distillate that will count as the "special time in our past" (as that Virginia restaurant's marketers phrased it)? In fact, how does this winnowing actually work? And even if there are many past homes from which to choose today, are they each some stable thing, a yesterday that's the same today as it will be tomorrow? Or are each prone to continual revision, adaption, and maybe even complete alteration, inasmuch as the historically situated, remembering subject him or herself is no less prone to revision, adaption, and yes, even complete revision?

Question: will I always remember tapping on that long past window? Given that my own father is now 94 (his birthday was yesterday, as I write this), and, though in fine shape, that I sometimes hear the same story repeated almost verbatim to me when I call home to chat, I know something about how fleeting the past can be and how we live more in the present than many of us may realize. After all, I'm likely not the same person now, fondly remembering some past occasion, as I was when I was a teenager unknowingly living it as some sort of all-consuming present, not yet in the position, as a 56-year-old man, to pick and choose from among what I happen to remember now. (And don't forget how the scientists now tell us that memory is more constitution than retrieval.) Might it all be much like how a favorite novel is somehow different each time it's read, all depending on the mood or situation of the reader? If so, then inasmuch as it makes no sense to ask what such a novel is really about, what it *really means* – for, as the reader-response theorists told us some time ago, its meaning is continually changing inasmuch as it's the function of an always-changing reader – it will make just as little sense to talk of definitive originary points to which we try to return or which we use as authoritative standards by which to judge the present.[4]

In fact, might there be, as the homesick Dorothy was so wisely instructed to recite by the charlatan wizard, no place like home at all, not because all others pale in comparison but, instead, because the reference point of home itself is an untrustworthy source, given that it is an unstable isotope that's continually created anew by means of the always-shifting needs of a continually decaying present? If so, then this might explain the pain of nostalgia: it's not just a longing for a home that, as I suggested at the outset, no longer exists, but, because we remember what we now either wish or happen to recall, and forget the rest, it may be a desire for an idea or image of home *that might have never existed to begin with*, a construct of the present. That would put it forever out of reach – except in the epic tales that we tell to ourselves, whether around campfires or in darkened movie theaters, when we vicariously return to a place of no place that we've constituted in the present moment, by flipping through an old photo album or, in my case, putting that old Holly Cole CD into the tray. (Yes, I still use the CD player.)

So the Saturday night of the song that I mentioned at the outset is, for me, a good place to start thinking about how the socially formative use of a longing for a past works, and to consider its link to what a number of us know as essentialism: that effort to boil down complex and ambiguous situations to an essence, a pristine distillate, leaving what we take to be a deeply significant, perhaps even definitive and thus all-powerful residue, much like in an experiment in a chemistry class that leaves an intense, concentrated powder as the lone trace of the ambiguous, cloudy liquid that once filled the laboratory flask. If you listen to Waits' lyrics, you may realize that from all that might have once characterized that weekend evening he's selected – and *choice*, and along with it, the *interests* that direct it, both of which are in the present and not the past, are the key issues here! – a series of discrete and condensed vignettes are offered, none more or less indicative of what any particular Saturday night surely feels like or ought to feel like. (Question: what *does* Saturday night feel like? And why does it feel that way?) But, when strung together in the right way, and conveyed in Cole's dreamy, sultry style, they begin to paint a picture where the gaps between past and present, us and them, *seem to be bridged*; and, even if you don't directly

---

4 See the introduction and afterword to McCutcheon 2015a for a more detailed, and directly related, discussion of the problem of origins.

identify with its specific parts, you might find yourself imagining a distant, alien moment as if it were intimately familiar, and longing for a long past and seemingly simpler time – and, along with it, a long past and seemingly simpler self.

The song opens:

> Well, you gassed her up
> Behind the wheel
> With your arm around your sweet one
> Your Oldsmobile
> Barrelin' down the boulevard
> Lookin' for the heart of Saturday night

From the outset, I should be clear to state one important thing: despite the nostalgia that I admit to be inspired by this song, this is *not* the sort of Saturday night that I grew up with, living in southern Ontario in the 1960s and early '70s; I state this so that I'm clear that an actual memory, or some actual but distant past, is not what this nostalgia is about. Much as with that Greek restaurant, it may instead be more about the particular present, and specific self that occupies it now, that we're each trying to legitimize and fortify, by persuading ourselves that all of our history anticipated it and led up to it. For I was not yet driving, didn't play pool, and I likely wasn't even sure just what a boulevard was. (To be honest, I'm still a little foggy on the difference between a lane, drive, avenue, and a street.) And besides, my dad was a Ford man – back in the day, when and where I grew up in Canada, the choice between Ford and Chev (which is owned by General Motors, as Oldsmobile was) plotted you no less than either reporting on whether you were Protestant or Catholic or that you spoke English or French.

And depending on which, it might even predict which hockey team you supported. Case in point: consider Roch Carrier's well-known and much-beloved (at least in Canada) 1979 children's book, *Une abominable feuille d'érable sur la glace* ("An abominable maple leaf on the ice," otherwise known in English translation simply as *The Hockey Sweater*); set in the 1940s, a little boy in the largely French-speaking Canadian province of Quebec receives the wrong hockey team's sweater from the mail-order catalogue. (Was it a mistake of his non-English speaking mother's poorly written English order? Or was it an error on the part of the department store? Perhaps the hegemony of English-speaking Canada?) While wearing it (though he strenuously resists putting it on, of course, for its blue and white colors defined not who *he was* but who *he was not*!) he has no choice but also to adopt the identity it connotes – in his own eyes and those of his friends at the outdoor rink – much to his disappointment, of course; for he's no longer seen as a member of the home team from Montreal (wearing their red, white, and blue) but, instead, as their arch rivals from Toronto.

Like the song, that story resonates with me, though I was born decades after it's set, never lived in Quebec (but, importantly perhaps, everyone else in my family was born there), and, when it was first published, I was 18 and thus hardly reading children's books. But I can easily imagine playing hockey on a rink outdoors in the winter or waiting, in the small living room of that gas station on Davis Street, about 90 minutes outside Toronto, for the theme from "Hockey Night in Canada" to come on TV precisely at 8 each Saturday night to announce the start of the Leafs game – making *my* home team and the sweater that *I* wore with pride (number 14, Davey Keon!) ironically a symbol of Carrier's alienation (given that he was a fan of what *I* considered to be *our* arch rivals: the Montreal Canadiens). So my Saturday night, at least as an adolescent and then teenager, did and did not overlap with these two models that I'm considering here: it involved being on the opposite end of the gas pump, as compared to Waits' song, for I was watching people gas up and drive off into the darkness and then, after we closed up shop, I went in to watch the Leafs game, which involved getting the TV trays out and a big bowl of potato chips, with some corn chips mixed in among them. Maybe some chip dip too. And a pop – yes, we called it "pop" and not "soda" – from the cooler, up front (and yes, we called the store part "the front") – the one with bottles of Coke and Pepsi, Orange Crush and Mountain Dew, all lined up in neat rows, like obedient soldiers, and submerged halfway in the cold water, gently tinkling from the compressor motor's vibrations when they stood too close to each other.

However, these details are all (predictably?) absent from Carrier's story and also from Waits' song – but does that matter? For into the space that each has opened, I've seamlessly added my own details, not unlike the supporters of then-candidate Donald Trump, perhaps, at his early 2016 campaign rallies, who responded so well to his own version of nostalgia. "Make America Great Again" (the "MAGA" written on their ball caps and used as hashtags to their online posts) was his catchy slogan (Reagan had already used it in his 1980 campaign, though), despite it being utterly devoid of all concrete detail. (It's the "again" that signals the nostalgia.) Some commentators at the time criticized him for this lack of specificity, of course, but thinking back on how easily, and without realizing it, I've personalized Waits and Carrier's tales with details of my own, I think the generality of the slogan, unencumbered by historical specifics, was the key to its success. After all, forming alliances across large numbers of people who have previously never met can likely only happen at the level of vague generalization (studies of nationalism have long told us as much), offered in just the right way, so that listeners populate the narrative with their own details. "Yes, we need to make America great again" they might say to each other, nodding in vigorous agreement, while never specifying for each other just what constitutes the historical referent for the claim – the 1960s? Perhaps the 1950s? Or what about the 1850s? The generalized rhetoric encompasses them all and its success is predicated on no one ever specifying, for the last thing we want is to put our cards on the table, or to see those of the others playing the game with us, for then we risk disagreement, and disunion, among our ranks. Simply put, we may come to realize that we're not playing the same game.

But, to return to the song, it continues:

> You got paid on Friday
> Your pockets are jinglin'
> And then you see the lights
> You get all tinglin'
> Coz you're cruisin' with a 6
> Lookin' for the heart of Saturday night

Cruising with your girl and a six-pack of beer in your Olds – a more particular Saturday night is being created, but it remains one with which, despite my affinity for the song, I have little in common – at least not when growing up and certainly not when Cole released the song and thus back when I first heard it. I was then working at the University of Tennessee, already uprooted from my "home and native land" (to quote the Canadian national anthem) in the Great White North (to quote the toque-wearing comedians and Canadian stereotypes, Bob and Doug McKenzie),[5] and I'd already grown used to hearing "Rocky Top," Tennessee's so-called fight song echoing all over campus in the late afternoon as the band marched around campus and rehearsed. Come to think of it, it's a song from 1967 that packs a nostalgic punch of its own; written by the married songwriting team of Felice and Boudleaux Bryant, its lyrics are easily read as a lament for simpler days in the Appalachian hills of east Tennessee (when, notably, strangers met a mysterious fate for bucking local habits). Its opening verses read:

> Wish that I was on ol' Rocky Top
> Down in the Tennessee hills
> Ain't no smoggy smoke on Rocky Top

---

5 For those either puzzled or alienated by my casual use of local jargon, in Canada a toque (pronounced to͞ok) – contrary to the good people of Tennessee and other parts of the American south, where the term toboggan was instead used – is a knitted winter cap, with or without a pom-pom on the top. The word comes into English from French but, as the label on the University of Tennessee winter hat that I once bought for my mother, to illustrate how strange my new home in Knoxville was (it was instead named as if it was a winter sled), made clear, unpoliced designations are never anchored all that well.

Ain't no telephone bills
Once I had a girl on Rocky Top
Half bear, the other half cat
Wild as a mink, sweet as soda pop
I still dream about that

Once two strangers climbed ol' Rocky Top
Lookin' for a moonshine still
Strangers ain't come down from Rocky Top
Reckon they never will

Corn won't grow at all on Rocky Top
Dirt's too rocky by far
That's why all the folks on Rocky Top
Get their corn from a jar

I've had years of cramped up city life
Wrapped like a duck in a pen
Now all I know is it's a pity life
Can't be simple again.

Rocky Top you'll always be
Home sweet home to me
Good ol' Rocky Top
Rocky Top Tennessee, Rocky Top Tennessee

But despite the specificity of the picture being painted, both here and in Cole's song, which is surely quite alien from the specificity of those who hear both today (after all, despite how fans from my own school might taunt them as hillbillies, it's more than likely that few college football fans from Tennessee today drink moonshine, no?), there's something here that grabs us, helping us to overlook the inevitable gaps.

But to return to Cole's song – it continues:

Then you comb your hair
Shave your face
Try to wipe out every trace
Of all the other days
In the week
You know that this'll be the Saturday
You're reachin' your peak

By means of the necessarily compact, distilled language of poetry (which is what gives it its ideological power), we know a surprising amount about this fellow – yet the danger, as already suggested, is that the more we know, the less affinity we might have for him, for the more distinct he becomes, in distinction from ourselves, our memories, our long-past Saturday nights.

Then, not long after, the singer asks about those very details:

> Tell me, is it the crack of the pool balls?
> Neon buzzin'?
> Telephone's ringin'
> It's your second cousin
> Is it the barmaid that's smilin' in the corner of her eye?
> The magic of the melancholy tearin' you right up

And then the song finishes:

> Makes me kind of quiver
> Down in the core
> Been dreamin' of those Saturdays
> That came before
> And now you're stumblin'
> Stumblin' onto the heart of Saturday night
> Right now you're stumblin'
> Stumbling onto the heart of Saturday night

So here we have a song trying to identify (meaning to describe an identity or, instead, to assert and thereby claim one? That's the question! – something "down in the core:" the essence or the heart of Saturday night) not any old weekday evening, mind you, or the expectation-laden Thursday or Friday nights (just when *does* the weekend actually start? On my campus it seems to start on Thursday night), and certainly not the workweek's somber eve (i.e., Sunday night). But, instead, we're working to understand the distilled and purified core of the weekend: Saturday night. But this is no easy task, of course; in fact, the difficulty is apparent in the lyric that begins "Tell me, is it the … ," for it could have had innumerable items listed after it, such as, in my case, "… the theme song from 'Hockey Night in Canada?'" or "… the sound of the corn chips pouring into the bowl?" – confirming that, as already suggested, there are surely as many Saturday nights as there are definers of what counts as definitive of that evening, which also confirms that a search for its heart, much like a homecoming, is a rather pointless quest. If anything, there are innumerable hearts, much as an infinite, boundless space has innumerable centers, all equally distant from an undefined and thus continually retreating margin. Case in point: I recall my late older sister, a nurse who worked shift work for pretty much all her career, and how the holidays – days that just inherently felt like a holiday to me as a young boy, due to a host of cues and prompts all around me – were, for her, not necessarily the holidays at all; hospitals, after all, have a schedule of their own, and are in business 365 days a year, so somebody's always on the job there. When you're sick, there's no weekend respite and so, for her, Saturday night was just another night shift and thus one step closer to getting back on days.

Or I think again of my father, with whom I joked, when he retired, that he'd never again have a Sunday night for as long as he lived – i.e., he'd never again have to mourn the end of the weekend's break from the workweek and thus never again have to get up for work on Monday morning. For from now on, despite retaining a daily schedule (though, significantly, not a *work* schedule), every night was a Friday night.

So, returning to the song, whose idea of that weekend night gets to stand in as definitive, its very heart? That's a far better question than asking what its heart is.

Now, if there are as many centers as there are definers making choices and drawing boundaries, then, the trick to making the heart you've selected stand out as if it's *the* center is in painting a picture that takes a stand (i.e., provides some details) but, as already suggested, is also just vague enough to allow a variety of listeners to connect with it in some unexpected way. Like how, for me, this song brings back memories of young guys (who, though, were older than me) driving their old cars up and down the streets of my small childhood town, hanging out in the early evenings, maybe in the parking lot of a grocery store, or over at the high school, and lifting the hoods to, well, just stare at the engines for a while and swap repair stories. Primatologists would no doubt study this as mating behavior. Oh, and of course, they were listening to Rush playing on someone's car stereo, cranked up loud – that's not a detail in Waits' 1974 song, of course (since the band had not even gone mainstream yet – that came a few years later), but I'm free to insert some details of my own into his rather minimal narrative, customizing it, filling in the gaps, and drawing on a repertoire of recollections that suit my interests, my needs, today. That's just how it works.

It's a summer night, the dusk sky still lit more than it ought to be while the store lights are just all coming on – the neon's buzzin' ... .

The lyrics therefore resonate with me not because they match some event in my past – i.e., assuming the correspondence theory of meaning illuminates everything is precisely the problem – but because they provide an opportunity for me, in the here and now, to pick and choose from my own archive of the past, its contents vague and disconnected, matching up items, in ways the songwriter never imagined, with Waits' own selections, even though each discrete memory has no necessary relation to the other elements of this nostalgic scene.[6] So

---

[6] The idea of an archive of the past, from which we pick and choose to suit our current needs, is one that I borrow from the late Michel-Rolph Trouillot (1997).

although I never did the things mentioned in the song, and though the memories it seems to evoke are not connected themselves, that's not exactly what the song is about; instead, the few minutes of that song are an occasion for a set of possibly random childhood memories of my own to get hooked together, on the spot, by means of something vague enough not to repel what it was that this one listener wanted to do with it when he first heard it sometime in the mid-1990s, and what he does with it each time he hears it again. That another listener would do something else should be clear – maybe they'd not even "like" the song at all (I'm assuming few readers even know the tune, let alone Cole's rendition); in its place they'd probably select another occasion to legitimize their happenstance present by means of a wrapping that conveys the power of what we take to be an authoritative past. All of which makes plain that there are as many hearts as there were Saturday nights, as there were people cruisin', workin', or just sleepin' their way through them – correction: as there are people today spinning yarns about them.

(As made plain by my earlier aside concerning Trump's attempt to become the Republican nominee for U.S. president, it should also be clear that this is the secret to good political campaigning. For if you're trying to build a broad coalition, then your specificity must be moderated by pithy vagaries with which listeners can do as they like – Hope, Change, A Stronger America, A Thousand Points of Light, Don't Stop Thinking About Tomorrow, Yes We Can [slogans all associated with so-called mainstream U.S. presidential candidates, indicating this is hardly a rhetoric of outsiders] – suggesting the strong correlation between social formation, generalization, and the acquisition of power.)

And so, this song *works* – at least for me, with memories of listening to it while having already moved to the U.S. from Toronto, but with the melody tethered to yet other memories, from other, disparate occasions, such as discovering what was then the Holly Cole Trio a few years before, in 1990, back when their first album "Girl Talk" came out, three years before I moved to Tennessee and five before her eventual album of Waits' tunes was released (no "Trio" noted on that later one, just her). There's also a memory of seeing her perform live in 1990 or '91, in a small bar, with a dirty bathroom, as I recall, out in the west end of Toronto, all of which indicates to me, now, that the song is an occasion for me to miss not the home that *it* spins but *my* current idea of a long past home, which I continually re-spin out of the raw materials of my always-changing memory. It captures – or, better put, by it *I* now capture, maybe even *create* – a dream of a forgotten Saturday that, if I'm being truthful, I've neither ever had nor likely ever will. What's more, inasmuch as it works with so few discrete elements, providing me with just so many opportunities to pair my own memories to its invitations, it can't help but suggest a simpler, condensed time (a more complex song, that put all the details into words, would make the seven minutes of "Hey

Jude" look pithy and succinct and would risk all of the perplexing problems of the exactitude of Borges' fabled cartographers as well as his never-ending library). Although when the past was the present (what some in our field today call lived experience, as if the immediacy of the moment is somehow naturally signified), it was likely just as complex or ambiguous as we take our current moment to be; when we tell tales about it later, it was always a simpler time when pocket change mattered, when second cousins lived around the corner and knew where to find you, and when driving up and down the streets was a sufficient pastime.

The trick of being a good essentialist, then – for, as you may have realized, this is what we've been discussing all along, not just nostalgia – is to select (and, as I signaled earlier, *choice, agency,* and *interested situation* are all crucial to keep in view, so that we recall that nostalgia is not something that happens to us but, instead, is a technique we use in the here and now) what champions your case. Then, while portraying it to your own advantage as emblematic of something universal, timeless, self-evident, offer details just open-ended enough for others to buy into it and latch onto it – *but for their own reasons* (thereby universalizing and, in turn, re-authorizing, your particular all the better). It's a simple but effective technique, with far-reaching consequences if done correctly; in fact, it's something marketers (along with those campaigning politicians I mentioned earlier) have long known.

Case in point: consider episode 13 from season 1 of the once-popular television series "Mad Men" from which my epigraph originated. Entitled "The Wheel," it involves Don Draper – an advertising executive who is representative of an early-1960s shift in how we sold products to one other – pitching his idea to the executives from Kodak for how their new slide projector, which they just call "the wheel," ought to be sold:

> Well, technology is a glittering lure. But there's the rare occasion when the public can be engaged on a level beyond flash, if they have a sentimental bond with the product. My first job: I was in-house at a fur company, with this old pro copywriter. Greek, named Teddy. And Teddy told me the most important idea in advertising is "new." Creates an itch. You simply put your product in there as a kind of [dramatic pause] calamine lotion. But he also talked about a deeper bond with the product: nostalgia. It's delicate [dramatic pause] but potent. Teddy told me that in Greek, "nostalgia" literally means, "the pain from an old wound." It's a twinge in your heart, far more powerful than memory alone. This device isn't a spaceship. It's a time machine. It goes backwards, forwards. It takes us to a place where we ache to go again. It's not called the Wheel. It's called a Carousel. It lets us travel the way a child travels. Around and around, and back home again [dramatic pause] to a place where we know we are loved.

Midway through his pitch – after calling out "sweetheart" over his shoulder to a woman at the back of the room, who then dims the lights (is this the America that some wish to make great again?) – Don calmly talks while clicking through family pictures projected from "the wheel" onto a screen at the end of the darkened boardroom: we see him and his new bride at their wedding, then their children, and a family vacation. The men swivel in their chairs to watch while they listen to his pitch. It's so effective that, before the lights come back on, one of his own colleagues quickly has to leave the room; it looks like he's going to cry. (Who among us has not felt teary-eyed at, say, a commercial that reminds us to call – "reach out and touch someone" AT&T called it in their late-1980s ads – the people we love?) That viewers already know that Don's marriage is far from perfect, that he regularly has affairs, that he himself, looking at the homey slides of his own presentation, knows there's no such home to which to return (and that there probably never was an actual Teddy), makes the moment all the more effective, for both the gaps and the technique for bridging them, and thereby minimizing them, are both apparent to us, the viewers.

Sure, it's just a recent TV show, deeply embedded in its own nostalgia for the 1960s, but the scene nicely captures what all of us have likely seen in ads and heard in speeches at both the dinner table and political rallies: nostalgias for a lost (or, better put, absent) home are thus effectively used for countless different contemporary purposes. For that 30-second commercial can somehow make us tear up – not to mention the tingles from hearing a national anthem or a host of other songs that conjure absence into presence.

Nostalgia, then, might best be understood as the effect of a set of social strategies, techniques whose analysis might be enhanced by a little attention from the sort of scholar of religion whom I have in mind. I say this, claiming that we have something to say about jazz tunes and longing, knowing full well that the academic study of religion was first instituted in public universities across the U.S. by means of an argument that the field was concerned with how *unique* and thus incomparable its objects of study were. As that old nugget went, religion (or what are often assumed to be its synonyms: faith, experience, or belief) was so utterly distinct that its adequate study required an equally distinct approach that was able to capture the *sine qua non* of its subject matter. After all, or so it was argued then, we can't expect the sociologists to do it, no matter how important religion's so-called "social dimension" might be, and the same goes for the psychologists, art historians, literary theorists, historians, folklorists, and anthropologists, and pretty much anyone else who might have already been employed in the university to study religion. They studied its various aspects (what our predecessors would have called manifestations, of course), to be sure, but none got to the ... well, I might as well just say it: none of them identified the *heart* of the matter. And that argument – or was it a nostalgia for a time, back during the Renaissance perhaps, when scholars transcended today's compartmentalized specialties and made grand, universal claims about the human condition? – was persuasive and won the day: departments of Religious Studies, whose members aimed to interpret what were portrayed as the deeply significant and, in many cases, long-lost meaning of religious expressions found in different historical and geographic settings (i.e., the troublesome world religions paradigm, complete with its no less problematic East/West taxonomy, reigns supreme, even to this day), sprang up all over the country in the mid- to late 1960s. This happened only once the U.S.' legal and political systems understood that studying religion didn't require one to promote or criticize it (thereby making studies *about* religion constitutionally sound in a publicly funded school). Although judged neutral on questions of religious truth, such an approach nonetheless presupposed religion's transcendental status (it was, after all, assumed by most to be a deeply personal, mysterious, transhuman experience projected outward, into the public domain, in countless forms – hence the importance of such terms as manifestation or expression throughout the history of the field). Religion, in the singular, was real and somehow eternal yet intangible, whereas religions, in the plural, were empirical yet merely derivative forms that it adopted here or there – hence the enthusiasm for studying religion *in context* as a way to see, feel, taste, or even hear and smell historical changes in this presumably invisible, eternal thing,[7] along with examining religion's interactions with that domain loosely collected together as "not religion," i.e., culture or politics (separate identities signaled by the conjunction in the still-common terms "religion *and* culture" and "religion *and* politics"). In many cases, the goal of such studies, then, was to use the comparative method to identify tangible, cross-cultural similarities (a technique our 19th-century predecessors perfected) all in order to infer the existence of the ever-present, ethereal essence that is assumed to animate it all. In fact, such a scholar of religion – and there are plenty around still, who practice the field in this manner – might not even recognize this very chapter as a contribution to their field – hence the incentive to see the alternative being proposed as no legitimate alternative at all.

But then along came the effects of structuralism, post-structuralism, semiotics, feminism, literary critical theory, and race studies in the second half of the 20th century, and, with them, a focus on difference and disruption, as well as a critique of such things as the canon, the author, intentionality, and an interest to

---

[7] Such as studying, for example, the history of Christianity, which many still narrate as unfolding in suitably Hegelian fashion, inasmuch as some modern idea of the thing is anachronistically presumed to have been there at its birth; thus we routinely refer to a subfield known as "Christian origins" while its members nonetheless argue that, at its beginning, there was no such thing as Christianity (for a longer discussion of this one example, see McCutcheon 2015b: chapter 6).

study meaning and identity as historical products or effects. Broaden that out and, instead, identify the role played over the past forty years (all across the human sciences) by that curious mix of Marxism and postmodernism, in which we forgo the quest for origins and essences and, instead, historicize the very efforts to identify a heart, seeing claims like "All Europeans believe ..." not as an innocently descriptive claim but as a situated act with socially formative consequences and practical interests. (This is all too apparent today, perhaps, what with the difficulties social actors in the EU are having with convincing their peers that there is such a thing as a common set of interests across that continent.) And so, not unlike other scholarly fields, in the academic study of religion, this has all had quite an effect; sure, there are all sorts of scholars in this field today who resist these influences and who, for instance, still look for the right way to interpret something self-evidently known to them as a ritual, those who tell us that the category Hinduism was a colonial-era invention but who yet somehow know that ancient things in the Indus River Valley were obviously set apart from others and therefore constitute Hinduism's origins, or who are very concerned with what the Apostle Paul *really meant* when he wrote such-and-such to so-and-so. But there are yet others who, for principled reasons, toss out these sorts of speculative inquiries and, instead, take seriously the findings of recent social theory, working hard not to fall into old habits concerning authentic sources and apolitical lived experiences versus derivative, symbolic expressions.[8] Instead, they look toward the operations, always in the here-and-now – like me, today, listening to that Holly Cole song, or Tennessee fans signaling their differences from the other team by singing along to "Rocky Top" – along with examining the situated, strategic effects of rhetorics and gestures, examining how authority (even our own, as scholars) is continually re-asserted, amidst a surprising number of always-present alternatives – a situation not unlike Odysseus dealing with Penelope's many eager suitors.

And perhaps it's because the study of religion is a field where it is so easy to find assumptions of transcendence and authenticity, or pristine meanings sadly polluted by their ineffective expressions and manifestations – assumptions found not only among the people we sometimes study but among colleagues as well – that the shift throughout the human sciences has had such a profound effect on

---

8 These are just the sorts who would, for example, question the traditional scholarly distinction, still in use today among some Bible scholars, between *exegesis* (drawing the meaning *out of* a text) and *eisegesis* (reading meaning *into* a text), for example. After the death of the author movement, this distinction is, of course, untenable – at least for many contemporary scholars; that it continues to be used is then the curious thing, suggesting some practical utility to the nostalgia for a day when a text's meaning was assumed somehow to be separate from a reader.

some. For it has produced a subgroup within the current generation of scholars of religion who hardly study religion at all but who, instead, *study what's at stake in designating something as a myth, a ritual, a symbol, a canon, an orthodoxy, a cult, and, of course, even a religion.* It has therefore resulted in a group of scholars attuned to what's involved in naming something *as* orthodox or *as* sacred or *as* tradition or *as* the past, and who are always keen to inquire as to what's at stake when we, as scholars who claim to be rigorously historical in our approach, fail to see such designations as the part of processes and competitions in which we are no less involved than are the others whom we may study. What cost is paid, they might ask, by our work when we take something as representative without asking for whom and against what alternative(s) – such as when we think that there is a single heart amid the cacophony of difference and possible arbitrariness that is historical existence and social life. It doesn't mean that we have to study it all, of course, as if the totality needs to be grasped or appreciated, but it does mean that we're willing to own the piece that we bit off to chew on for a while.

Sadly, though, too few outside the study of religion seem to understand that such a shift has taken place in this field; perhaps it is because the personal and familial lives of many in other fields are deeply implicated in those very rhetorics of authenticity and origin and, because of this, they remain uninterested in entertaining the implicated and situated historicity of it all. For instance, in my experience, we often find experts in other fields who, in their own work, are finely attuned to critiques of essentialism, perhaps as applied to those other widely used fabrications of gender or race, but who, when they turn their attention to that domain they (in an act of folk designation, since the term is commonly used all throughout our culture) know as religion, suddenly lose their critical edge altogether. They end up repeating what might as well be termed commonsense truisms or even platitudes – completely incapable of seeing this domain as being just as historically constituted as they might usually argue gender to be, or class, or race, etc. If there's no substantial there "there" to such things as, say, citizenship or one's familial identity, and if, instead, they are both performed and continually reconstituted in situationally specific networks of power and negotiation, then so too with those "things" called religiosity or spirituality, no? But for too many, the answer is indeed an emphatic and unironic "No," since this apparent aspect of the human is still thought by many to be the totalized place where history stops and the gaps are not just smoothed over but, rather, completely nonexistent.

And that's where, at least to me, the shift represented in this volume comes in; those outside the study of religion (not to mention many within) ought to be reading scholars of religion, or at least reading those who are game to ask tough questions about identity and place, about power and contest, those who do so at a variety of seemingly mundane sites in our contemporary world – like an old Tom

Waits song, for example. For if (drawing here on the work of Jean-François Bayart, for example, but I could easily also name Rogers Brubaker and others) we're serious about how identity is an ongoing work in progress, made possible by an assortment of basic, culture-wide techniques, then no matter which sort of identity we're talking about, an understanding of agency and structure as continually co-mingled and mutually informed domains is necessary, one that then prompts us to rethink claims of experience and meaning as just that – claims! – and thus something other than a reflection of a pristine, inner impulse easily pushed out into the world like an innocent baby being born. Instead, amidst the claims, we'll now be listening for all the kicking and screaming that comes with not just delivery but, as Bayart terms them, the "operational acts of identification" we each use every day to make ourselves into particular sorts of selves and our social worlds into particular sorts of worlds – rhetorics of nostalgia among them. And if this is the shift we're willing to entertain making, then the sort of reinvented scholars of religion who I have in mind each sit atop a rich archive where this move from necessary, ahistoric essence to the historical (and by historical, I mean contingent, negotiated, happenstance, accidental, etc. – along with social actors' responses to the unanticipated) can be illustrated quite nicely.

What's so exciting in this still young but promising branch of the contemporary study of religion, then, at least to me, is that once we leave behind assumptions of the inherent specialness of just some objects of study – the so-called sacred ones – and, instead, turn our attention toward the identification process of, shall we say, sacralization itself (which might as well just be a synonym for signification, as least as a Durkheimian scholar would approach it), then we're able to use as an example any number of mundane sites where people, to use an apt metaphor, stake a claim. Regardless the site and regardless the intensity of the claim, we'll make the move toward seeing not the object as having agency or meaning (as if some item compels us to do this or that or just means this or that) but focus, instead, on those doing the signifying and the otherwise generic items in the world – like a Saturday night, perhaps – that seem to become animated by means of those acts. For "the song evokes nostalgia," as some might phrase it, strategically bestows agency on the object and merely passive receptivity on the listener, thereby passing the buck (much like the use of passive language in general) by absolving us – the song's writers, as well as the singers and listeners – from the consequences for the choices we've made and the settings in which we've not just found ourselves but which we've helped to create; instead, the situated social actor, the chooser, and the situation that limits or empowers their choice, becomes our new focus. We easily fall back into old habits when we fail to see that the text, in and of itself, means nothing – is not even "a text" but, instead, a collection of incoherent jots and scribbles on some surface that might be indistinguishable from its surrounding (as Derrida asked so long ago, where do texts start and end, after all?) – without readers trained in a grammar and a vocabulary not of their making, which resulted from structures imposed upon them (i.e., us) by their elders that are themselves historical phenomena (accidents, in the technical sense), prone to change with the introduction of yet more agents with unanticipated goals. So what I think is so encouraging about this shift – and thus why I hope that making it is entertained by those who are open to rethinking what the study of religion has to offer to the human sciences at large – is that it makes evident what is to be gained when we turn our attention away from self-evidently interesting objects and, instead, ask some tougher questions – at any and all points where we mark our place and claim to be something – about why we become so curious to begin with, inquiring for whom something is seen as interesting, and under what circumstances might that interest continue or depart.

So it was in that spirit that, as the careful reader hopefully understood, I elected to open *not* with an obviously nostalgic song that tugs at me whenever I hear it (which it does, yes) but with an attempt to historicize myself, the listener, as an interested, even alienated and displaced, agent, in order to examine the potent thing that's transpiring when I slide that CD into the player – or, better put, why and how I use that song in just that fashion on just those occasions. In fact, it's playing as I first write these very lines (for inspiration, perhaps). Her slow hum that starts it off and that long lost / never was Saturday night begins to unfold:

> Stoppin' on the red
> Goin' on the green
> Tonight'll be like nothin'
> You've ever seen

And so, if the shift I'm describing is made, it turns out that the song is more correct than I'd imagined, for this nostalgic night, and the melancholy that surrounds it, is indeed "like nothing you've ever seen." In much the same way, Glinda, the Good Witch of the North, was also right: *there's no place like home* – for not even home itself is like our idea of home. (Thomas Wolfe made that evident in his well-known posthumous 1940 novel, *You Can't Go Home Again*.) Yet, if sung correctly, listened to in the right setting and on the right occasion, and if the heels are tapped in just the proper way, it all works, like magic – Don Draper's colleague cries and leaves the room. It's potent, after all. And that's the fascinating thing that needs our scrutiny; for it isn't magic at all but, instead, a finely tuned, delicate technique that, not unlike how nationalism itself works, provides a widely divergent group with a series of discrete opportunities for identification and the production of affinity. We see just this happening, or at least I do, in that Holly Cole / Tom Waits song – but if we look in the right way, and ask the right questions, we also see it in far more places than just that (as my various asides should have just made clear and as the final chapter makes even more explicit). In fact, readers for whom this shift (from focusing on products to scrutinizing modes of production) is new may want to step back for a moment and follow-up by considering where they can put it to work for themselves. They might want to consider something like Cole's slow jazzy rendition and the melancholy it somehow inspires (at least in me); if we can't understand its workings there, then we'll never understand it in those many other places where the stakes may be far higher and its workings far less transparent (such as in a presidential campaign or a TV commercial, perhaps? – occasions when long-past events are cited as authorizing anchors for contemporary actions, to rally groups, or when used as points of comparison to paint a disenchanted present that's somehow lacking a magic that the past supposedly once had).

Memories and nostalgias, no matter how exotic or special, are magical and potent, to be sure, but also mundane, consequential, and implicated. It's a lesson that might be new to some readers, but it is one that I learned long ago; for – if you'll bear with me and one more recollection – I once again recall my dad, when I was a boy, talking to a customer at that gas station my parents owned and operated. The fellow was complaining about the price of gas going up and up and waxing nostalgic for how much it was years ago. Now, my dad, who was born in 1923, also remembered plenty of things about the past, but his memories ran counter to his customer's – or at least he selected (and there's that *choice* again) one that did; so I recall him replying by stating how much a quart of milk used to cost (yes, my dad once was a milkman, going door-to-door with a horse and wagon), pointing out that no one today seemed to complain about its astronomic rise in price. If we use the early 1930s as our benchmark, when he was a kid, then the cost of milk has increased somewhere around 800%. So it seemed pretty evident that the customer's concern with gas prices in his present drove his selective memory concerning what it was in the past that ought to be marked and remembered. And it was equally obvious, judging from how my dad himself used the past on that occasion, that a duel in the present, over current issues, could be fought based on which past was recounted – such as my father defending his business from a complaint.

It was an early lesson for me (at least as I sit here now, many years later, and think back on it) in ideology analysis and in how signification and discourses on the past function – i.e., on how the past is created in the very act of seemingly remembering it. So when I find myself in classes today, trying to make points similar to this – such as bringing to the students' attention that we are right now living someone else's good old days, someone who will come along after us and wax nostalgically about an early 21st century that we ourselves might no longer even recognize despite supposedly living through it – well, I often think back on that lesson that I learned that day in the gas station, surely completely unaware at the time of just what I had been taught.

Which is itself an interesting little moment of nostalgia too, no?[9]

References

Carrier, Roch (1985). *The Hockey Sweater*. Sheldon Coher (illust.). Sheila Fischman (trans.). Westmount, Quebec: Tundra Books.
Detienne, Marcel and Jean-Pierre Vernant (1991). *Cunning Intelligence in Greek Culture and Society*. Janet Lloyd (trans.) Chicago, IL: University of Chicago Press.
McCutcheon, Russell T. (2015a). *Fabricating Origins*. Sheffield, UK: Equinox Publishers.
— (2015b). *A Modest Proposal on Method: Essaying the Study of Religion*. Leiden, NL: Brill.
Rushdie, Salman (2012). *The Wizard of Oz*. 2nd ed. BFI Classics. London, UK: The British Film Institute.
Trouillot, Michel-Rolph (1997). *Silencing the Past: Power and Production of History*. Boston, MA: Beacon Press.

---

[9] The opening to this essay, relying on the illustration of Waits' song, was originally posted, in an earlier and far shorter version, on April 4, 2014, at http://edge.ua.edu/russell-mccutcheon/magic-of-the-melancholy/ (accessed July 3, 2015), while the closing anecdote derives from a different post, dating from Jan. 5, 2016, at http://edge.ua.edu/russell-mccutcheon/coz-these-are-the-good-old-days/ (accessed Jan.10, 2016).

9 Fanfare for the Common e.g.: On the Strategic Use of the Mundane

For those who saw flyers advertising the public lecture where I first delivered this talk, on which was pictured the image of a roll of toilet paper with a neatly folded point along its leading edge, I had hoped that, by its end, I might have answered for them why I went with that probably unexpected graphic for this talk. But for those reading this just now, I'm hoping that I've piqued your curiosity enough not just to wonder where I'm going but to agree to go along for the ride.

But to start: I don't happen to think that social groups have tangible boundaries. Instead, as social theorists have argued, criteria for membership are always fluid while also always being policed, thereby allowing people to move in and out, through the ranks, and negotiate or even deny membership to others; recent debates in the U.S. over the future of Amendment XIV (which discusses naturalized citizens) and possibly deporting children born here to "illegal," i.e., undocumented, parents makes this all too apparent. Despite seeming to be a settled item, the very definition of citizenship is apparently up for grabs (so long as three-quarters of the state legislatures agree [as detailed in Article V of the U.S. Constitution]). What strikes me as so interesting, then, is that what can be rather easily demonstrated to be permeable, ad hoc boundaries – and, by extension, the sense of subjectivity that is made possible by our place within such contingent social worlds – can instead be understood by members as being so absolute, homogenous, and unambiguous. So it has long seemed to me that, instead of studying identity as so many do – as an expression of some pre-social sentiment, buried deep in our hearts – scholars ought to be examining how this

---

Note: This chapter began life as a public lecture written to be delivered at the University of Rochester (Sept. 3, 2015) – my thanks to Aaron Hughes for the kind invitation to visit his campus and speak with his students and colleagues. But its argument goes back much further than this, at least twenty years or more, to when, taking seriously my own critique of the field's preoccupation with defining religion as a *sui generis* phenomenon, it occurred to me that we not only ought to be studying the processes whereby groups made things appear to be unique or set apart (thus leading to the shift toward a model for the modern field based on semiotics rather than theology and intellectual history) but that we also ought to be doing this at sites that were utterly mundane and everyday (thereby swimming against our own group's devises for making things stand out as self-evident, authorized, etc.). As I've noted elsewhere, this may be thanks to the early influence on my thinking of Roland Barthes' *Mythologies* or, while reading for comprehensive exams, such other works as Michel de Certeau's *The Practice of Everyday Life*. Or, to put it a little more simply, it's likely the line from Émile Durkheim to Mary Douglas that has interested me in looking at implicated human inventiveness, at discrete sites, rather than merely focusing on the fanciful products that our groups come to take for granted.

https://doi.org/10.1515/9783110560831-010

nifty little trick is accomplished: that of persuading ourselves and others, over and over again, that history is uniform, that identities are enduring, and that the way things "happen to be" is none other than the only way things ever could have been.

In a word, I'm interested in studying not *identity* but, instead, *identification*. The distance between these two obviously related terms is great, I think. Whereas the former, a noun, names a product – i.e., the experience that we each seem to have in which we perceive ourselves *just to be* male or female or as obviously possessing a discernable race and class position or a nationality, etc. – the latter, though also a noun, names an *act* of identifying – i.e., to make an identification – thereby making the term "identification" far closer to a verb, inasmuch as it names a series of inter-related and specific historical and social procedures (i.e., acts) that made this thing we call an identity possible to experience, to perform, and to witness. Focusing on what he terms "operational acts of identification" (in order to highlight their situationally specific nature), we might therefore follow the work of Jean-François Bayart (currently the chairman of the Fonds d'analyse des sociétés politiques and a senior research fellow at the Centre national de la recherche scientifique [CNRS]). In particular, I have in mind his 1996 book, *The Illusion of Cultural Identity*. There, Bayart prompts us to consider moving from studying identity as an inner sentiment that is projected outward and somehow externalized in the public domain and, instead, to scrutinize this common way of understanding identity by seeing all social actors as continually involved in a series of techniques that fabricate the impression of such things as authenticity, autonomy, individuality, authority, and primordiality. Although these operations create an impression of continuity with all other moments and all other situations, they are (at least for the historically inclined scholar) inevitably discrete, tactical, in the here-and-now, and thus always in the public domain. They are, after all, *acts* and *claims* of identification. In this way, what is commonly described as an identity is redescribed as being the result of a series of practices, made by situated actors and claimants, all of whom are operating in a competitive environment of counter-claims. And so, one simply is not an American, but, instead, one acts *as if* one is an American, *claims* oneself to be Italian, and is, more importantly perhaps, treated by others *as* an Argentinian – that these actions, claims, and treatments can vary so widely, leading to innumerably different senses of what it means to be, say, British, Kenyan, or a Kiwi, should make evident just how competitive this hectic identity economy is. In turn, this should also make clear just how much is at stake for social actors seeking to normalize but one sense of that national identity – a sense they themselves take for granted, perform, or from which they benefit. Regulating that busy economy of competing identifications, and thereby setting the limit on what gets to count as – to stick with this one arbitrary example – a citizen is therefore, understandably, something with which many of us are preoccupied.

In the background of my lecture, then (and, yes, I'll eventually get around to that roll of toilet paper on the flyer), was this basic but crucial move from studying identity *as an expression* to identification *as a practice*; jumping ahead, I will argue that we fail as rigorously redescriptive scholars if we content ourselves with studying, as so many scholars of religion still do, the so-called sacred and the many sites where it is manifested. Instead, we should be studying the common but nonetheless intriguing procedures that – again, by means of a series of discrete and always public operations – sacralize (or, better put, signify) aspects of the contestable and ambiguous everyday *as if* they were inherently noteworthy and thus of enduring value. Failing to do this, failing to study the *means* by which significance is created, allocated, regulated, and contested, means that we have fallen under the sway of the authority systems we study by accepting other people's claims at face value. As I hope to demonstrate, our work can be so much more than that.[1]

Yet too often, scholars in our field begin their work with a very different presupposition, assuming that their subject matter – something they call a ritual, a myth, a symbol, a belief, a tradition, a heritage, an institution, etc. – is self-evidently and obviously interesting, a special case necessarily removed from all the tactical ad hocery of day-to-day social life, and thus requiring a special interpretive method to carefully understand its special and timeless meaning. (We have theories of myth, after all, which are distinct from how we approach the study of other sorts of narratives.) And so, whether intent on cherishing it or, instead, explaining it away, that part of life that many of us commonly name *as* religion is usually presumed to be essentially different from the rest of the mundane world (which we generally name as the secular or the profane) – for we often see it to comprise unique moments that defy our usual modes of understanding and explanation; after all, even so-called naturalists and reductionists devise theories specifically tailored to explain religion – it's just *that* different from everything else.

Such assumptions of the obviously set apart nature of our object of study are not new to the field, of course; there was a time, about fifty years ago, when the academic study of religion was first being instituted in public universities across the U.S., back when the rationale used to justify the establishment of autonomous

---

[1] See McCutcheon 2012 for the rejoinder in an exchange with Ann Taves concerning her call (2011) for studying how specialness is ascribed to things – an approach that, despite seeming to focus on human agency and society, strikes me as inconsistently implemented, possibly leading back to studying *expressions* rather than *fabrications*.

(i.e., set apart) departments of Religious Studies (as they were mostly called) was based on how utterly unique and unexplainable their object of study was; its adequate study, as already discussed, therefore was said to require an approach that was up to the task of capturing its elusive *sine qua non*.

But should we make the shift advocated in earlier chapters, then there are those today who now see that broad domain that we know as culture or even history as being comprised of contingent sets of situated signifiers (people like us, that is, busy making meaning) working within no less contingent structures that make the so-called experience of certain sorts of meaning, value, and identity possible and persuasive – such as that structured technique whereby some of us collect up and order certain elements of social life and treat them as uniformly religious and private in contradistinction to yet others that we understand as secular and public. If *this* was our object of study – *not* the description of an already constituted identity or domain, *not* the interpretation of some timeless meaning found here or there, and certainly *not* the detailed documentation of an already constituted specialness but, rather, an examination of the prior, always contingent (i.e., historical) conditions that make the appearance of enduring identity, the constitution of meaning, and perceived value possible – *then* we would likely expect to find curious systems worth studying anywhere that we find human communities engaged in the ongoing activities of forming and continually reforming themselves. In swimming against the currents of exoticization that we still find all throughout academia, we might rethink the seemingly benign aspects of our own day-to-day lives, seeing in them the very mechanisms that others seem only to see in far-off lands or in ancient times. And so, perhaps, the apparently mysterious and counter-intuitive snake handling of some rural, Appalachian Pentecostals (to select an arbitrary example that, however, always seems to catch our attention) will attract no more scholarly attention than, say, people merging their cars onto far more deadly interstate highways; for (back in my days at what was then called Southwest Missouri State University, a student, Stephen Hopkins, once astutely commented in class) given that the National Highway Traffic Safety Administration reported that there were 18,630 traffic deaths in the U.S. from January to June 2015 alone, the seeming irrationality of voluntarily handling deadly snakes during a church service might pale in comparison to voluntarily going for a Sunday drive – a fact that calls into question why some of us are so fascinated by the former while thinking nothing of doing the latter.

But to pull back from snakes and interstates, I think that we ought to start by considering our propensity to name an apparently distinct part of social life *as* religious as a good place to start this sort of rethinking. For this shift in focus from some seemingly distant "them" to the manner in which *we* make the no doubt mundane lives of ourselves and others interesting accomplishes what many before us have recommended as the main contribution of our cross-culturally comparative field: to make the strange familiar and the familiar strange. And, thinking about where I started this chapter, I would add that, in doing so, we lay bare some of the shared techniques that always fragile and transitory communities worldwide likely employ to reproduce the impression of themselves as permanently set apart and thus distinct from all others (i.e., the constitution of identity). Given this aim, the challenge is to find a sufficiently common, even uninteresting collection of data – possibly like pristine and pointed toilet paper rolls in hotel rooms? – where one can demonstrate that claiming something to be religious or sacred or spiritual is but one more mundane instance of social categorization and thus signification.

I recall first thinking about this back when I taught in southwest Missouri in the mid- to late 1990s. Dissatisfied with the traditional world religions approach, I saw all sorts of curious things around me that suggested that classifying anything *as* religion was about something other than recognizing that it was inherently religious – like the nearby city of Republic, Missouri, being taken to court in the late 1990s by the American Civil Liberties Union (ACLU) over displaying a simple line drawing of a fish, commonly signified as the Christian "ichthus" symbol, in one quadrant of its town seal. The crest dated to about 1990 and also included an outline of the State of Missouri (with a star in the southwest corner denoting the city of Republic), an outstretched hand, and a silhouette of a family.[2] If one is able to see the very act of designating that fish *as* religious as being the curious thing (regardless whether it is then seen as desirable and to be protected or unconstitutional and thus unlawful), then suddenly an academic field like our own, thought only to entail the examination of a small domain of the human, becomes far more relevant. For how is this one e.g. – say, that little Missouri town's coat of arms and the controversy that arose around it – not a fascinating moment of ongoing boundary contestation and identity formation, a specific site (yet one among many) where a certain way of making the ambiguous present knowable (by delimiting and thereby distinguishing it) was grinding against another, with high stakes for both sides?

So, it occurred to me back then that if you can't find the social mechanisms you're looking for in your own back yard – since we're all human, no? – then finding them only to be operating in some distant, exotic land, or only in the yellowed, ancient past, will result from an ethnocentric scholarship that's of little use to anyone but you and the like-minded members of your own in-group. This

---

[2] Read the complaint here: http://law2.umkc.edu/faculty/projects/ftrials/conlaw/republiccomplaint.html (accessed Sept. 3, 2017). In July 1999, the city was ordered to remove the fish from the crest.

means that, despite our indebtedness to Émile Durkheim's early work in sociology, we must invert his effort to study the function of religion in "our" complex society by first studying its role in the ostensibly simpler social worlds of other (aka primitive) people. Instead, we ought to consider studying what seems to be the less than interesting local and the boringly familiar, in order to de-exoticize what we can't help but see as alien or unique, thereby finding significance in the irreverent, rough-and-tumble profane – something that will help to desacralize that other sphere of culture and history that we now treat so delicately, as if it were essentially set apart. For, much as with those snake-handling Pentecostals who report being puzzled as to why others find what they do to be so curious, *it's all commonplace to someone*.

What we therefore need, I would argue, are *not* more careful studies of "the sacred" but, instead, more careful studies of how different groups signify and manage their otherwise mundane worlds. Lest you think that this term, the sacred, is part of our field's distant past and that I'm tilting at windmills, as they say, consider an article entitled, "The Sacred in Hittite Anatolia: A Tentative Definition" (which appreciatively cites the work of Rudolf Otto and Mircea Eliade among others), which I recently found not in my library's dusty archives but, of all places, in a recent issue of Chicago's well-known peer-review journal *History of Religions*. Written by a European scholar, Alice Mouton, it is interested in "the different ways to protect sacred or consecrated elements from possible profanization" (Mouton 2015: 42); like so much work in our field's history, it satisfies that interest by merely adopting a phenomenological stance all throughout (thereby privileging supposed participant viewpoints by doing nothing but assuming the internal logic of their imagined position), and thereby concludes that "the sacred allows human beings to reach their gods (principally through rites and divination)" (48). Instead, it might have moved the analysis from this initial description of a system's internal logic to examine not only how social actors sacralize mundane items in the first place but then also to investigate what is socially and politically at stake in those very acts – both for those who wrote the texts and the inscriptions we interpret today as well as for those who did not have access to those ancient purity rituals. To be fair, Mouton's essay is not far from making this move; for instance, toward its end, after examining how formerly sacred items could be re-consecrated, she goes so far as to note, "The purification of a profaned element is logical when we remember that any disruption of the established order brings about some form of impurity" (59). But nowhere does she take seriously that such actions are indeed connected to this wider thing she vaguely terms "the established order," something that could be done if we asked – along with Bruce Lincoln in his still important "Theses on Method" – what that order was, who instituted and who benefited from it, who did not, let alone how that order was perpetuated and what role this act called purification played in all this. For it may turn out that, much like someone claiming "All Americans believe" such and such, this established order might have been fabricated in the doing of these very actions.

Instead, in her study, these ancient rituals, the ritual participants, and the ritual beneficiaries all exist in a bubble of their own (including ancient ritual experts, diviners, priests, and, of course, members of the Hittite royal family), inasmuch as purity is merely understood as providing for them alone access to the sacred (60) – whatever that may in fact be. So rather than using such amorphous terms and instead of imaginatively conjuring up a world as some far-off elite participant may have thought it worked, I'd argue that we instead require a redescriptive, general theory of signification that's capable of accounting for not just *how* we signify the world but *why* just some of the items in our world are signified by us in this or that manner, which includes examining the practical effects of signification. This is something we could accomplish if the *History of Religions* article that I've just referenced theorized its key terms (e.g., purification, consecration, dedication) as socio-political techniques or maybe even if we investigated the possible assumptions made about a supposedly backwoods place like the Ozarks that might have helped the big-city editors of *The New York Times* to decide that the story about that Missouri city crest was worth covering as national news.

It ought to be evident by this point in this volume that – despite what participants in the groups that we often study may themselves say when queried by us – for the sort of scholar whom I have in mind, there is nothing particularly religious about any of the sites examined in this way. In other words, religion – itself but one among many folk taxons used by groups to make sense of their world – isn't about being religious any more than thanking God at the Grammy awards is about being holy (an example I've sometimes used in class over the years)[3]; instead, calling something religious or spiritual, like any social designation, is all about the act of designation itself, the means whereby otherwise generic, indistinguishable items are (to borrow Durkheim's well-known words, yet again), set apart, by us and for our purposes, whether to be privileged or criticized – in a word, signified. That is, while all of the objects and situations that we arrange are irreducibly humdrum, the system of arrangement and distinction, its rules, users, and effects begin to attract our attention because it is through their controlled relationships

---

3 Note: I hope that it is evident that I am not reserving these terms (or inserting new ones, like faith or belief) to later name some more authentically deeper value that is rightfully our object of study (like so many who now offer critiques of the category religion). Instead, these terms, and the identities which they help to create, are seen as rhetorical through and through.

of similarity, difference, and rank that significance is made and managed. So I hope it's evident that I'm not arguing that we ought to widen the already big tent of religion so that we can start studying, say, baseball as religion, as some scholars now do. As Tweed describes the turn to the everyday, it is usually driven by the "intent to broaden the analytic scope of their studies of selves, societies, and the sacred" (2015: 367). Instead, I'm arguing just the opposite: that instead of expanding membership to the big tent, we ought to be studying why we even have this particular grouping in the first place and what is accomplished when admitting a new member or barring something from membership in that particular family.

If this is our approach then, for example, something so seemingly ordinary as the opening verse from that classic 1989 rock song, "Free Fallin'" (performed by the late Tom Petty and co-written with Jeff Lynne) might catch our attention in a whole new way. (I give away my age by using this as an example, I know.) For those of a younger generation who have somehow escaped being forced to listen to their baby boomer parent's music, the words are as follows:

> She's a good girl, loves her mama,
> Loves Jesus and America too.
> She's a good girl, is crazy 'bout Elvis,
> Loves horses and her boyfriend too.

Here we see that discourses on Jesus exist on a par with discourses on Elvis: although each obviously takes place at a different site, they both employ the same rhetoric of nostalgia and personification, all in an effort to reproduce a specific sort of social world today, whether that world is dominant or marginal, high-class or low. And, to press this further, that institution that we commonly call a church can now be seen to be an architectural site of social formation no different from Graceland – and it is *our* propensity to call only one religious, and thereby treat it differently (whether to support it [e.g., by providing tax breaks] or criticize it) that now becomes our object of study, for this act of distinction can now be understood as but one of the ways that we make our own social worlds habitable and meaningful. So, if, in that lyric, we see each of the objects of this unnamed young girl's affection as a node in an intertwined web of significations (i.e., what we often call culture), then the opening words from that song wonderfully capture the moment when a specific locale is produced and made to seem normative, sensible, and thus natural – i.e., as worth conjuring up in the mind's eye of your listeners, perhaps even worth yearning for. From those seemingly separate domains we call motherhood to religion, from nationalism and rock 'n' roll to a young girl's stereotypical love of horses and her preoccupation with dating – a specific idea of gender, generation, and nation is made by just these distinctions and just those associations. (Case in point, consider how this may have all spun out of control for some listeners had the song's protagonist expressed love for "her girlfriend too.") For segmenting and then arranging the ambiguous, unending domain that we might otherwise call social life is something that is surprisingly ordinary, though we don't all do it in the same way, of course, and the consequences of doing it in this and not that way are far-reaching.

As suggested in my opening note, this shift in my focus (from studying products to processes) began not long after the publication of my first book (McCutcheon 1997). It was probably around the time that I was reading the French author Roland Barthes, writing on margarine and whatever it was that made some cars "look" fast.[4] It was not long after reading Michel de Certeau on just how exotic the practice of everyday life can be if looked at in the right way. Or maybe it was when I first read Bruce Lincoln's commentary on the social processes exemplified in the various tales of origins found in Barry Levinson's wonderful film, *Avalon* (Lincoln 1996b) – a story of early 20th-century immigration from Europe to the U.S. and the changing familial identities that resulted. It struck me that Lincoln, in seeing this film as no less useful a site to make his case than the obviously religious texts he usually studied, had here made a tactical move that, in my reading, allowed me to operationalize my own critique of the discourse on *sui generis* religion: for if there's nothing inherently unique about what we call religion, then you'd think that the items in a reconstructed scholar of religion's tool box could be applied far wider than we usually do. So I started using, for instance, then-popular music videos as data in my classes (e.g., see the discussion in McCutcheon 2001: 210–211). I did this not to illustrate the unexpected appearance of the religious in places where we least expected it (the move made by the "religion of baseball" crowd or, for example, the late Edward Bailey's interest in this category "implicit religion") but, instead, as a way to de-exoticize the presumed uniqueness of what we usually study in our scholarship or teach in our classes. This use demonstrated the analogical relationship to the common and, by so doing, invited a fascination with the techniques that we (scholars included) routinely employ to make it seem that just some things are serious, meaningful, and thus worth our while as scholars. So, why not pair up the late Frits Staal's classic analysis of the meaninglessness of ritual (1979; in which he concludes that, in the doing, ritual is all about form and that the content, the meaning, comes only later, in hindsight reflection on the past, structured act) with Blues Traveler's song "Hook" (1994) – a hit song about the proper way to write a hit song. For those unfamiliar with it, the opening verse goes as follows:

---

[4] I elaborate on what I think to have been the influence of Barthes on my work in a chapter on why I blog in McCutcheon 2018.

> It doesn't matter what I say
> As long as I sing with inflection
> That makes you feel I'll convey
> Some inner truth or vast reflection
> But I've said nothing so far
> And I can keep it up for as long as it takes
> And it don't matter who you are
> If I'm doing my job then it's your resolve that breaks

Now, it wasn't that the song was implicitly religious, and thus naturally comparable to the ritual; instead, both the supposedly religious (e.g., the Vedic priest making a sacrifice, as studied by Staal) and the apparently nonreligious (e.g., a song about songs needing to have a good hook) exemplified the same basic social technique (i.e., the creation of significance through the careful management of structure), suggesting that *we*, the ones who distinguish religious from nonreligious, might be the ones in error when thinking that the one was sacred and necessarily distinct from the other, which was secular. Instead, it was all just ordinary signification taking place – and our binary efforts to set these two apart, by worrying over the right definition of religion and thus the proper sort of data to be studying, *was itself the curious thing*!

Consider another case in point: I recall a U.S. conference of sociologists and psychologists of religion that I attended sometime in the late 1990s at which a paper was presented on some Hollywood movie that had recently been released and, more importantly, the controversy that it inspired among some so-called religious conservatives in the U.S. It may very well have been Kevin Smith's film *Dogma* (1999) whose release in the early fall pre-dated the conference by a month or so.[5] Back then, what stood out for me was the muffled laughter in the audience at various points in the paper, during which it was tacitly agreed that the protestors were just a little bit silly to react as they did. I think I've written a bit about this episode before, inasmuch as it seemed to illustrate nicely how a generally liberal (whether politically or theologically) position is dominant in our field, whereby "we" have confidence that we somehow know what really should or should not matter to "them," thereby allowing a surprisingly large number of scholars of religion to chuckle mildly to themselves at this or that group's behavior, all the while knowing to take with stern seriousness, even hushed reverence, some other group's preferences. In other words, I find it hard to imagine such chuckling taking place at a conference session on, say, Tibetan Buddhist ritual or the rise of Hindu nationalism.

---

5 Consider this example of a newscast from Nov. 12, 1999, covering one such protest, at which Smith himself participates: http://www.youtube.com/watch?v=QepgKVOVfZ8 (accessed April 10, 2014).

That I find this double standard, this scholarly confidence in just certain norms, problematic should, I hope, be evident. If nothing else, we ought to pass the test of methodological equal opportunity, as I've phrased it elsewhere, if we're to take on the badge of participating in an activity we call a science Whatever else a science may or may not be, it is at least a disciplined effort to study processes in an evenhanded way and not, instead, to invoke a so-called critical attitude only when it suits our purposes. What we do after hours is our own business, of course, but when we're on the clock, when we're making claims in our classrooms or in our writings, claims that trade on the authority that is represented by those framed credentials hanging on our office walls or listed on our C.V.s, then chuckling at just some of the people whom we study is a sign of a rather undisciplined, self-serving, and, I would say, ethnocentric and thus unscientific pursuit.[6]

But something else was also operating back then, when I heard that audience chuckle, other than the typical way in which so-called political or theological conservatives are often presented by scholars as if they are a problem to be solved – a point nicely made in Leslie Dorrough Smith's book, *Righteous Rhetoric* (2014), by the way, in which she ends the book by identifying the way scholars of American religion studying so-called Fundamentalists often implicitly contest the claims of the people whom they study *rather than* simply documenting and analyzing them. In just such a way, we often play either intentional or, at least, accidental favorites – the latter being the title of what I consider to be an important paper by my Alabama colleague Steven Ramey (to which I've already referred in this volume), which he delivered in 2013 as his Presidential Address at the Southeast Commission for the Study of Religion (SECSOR), our regional American Academy of Religion group.[7] But, as I said, I now think that more than this common sort of implicit favoritism was going on at that conference session on religion and film; for the fact that this case involved people's heated reactions to a Hollywood movie was probably also directly relevant to the academic audience's ease at laughing, just a little, at people getting so worked up over what was, for the members of the audience at least, merely a "popular" film. Despite the gains made over the past few academic generations by social historians – those who are interested

---

[6] On past occasions I've noted that I have failed to observe such laughter at academic meetings where so-called reductionists are presenting their research but have often experienced it where a predominance of humanist scholars of religion – not to be confused with outright theologians, of course – are in attendance. The irony here is rich, of course, since a generation or more of humanists have scolded scholars interested in naturalistic, explanatory theories for not "taking religion seriously" – which is, of course, a code word for taking seriously only what they wish to take seriously.

[7] Although it is published in Miller 2015, you can watch the original lecture at http://edge.ua.edu/steven-ramey/accidental-favorites/ (accessed Sept. 3, 2017).

in writing history from, as we say, the bottom up, so as to reflect the worlds of non-elites – and also by semioticians – those who, much as a linguist can study any language sample, find *any* instance of signification to be no less deserving of study – I think that there is still a class- and an orthodoxy-based tendency or preference among many scholars of religion, prompting them to have great trouble taking so-called low brow or socially and politically marginal culture as seriously as they take its elite or mainline counterpart. After all, we have all been schooled so long and so well in understanding religion to comprise "a system of beliefs and behaviors" that, sooner or later, our seemingly natural tendency is to study those systems themselves, often failing to understand them as the authorized reproductions of a class of authorized speakers and actors. For those are the systemitizers, propagandists, and the bureaucrats (which I offer as possible redescriptions of what we usually call theologians), all of whom are involved in local skirmishes of their own (otherwise, why write something down at all or why try to systematize the world?) and all of whom therefore have much to gain when their fingerprints are removed from the creations that we then come to study, as if they were independently existing and thus self-evidently interesting entities that we then name as scripture, canon, ritual, theology, myth, institution, etc.

Now, I fully realize that, to some, what I have just said will not come as news. They will quickly reply that I'm late to the party and then cite the rapidly growing body of scholarship (surveyed in that article by Tom Tweed that I mentioned earlier) on such things as material religion, lived religion, embodied religion, and, of course, religion and popular culture – what some call religion on the ground. All of this, they might claim, represents a long-overdue turn away from the presumed relationship between religion and belief or religion and high culture, and, in its place, marks a hard turn toward applying the techniques of social history in our own field. After all, the University of Toronto Press's *Journal of Religion and Popular Culture* is, for example, now about thirty years old – so, they might reply, there's nothing much new to be announced by my fanfare for the common. So, like changes that have impacted anthropological fieldwork over the past few generations, scholars of religion, we're told, are no longer content with merely studying the orthodox, but, instead, they now write on everything from comic books to zombies. After all, apart from both of these, the Religion and Popular Culture group of the American Academy of Religion (our main professional association here in the U.S.) also lists such areas of focus as alternate reality games, religion and play, and even Frankenstein himself (or, more broadly, Gothic monsters throughout history) as possible research areas in a recent call for papers.

But, despite the drive to redefine our data in ever broader terms (i.e., what I earlier termed the big tent approach – in which, for example, some critics of the category religion turn out to be more conservative than they seem for they simply wish more things, like baseball and now even zombies, to be included), the problem is *not* with how widely we do or do not pitch our tent. Instead, it is with why its contents are grouped together as they are, in contradistinction from all other things. Simply put, the problem is the tent, regardless how big. Despite the apparent differences between a gritty, engaged scholar studying football as religion – a common enough topic on my own campus (Roll Tide) – and an apparently aloof one still studying, say, the High Anglican Eucharist, both rely on the same surprisingly conservative conception of their object of study (e.g., given that both football and communion are understood as material sites where inexplicably deep and enduring sentiments are being expressed). It turns out that making the switch from studying one object to the other, no matter how high or low their cultural placement seems to be, is of far less methodological consequence than we might at first think. And that's why I can't join Tweed in holding that this "redirecting of scholarly attention is a praiseworthy accomplishment" (2015: 370) and an "important corrective" (379). Despite the greater inclusion, I see not a redirection but a misdirection.

For instance, take a blog post from Brent Plate (well known for his work on material religion and editor of *Key Terms in Material Religion* (2015), on what was then the newly opened 9/11 museum in New York City:

> We secular people may not believe we are fetishists, bowing to divine sculptures for help in fertility and war, but our responses at memorials and museums show that we at least continue to be functional animists. *There is an animating force at work within the material realm.* Objects may or may not be living beings, but they do a very good job of conveying information, evoking emotion, and triggering memory. (emphasis added)[8]

The trouble here is that despite the appearance of novelty in this scholarly turn, we continue to find the same old lack of *analysis* for how signification takes place; instead, significance, like Mouton's value of sacredness in ancient Hittite culture, is already present and, rather than studying the *claims* of presence as *constitutive* of the value they purport to *describe*, we simply take great care to describe the world *as the imagined participants themselves might claim to experience it* in which the sacred "manifests itself" (as Mircea Eliade so often [and, I'll add, so problematically] wrote). Instead of focusing on the benign, material sites which *we* actively signify to one another, people are here portrayed as being rather passive, as "responding to" pre-existent stimuli that possess their own "animating force." And thus, the apparently provocative and now popular move of including not just zombies and baseball but also the Nones (those who

---

8 See http://www.religiondispatches.org/archive/culture/7893/the_sacred_objects_of_9_11 (accessed May 26, 2014).

report, in polls, having no religious affiliation but nonetheless seeing themselves as spiritual), and even the irreligious in our studies turns out to be not a *corrective* but an *extension* and thus a reinvigoration of a very old, conservative theory of signification that some of us thought had long been retired from our field. The hills, or so it is claimed, may indeed seem to be alive with the sound of music; I'm simply suggesting that we go looking for the musicians instead of listening appreciatively to the tune.

Or, as another example, let's return to the above-mentioned Religion and Popular Culture group at the American Academy of Religion, which describes itself as follows: "This Group is dedicated to the scholarly exploration of *religious expression* in a variety of cultural settings ..." (emphasis added).[9] This is surprisingly close to the earlier named journal's own self-description, which reads:

> The *Journal of Religion and Popular Culture* is ... committed to the academic exploration, analysis and interpretation ... of the interrelations and interactions between religion and *religious expression* and popular culture ... (second emphasis added)[10]

What I find curious in both descriptions is the use of the word "expression" – i.e., "the scholarly exploration of religious *expression* in a variety of cultural settings meaning ..." and "the interrelations and interactions between religion and religious *expression* and popular culture ..." (emphases added) – which, in my understanding, denotes a teleological pushing outward, squeezing, or even extruding. Linked with a philosophically idealist conception of the self, of subjectivity, of meaning-making, and of identity, etc., it isn't difficult to see why, in English, we quickly and commonly come to talk about *expressing* an idea, *expressing* an opinion, *expressing* a belief, or naming a figure of speech "an *expression*" and calling a fundamental legal right the "freedom of *expression*." For the folk model that governs day-to-day life – and the problem here is that this model is often simply and uncritically adopted wholesale by scholars in certain cases (generally in cases where the scholars takes the participant claims as familiar, commonsense, and, perhaps, agreeable), as if it is a fact, as if it provides the grounds upon which their analyses are then build – presupposes the classic (and hierarchically arranged) mind/body, individual/group, and origin/destination dualisms. These are mechanisms whereby a dynamic inner life is thought not only to animate us (i.e., "I think therefore I am") but also to be mediated publicly via such presumably secondary things as

---

[9] See http://papers.aarweb.org/content/religion-and-popular-culture-group (accessed April 7, 2014).
[10] See http://muse.jhu.edu/journals/journal_of_religion_and_popular_culture/ (accessed April 9, 2014).

language (conceived as a neutral domain that carries prior messages, meaning, intentions, etc.). Thus, calling a particular use of language "an expression," as we routinely do, betrays an approach that presumes meanings are somehow originally in the isolated individual's head (or is it their heart?) and are only later projected outward and thereby put into play publicly, in the socio-political world of history.

But what if we started, instead, from the position that assumes that it's all history, and thus all public, all the way down and all the way up? What if we assumed that the world was not naturally divided between sacred and profane but that social actors made use of such coordinated terms, variously defined and applied, in their attempts to manage what seemed to them to be an unruly world in need of some sort of order? What if we assumed that language is not a neutral, secondary medium that passively conveys prior and thus private experiences outward but, rather, is a public structure through and through, one that creates the conditions in which that thing that we commonly call experience takes place, one that was either taught to us by others who came before us or, with a nod to those linguists whose work draws on genetics, encoded in us by others who, yes, also (quite literally) came before us. Then what sort of new questions will we ask and where will we go looking to answer them? But, as I have also written on various past occasions, rather than theorize and thereby historicize language, meaning, identity, etc., the well-known "I can't quite put it into words" approach is instead our (and I include many scholars in this grouping) default starting point, comprising evidence of this widespread folk model, as if meaning is private and personal, thereby predating language, society, and history – in a word, predating its eventual (and usually flawed) *expression*. After all, "words just don't do it justice."

With the study of religion in mind, the field in which I do my own work, this supposedly progressive turn toward material religion, embodied religion, and religion in popular culture therefore strikes me as nothing more than a rebirth of what I consider to be a long-discredited (e.g., see the critique of the late Hans Penner [1970]), and thus rebranded, phenomenology of religion. The current preference for such terms as "expression" or "embodiment" are synonymous for what was once simply termed "a manifestation" (see McCutcheon 2014: 8, 93, for elaborations on this critique). In all cases, I would argue, the material, historical object under study is simply seen as a proxy, a stand-in for the non-empirical and thus the unnamable, whether we term it elusive *meaning* (note: according to this approach, we are often trying to "find" or "interpret" the meaning, not "make" it) or whether, as we once might have, we instead call it an *essence* (presumably that immaterial item that is being put into the body, i.e., *em*-bodied religion). It is for this reason that, from where I sit, the turn away from high culture that we now see all across the field is really not much of a turn at all. In expanding the tent, it nonetheless conserves what I find to be a problematic, philosophically idealist approach to the study of signification, inasmuch as this thing we call meaning or identity is still presumed to be a pre-social, pre-linguistic, and thereby ahistorical *something or other* that is, in fact, *no thing* at all, for it somehow *animates* matter (i.e., quite literally, breathes life into the inanimate, making it special) but which, of course, is not reducible to matter. That we can only study the intangible "it" – whether found in zombies and baseball or in dusty volumes of on library shelves – by reference to tangible, historical items (an acknowledgement that Mircea Eliade himself was well known for making[11]) does not make this approach any more empirical or historical, however.

So let me be clear: it should be obvious that it is not this particular reason for studying the mundane and the common that I had in mind when selecting the title for this closing chapter and the subtitle for the book (which I obviously pilfered from the American composer, Aaron Copland [1900–1990], of course, and his 1942 symphonic effort to exalt the everyday).[12] If anything, my hope was to swim directly against this now-popular current by suggesting that we have good theoretical warrants for challenging the longstanding formality and class-based assumptions that are found in much of our data, but doing so without either reproducing a problematic (because it is nothing but a folk or intuitive) theory of meaning, on the one hand, or trying to reanimate a no less troublesome phenomenological quest for pristine origins, timeless meanings, and unexplainable essences, on the other. Instead, I had in mind a quotation from the late French social theorist Pierre Bourdieu that I have cited on a variety of past occasions and which, I think, is worth repeating here:

> There is nothing more difficult to convey than reality in all its ordinariness. Flaubert was fond of saying that it takes a lot of hard work to portray mediocrity. Sociologists run into this problem all the time: How can we make the ordinary extraordinary and evoke ordinariness in such a way that people will see just how extraordinary it is? (1998: 21)

---

11 For example, he famously wrote: "Obviously there are no *purely* religious phenomena; no phenomenon can be solely and exclusively religion. Because religion is human it must for that very reason be something social, something linguistic, something economic – you cannot think of man apart from language and society. But it would be hopeless to try to explain religion in terms of any one of those basic functions which are really no more than another way of saying what man is." (1996: xvii)

12 For background on the song, such as the currency of the once popular rhetoric of "common man" or "common people" (such as articulated in a famous speech by onetime U.S. Vice President Henry Wallace (1888–1965), see the engaging podcast at http://www.wnyc.org/story/common-man/ (accessed Aug. 30, 2017).

What I therefore wish to emphasize is that our interest in studying culture-wide signification and identification practices, an approach that works against simply adopting and using indigenous systems of valuation, requires us to define and examine our data in a whole new way. We must see it as material items that are not proxies for the expression of ineffable sentiments but which are, instead, the products of wider procedures and rules that previous social actors invented and which, in turn, continually reinvent us (think again of language as the example here, or maybe, instead, the inherited structure of something as simple as setting the table to eat). These are processes whereby we collectively manage what it is that we focus on and thus who we end up thinking ourselves to be in relation to others, all within the otherwise hectic domain that is history and social life. Precisely because of the ease of falling under the sway of the taken-for-granted, the dominant, the accepted – after all, we, as scholars, are all social actors as well, accustomed to the daily worlds in which we live and move and, quite literally, *make* sense – I suggest that those who wish to make this methodological move must seriously consider leaving behind the pre-signified data most scholars of religion study (scriptures, canons, myths, rituals, etc.) and opt instead for the more challenging study of the routine and the mundane.

But examining the limitless ordinary and, by doing so, owning the role that our *own* curiosity, *our* assumptions, and *our* tools play in making whatever portion of the unsignified "it" stand out *as if it were* interesting (recognizing, of course, that there is no unsullied domain of pure present since even "the common" is itself a signified item), pays dividends for the study of what is was formerly known as the extraordinary, too. This approach presupposes that both are just as fabricated by us, and all those other people out there who are just like us, and so both are no less items of social life, markers we produce and use to try to orient ourselves in distinction from others. Thus, if we are able to suspend our bias toward the exotic and the sacred, the insights that we might gain concerning the functioning of commonplace systems of signification will be applicable to all other instances as well – if, to repeat, we begin from a position that refuses to play favorites when it comes to how such things as significance, identity, and focus work. For then, whatever cultural, historical, social moment of identity formation that we chose to examine will be seen as but one among many e.g.'s, a discrete but possibly generalizable instance of ongoing social governance and self-management that is illustrative of a larger point we wish to make.

And in this way, we may come to realize that (as I regularly do in my classes) showing students a picture of a freshly cleaned, North American hotel room's usually innocuous toilet paper roll, with its neatly (or sometimes elaborately) folded point, can be the start of a fascinating conversation on this usually invisible item in a student's world. It's a conversation that has application to innumerable other instances in which our labors (those toilet paper rolls don't fold themselves, after all) help to signify what might otherwise strike us as chaotic, unfamiliar, and unknown *spaces* (like newly occupied hotel rooms into which we know that innumerable other people before us have also walked and, shall we say, done their business?) as if they are settled, safe, and habitable *places* that are all our own (a useful distinction I long ago borrowed from Michel de Certeau). A children's story helped me to see all this – David Macaulay's 1979 book, *Motel of the Mysteries*, a fun little tale, taking place in the year 4022, of people trying to make sense of what remains from *our* civilization. It's a story that, among other things, draws attention to that curious little point on the fresh toilet paper roll – something that utterly stumps the book's fictitious amateur archeologist (modeled after a Victorian gentleman scholar) who stumbles upon the ruins of what readers know to be a motel room but which he classifies as an exotic burial chamber. But what's most curious is that whenever I ask students why we do that with rolls of toilet paper, or what those folds communicate to them when they see it while first entering their hotel room, this point – which is dubbed "the Sacred Point," in Macaulay's story, about which his intrepid scholar says the following: "Very little is actually known about the origin of the Sacred Points except that they were very rare and were only ever found on the ends of sacred parchment scrolls. Carson [the archeologist of the story] believed that they simply pointed the way to eternal life" – well, this point also stumps my students, who have nonetheless seen it countless times without ever really "seeing" it. The conversation that results therefore starts from something commonplace to us, something toward which we've never paid much attention, if any, but eventually works its way to figuring out that doing this in hotels and *not* in our homes (even if guests are coming over) is likely important to recognize. The discussion usually ends in seeing those crisp folds as a coded signal to the room's next occupant (like "Sanitized for Your Protection" strips of paper around the toilet lid and seat once did), telling them that the room has not just been cleaned with soap and water but has been cleansed of any trace of the previous occupant. It's been purified, reset, and thereby returned to some mythical, initial state, ready for us to put out *our* toothbrush and *our* toothpaste by the sink, to put *our* socks and pants in the drawers, to put the TV remote by *our* bed and to hang *our* shirts in the closet, thereby bringing our own idiosyncratic order and thus identity to that generic space and, in so doing, making it into a place of our own, our "home away from home." And if we can understand this intertwined process of signification and identification there, in that seemingly inconsequential toilet paper roll, and if we can understand how we each regulate the hectic economy of how things could have been (had others been in charge or registered in that motel room), then maybe we can find this set of techniques being used elsewhere, in other, no less ordinary locales, establishing yet other orders, continually making the common seem exemplary and interesting – at least until we pack up our toothbrush and socks and check out.

The turn to the common that I'm recommending, then, is not, as Tom Tweed has argued, about finding "meaning-making practices we otherwise might have overlooked or undervalued," (2015: 373) and so it's also not about, as Robert Orsi puts it (another prominent scholar of religion in America who is also very interested in everyday religion), studying usually overlooked, "everyday miracles" (1997). Instead, I think that it is all about accepting that *our* choices and actions as scholars, no less than the choices and actions of the people whom we might study, are what animate the world with the *appearance* of meaning, making any old thing into a thing that seems to be worth paying attention to or fabricating the miraculous from the, as we say, run-of-the-mill. The turn to the common, as I understand it, is therefore not about discovering the otherwise ignored – such as some previously undetected home shrine or the overlooked symbolism of food – but, instead, about teaching us, as scholars who are usually so preoccupied with what is presented to us as extraordinary and obviously sacred, a lesson in how discourse and signification presuppose a set of techniques to set something apart, thereby requiring us to ignore most of what's going on at any given moment.

References

Bayart, Jean-François (1996). *The Illusion of Cultural Identity*. Steven Rendall, Janet Roitman, Cynthia Schoch, and Jonathan Derrick (trans). Chicago, IL: University of Chicago Press.
Bourdieu, Pierre (1998). *On Television*. Priscilla Parkhurst Ferguson (trans.). New York, NY: The New Press.
Certeau, Michel de (1988) [1984]. *The Practice of Everyday Life*. Steven Rendall (trans.). Berkeley, CA: University of California Press.
Eliade, Mircea (1996) [1958]. *Patterns in Comparative Religion*. Rosemary Sheed (trans). John Clifford Holt (intro). Lincoln, NE and London, UK: University of Nebraska Press.
Lincoln, Bruce (1996a). Mythic narrative and cultural diversity in American society. In Laurie Patton and Wendy Doniger (eds.), *Myth & Method*, 163–176. Charlottesville, VA and London, UK: University of Virginia Press.
— (1996b). Theses on Method. *Method & Theory in the Study of Religion* 8 (3): 225–227.
Macaulay, David (1979). *Motel of the Mysteries*. Boston, MA: Houghton Mifflin.
McCutcheon, Russell T. (1997). *Manufacturing Religion: The Discourse on Sui Generis Religion and the Politics of Nostalgia*. New York, NY: Oxford University Press.
— (2001). *Critics Not Caretakers: Redescribing the Public Study of Religion*. Albany, NY: State University of New York Press.
— (2012). A tale of nouns and verbs: Rejoinder to Ann Taves. *Journal of the American Academy of Religion* 80 (1): 236–240.
— (2014). *Entanglements: Marking Place in the Field of Religion*. Sheffield, UK: Equinox Publishers.

— (2018). *"Religion" in Theory and Practice: Demystifying the Field for Burgeoning Academics*. Sheffield, UK: Equinox Publishers.

Miller, Monica (ed.) (2015). *Claiming Identity in the Study of Religion: Social and Rhetorical Techniques Examined*. Sheffield, UK: Equinox Publishers.

Mouton, Alice (2015). The sacred in Hittite Anatolia: A tentative definition. *History of Religions* 55 (1): 41–64.

Orsi, Robert (1997). Everyday miracles: The study of lived religion. In David D. Hall (ed.), *Lived Religion in America: Toward a History of Practice*, 3–21. Princeton, NJ: Princeton University Press.

Penner, Hans H. (1970). Is phenomenology a method for the study of religion? *Bucknell Review* 18: 29–54.

Plate, S. Brent (ed.) (2015). *Key Terms in Material Religion*. London, UK: Bloomsbury.

Smith, Leslie Dorrough (2014). *Righteous Rhetoric: Sex, Speech, and the Politics of Concerned Women for America*. New York, NY: Oxford University Press.

Staal, Frits (1979). The meaningless of ritual. *Numen* 26: 2–22.

Taves, Ann (2011). *Religious Experience Reconsidered: A Building-Block Approach to the Study of Religion and Other Special Things*. Princeton, NJ: Princeton University Press.

Tweed, Thomas (2015). After the quotidian turn: Interpretive categories and scholarly trajectories in the study of religion since the 1960s. *The Journal of Religion* 95 (3): 361–385.

Author Index

Abu-Nimer, Mohammed 123, 124
Albanese, Catherine 131
Alles, Greg 2, 41
Almond, Philip 66
Althusser, Louis 17, 22, 59, 63, 92, 116
Altman, Mike 44, 134, 137
Armstrong, Karen 27
Arnal, Bill 13, 21, 105
Arnal, William 137
Arvidsson, Stefan 85
Asad, Talal 13, 18, 28, 96, 105
Aslan, Reza 34, 47

Bailey, Edward 169
Balagangadhara, S. N. 105
Baldwin, Matthew 43, 46
Barthes, Roland 161, 169
Barth, Karl 107
Barton, Carlin A. 33–42
Bayart, Jean-François 16, 64, 85, 157, 162
Bazzano, Elliott 86, 89
Bhaskar, Roy 96
Biale, David 83
Blum, Jason 115
Boer, Roland 100, 101
Borges, Jorge Luis 39, 122, 152
Bourdieu, Pierre 75, 76, 85, 176
Boyarin, Daniel 33–42
Boyarin, Jonathan 96, 100, 101
Braun, Willi 117, 137
Brockopp, Jonathan E. 82, 90–92
Brubaker, Rogers 15, 20, 157
Bush, George W. 55
Bush, Stephen 115

Caplan, Mariana 47
Carrier, Roch 145, 146
Cavanaugh, William 26, 27
Chamberlain, Neville 124
Chartier, Roger 75
Chidester, David 13, 14, 17, 18, 25, 67, 111
Childers, R. C. 133
Chomsky, Noam 1, 63
Clifford, James 14

Cole, Holly 141, 144, 151, 155, 158
Cone, Patricia 84
Cook, Michael 84
Cooper, Frederick 20
Copland, Aaron 176
Cotter, Christopher 51
Cunningham, Lawrence 83

de Certeau, Michel 161, 169, 178
Derrida 158
Dewey, Jon 63
Douglas, Mary 161
Draper, Don 152, 158
Dressler, Markus 28, 29
Dubuisson, Daniel 18, 99
Dundas, Paul 136
Durkheim, Émile 22, 37, 61, 161, 166, 167

Eagleton, Terry 97
Eliade, Mircea 7, 86, 101, 135, 166, 173, 176
Elvis 168

Fitzgerald, Tim 13, 18, 25–27, 34, 96, 99, 103, 105, 107
Foucault, Michel 62, 75
Freud 38
Führding, Steffen 87

Gafni, Marc 47
Gale, Dorothy 88, 93, 142, 144
Geertz, Clifford 13
Goldenberg, Naomi R. 18, 29, 43, 96, 99
Goldstein, Warren S. 96, 100, 101
Grewal, Zareena 86, 87, 89, 90, 92

Hagenston, Richard 4
Hall, Tamron 80
Hammer, Juliane 81, 86, 88, 90
Herman, Jon 43
Hermann, Adrian 87
Hick, John 2
Hinnells, John 5, 6
Hughes, Aaron 24, 25, 27, 79, 82, 83, 88, 90, 91, 137, 161

James, William 48
Jensen, Jeppe Sinding 11
Jensen, Tim 79
Johnson, Greg 137
Jones, Robert 79
Josephson, Jason Ānanda 20–22, 27–29, 34, 85, 108
Josephus 34

Kavka, Martin 103, 104
King, Rebekka 96, 101
King, Richard 18
Kirsch, Anja 55
Koch, Anne 123, 124, 134

Laborde, Cécile 99
Larsson, Göran 79
Lawson, Sierra 43
Lease, Gary 109
Lehmann, Karsten 123, 124, 134
Lehrich, Chris 15
Levinson, Barry 169
Lewis, Thomas A. 87, 88
Lincoln, Bruce 9, 21, 60, 68, 75, 76, 85, 99, 121, 122, 126, 134–137, 166, 169
Lofton, Kathryn 15
Lopez, Donald 20, 122
Luhrmann, Tanya 16, 17
Lynne, Jeff 168

Macaulay, David 178
Mack, Burton 75, 99, 102
Mandair, Arvind-Pal S. 28
Marcus, George 14
Martin, Craig 95, 101, 104, 107, 113, 115, 117, 118, 122
Marx, Karl 38, 86, 98
Masefield, Peter 126, 127, 131, 133
Masuzawa, Tomoko 18
McAuliffe, Jane 82, 84
McCormac, Gerry 100
Meylan, Nicolas 111
Moore, Clement Clarke 127
Mouton, Alice 166, 173
Müller 50

Neusner, Jacob 2, 121
Nongbri, Brent 17–20, 22, 27, 34, 35, 41

O'Connell, Joseph 43
Orsi, Robert 179
Otto, Rudolf 166
Oxtoby, Will 43

Patton, Kimberley 43
Penner, Hans 175
Penniman, John 47
Pennington, Brian 66
Peterson, Derek 28
Petty, Tom 168
Plate, Brent 173
Popper, Karl 37
Prothero, Stephen 51

Ramey, Steven W. 3, 24, 25, 43, 51, 82, 98, 99, 121, 137, 171
Read-Wahidi, Mary Rebecca 20
Reisebrodt, Martin 18
Reynolds, Frank 2, 41
Robertson, David 51
Robertson, William 43
Rudolph, Kurt 97, 98
Rushdie, Salman 142

Safi, Omid 24
Said, Edward 20, 66
Sawyer, Dana 43
Saxe, John Godfrey 127–129, 131–136
Schilbrack, Kevin 18, 95, 104
Schleiermacher, Friedrich 28
Searle, John 109, 110, 112
Sharf, Robert 123
Sharma, Arvind 43
Simmons, Merinda 137
Smith, Cantwell 29
Smith, Christian 113, 117, 135
Smith, Huston 43
Smith, J. Z. 1, 2, 14, 15, 18, 34, 37, 39, 41, 46, 75, 108, 117, 118, 135
Smith, Leslie Dorrough 87, 171
Smith, Wilfred Cantwell 1, 18, 28, 34, 43, 79
Staal, Frits 16, 169, 170

Stausberg, Michael 21
Strenski, Ivan 106, 107
Stroumsa, Guy 70
Sullivan, Winnifred F. 99
Swidler, Leonard 123–125

Tertullian 34, 40
Tiele 50
Touna, Vaia 3, 18, 19, 22, 41, 43, 110, 137
Trouillot, Michel-Rolph 39, 150
Trump, Donald 69, 79, 81, 146, 151
Turner, Alicia 13, 14, 20, 25
Tweed, Thomas 168, 172, 173, 179
Tylor, E. B. 36

Uehlinger, Christoph 55
Urban, Hugh 136, 137

Waardenburg, Jacques 8, 12, 29, 50, 53
Waits, Tom 15, 141, 144, 146, 150, 157, 158
Walhof, Darren 28
Wansbrough, John 84
White, Hayden 36
Wiebe, Donald 43, 98
Williams, Raymond 97
Wolfe, Thomas 158

Zaehner, R. C. 49
Žižek, Slavoj 59
Zoloth, Laurie 89

Subject Index

anachronism 17–19, 34, 66, 76, 84, 91, 92, 136, 154
–identifications 110
assessment measures 55
authenticity 13, 16, 35, 38, 47–49, 63, 72, 81, 84, 102, 136, 155–156, 162, 167

bias 29, 177
binary 26, 80, 112, 170
–pairs 13
–systems 12

category "religion" 11–29
classification 4, 6, 8, 13–15, 18, 20–22, 29, 63–66, 75, 80, 81, 97, 106, 109, 113, 115, 116, 121, 136, 165, 178
construction 21, 36, 41, 73, 75–77, 91, 92, 104, 105, 107, 109, 123, 135, 144
–requirements, minimum 43
critical realism 95, 96, 104, 109, 111

dehistoricized 25, 73, 82
desacralize 166
description 7, 11, 17, 19, 24, 26, 34, 36, 37, 108

embodied religion 12, 172, 175
example 2, 6, 11, 12, 14, 18, 19–24, 28, 34, 37, 38, 40, 43, 45, 47, 52, 57, 58–60, 63, 64, 66–73, 75, 81, 83, 85, 87, 91, 95, 97, 99, 105, 106, 108, 110, 113–116, 123, 124, 157, 163, 164, 167, 168
experience/expression 7, 13, 14, 16, 17, 26, 38, 42, 64, 75, 95, 100, 109, 111, 116, 123, 127, 152–155, 157, 162, 164, 173, 175
expression 13, 14, 28, 38, 59, 63–64, 75, 154–155, 161, 163, 173–175, 177
extraordinary 7, 75, 176, 177, 179

fabrication 2, 3, 7–9, 24, 29, 35, 42, 61, 64, 65, 67, 70, 91, 137, 156, 162, 163, 167, 177, 179

historicization 13, 22, 23, 51, 60, 71, 73, 81, 99, 101–103, 117, 121, 125, 137, 155, 158, 175
human nature 7, 51

idealist 1, 2, 5, 11, 41, 107, 115, 124, 174, 176
–rhetoric 122
identification 4–6, 16, 22, 24, 29, 48, 49, 57, 60–62, 64, 69–71, 88, 96–99, 108–110, 113, 115, 116, 122, 123, 125, 133, 134, 145, 149, 154, 155, 157–158, 162–163, 171, 177–178
induction 36, 37

lived 34, 38, 81, 143, 146, 150, 155
lived religion 172

materialist 2, 115
material religion 172, 173, 175
mundane 7, 20, 22, 40, 84, 100, 108, 113, 156, 157, 159, 161, 163–166, 176, 177

naturalize 13, 19, 40, 161
nones 40, 116, 131–133, 173
nostalgia 80, 141, 142, 144–146, 152, 153, 155, 157, 159, 160, 168

observation 57, 114
ordinary 8, 57, 168, 169, 176–178
–signification 170
oriental religions 55ff
origin 1, 4, 39, 40, 50, 64, 65, 73, 83–85, 87, 88, 127, 141, 142, 144, 154–156, 169, 174, 176, 178
original 13, 28, 72, 107, 121, 136
originary 36, 91, 144

post-secular 96
protagoras 55, 62, 74

realism 11, 96, 104, 105, 109, 111
realist 22, 95, 104, 107, 110, 114, 115, 117, 118, 125, 143

redescription 19, 49, 80, 81, 83, 103, 106, 108, 113, 117, 162, 163, 167, 172
religion on the ground 38, 172
rhetorical 4, 5, 7, 20, 22, 24, 26, 27, 29, 39, 87, 88, 90, 101, 103, 104, 107, 112, 123, 124, 131, 134, 147, 151, 155–157, 167, 168, 176

sacralization 37, 157, 163, 166
sacred 7, 13, 27, 48–50, 57, 80, 156, 157, 163, 165–168, 170, 175, 177, 179
sacredness 173
scholarship 6, 14, 25, 49, 66, 70, 71, 76, 77, 81, 83, 84, 86, 87, 90, 92–93, 95, 98, 101, 117, 165, 169, 172

secular 6, 13, 23, 26–28, 86, 97, 100–103, 163, 164, 170, 173
secularism 12, 13, 21, 87
self-reflexively 7, 12, 73, 75
signification 7, 29, 34, 58, 60, 63, 75, 103, 106, 108, 109, 111, 113, 123, 132, 142, 152, 157, 159, 163–165, 167, 168, 172–174, 176–179
spirituality 12, 23, 46, 47, 57, 82, 122, 125, 141, 156, 165, 167, 174

translation 19, 34–36, 55, 66, 108, 122, 125, 126, 133, 136, 141, 145

unbiased observation 36–37

CPSIA information can be obtained
at www.ICGtesting.com
Printed in the USA
LVHW111435200620
658100LV00008B/456

9 783110 676709